Strive and Thrive with the Psalms

A fresh look at the Psalms
in 365 bite-sized pieces

PAM POINTER

kevin mayhew

kevin
mayhew

First published in Great Britain in 2020 by Kevin Mayhew Ltd,
Buxhall, Stowmarket, Suffolk, IP14 3BW
Tel: +44 (0) 1449 737978 Fax: +44 (0) 1449 737834
E-mail: info@kevinmayhew.com

www.kevinmayhew.com

© Copyright 2020 Pam Pointer.

The right of Pam Pointer to be identified as the author of this work has been asserted by her in accordance with the Copyright, Designs and Patents Act 1988.

Unless stated otherwise, Scripture quotations are taken from The Good News Translation (GNT). Copyright © 1992 by American Bible Society.

Scripture quotations are also from: The King James Version and
The Holy Bible, New International Version® Anglicised.
NIV® Copyright © 1979, 1984, 2011 by Biblica, Inc.®.
Used by permission. All rights reserved worldwide.

All rights reserved. No part of this publication may be reproduced, stored in a retrieval system, or transmitted, in any form or by any means, electronic, mechanical, photocopying, recording, or otherwise, without the prior written permission of the publisher.

9 8 7 6 5 4 3 2 1 0

ISBN 978 1 83858 052 0
Catalogue No. 1501642

Cover and layout design by Rob Mortonson
Edited by Linda Ottewell

Printed and bound in Great Britain

Contents

	About the Author	15
	Introduction	16
1	Growth	18
2	Contrasts	20
3	Plots	22
4	Warning	24
5	Night and day	26
6	Worth	28
7	Bedtime peace	30
8	Sunrise	32
9	Reverence	34
10	Safety	36
11	Exhaustion	38
12	Weeping	40
13	Torn to bits	42
14	Judgement	44
15	Justice	46
16	Baby praise	48
17	Sky at night	50
18	Man's dignity	52
19	Wonder	54
20	In charge	56
21	Refuge	58
22	Testimony	60
23	Hope	62
24	Questions	64
25	Pride	66
26	Unseen?	68

27	Commitment	70
28	Confidence	72
29	Flattery	74
30	Help me!	76
31	How long?	78
32	All bad	80
33	Humility	82
34	Sincerity	84
35	Pleasure	86
36	Security	88
37	Delight	90
38	Innocence	92
39	Shadows	94
40	Fortress	96
41	Thunder and lightning	98
42	Rescued	100
43	Faithful	102
44	Sure-footed	104
45	Rebellion	106
46	Victorious	108
47	Heaven's glory	110
48	Words	112
49	Blessings	114
50	Trust	116
51	Royal humility	118
52	Royal praise	120
53	Abandoned	122
54	Bullied	124
55	Dependence	126
56	Bulls, lions and dogs	128
57	The bigger picture	130
58	Global testimony	132
59	Shepherd's goodness	134
60	Foundations	136

61	Purity	138
62	Triumphal entry	140
63	Teach me!	142
64	Friendship	144
65	Your ways	146
66	Desires	148
67	Glory	150
68	Light and salvation	152
69	Parental care	154
70	This present life	156
71	Deception	158
72	Shepherd's care	160
73	God's voice	162
74	Sadness and gladness	164
75	Fear and favour	166
76	Dance for joy	168
77	Shelter	170
78	Weak bones	172
79	Whispers	174
80	Courage	176
81	Defiance	178
82	Open and hidden	180
83	Unbridled	182
84	Skill with strings	184
85	Full earth	186
86	Endurance	188
87	Freedom from fear	190
88	Find out	192
89	Goals for the young	194
90	Preservation	196
91	Deep hole	198
92	Lies and leers	200
93	Rouse yourself, Lord!	202
94	Wickedness	204

95	Goodness	206
96	Don't worry	208
97	Waiting	210
98	Little and good	212
99	Old age	214
100	Observe	216
101	Struck down	218
102	Suffering	220
103	Head below parapet	222
104	Anxiety	224
105	Patience and loyalty	226
106	Aid	228
107	Illness	230
108	Heartbreak	232
109	Longing	234
110	Exile	236
111	Assurance	238
112	Accusation	240
113	Low notes and high notes	242
114	Euphoria	244
115	Royalty	246
116	Shelter and strength	248
117	Applause	250
118	Cityscape	252
119	Priceless	254
120	You can't take it with you	256
121	Mine!	258
122	Reprimand	260
123	Wash day	262
124	Snow white	264
125	Pure heart	266
126	Proper worship	268
127	Razor tongue	270
128	Wicked!	272

129	Atheism	274
130	Attack and defence	276
131	Escapism	278
132	Betrayal	280
133	Let it go	282
134	Mere humans	284
135	The list of tears	286
136	Companionship	288
137	Supply and demand	290
138	Glory in the skies	292
139	Slimy snails	294
140	Snarling dogs	296
141	Growls and songs	298
142	Earthquake	300
143	Despair	302
144	Broken fences	304
145	Weight	306
146	Feast	308
147	Clinging	310
148	Mobs	312
149	The whole world	314
150	Harvest	316
151	Come and see	318
152	But now	320
153	Everyone praise God	322
154	Provision	324
155	God our porter	326
156	Procession	328
157	Majesty	330
158	Mud	332
159	Multiple enemies	334
160	Insults	336
161	Revenge	338
162	Answers	340

163	Dismay	342
164	A good example	344
165	Tell it how it is	346
166	Lifelong learning	348
167	The kingdom	350
168	King for ever	352
169	God won't know	354
170	Too difficult	356
171	Bitter thoughts	358
172	Weakness and strength	360
173	Hands behind back	362
174	Mighty creation	364
175	Rouse yourself!	366
176	Fairness	368
177	Silence	370
178	Sighing	372
179	I will	374
180	Past presence	376
181	The generation game	378
182	Commandments	380
183	Miracles	382
184	Demands	384
185	Angel food	386
186	In spite of . . .	388
187	Mere mortals	390
188	Sat Nav	392
189	Anger	394
190	God's choice	396
191	Burning fire	398
192	Pay back time	400
193	A plate of sorrow	402
194	Deep roots	404
195	Grapevine	406
196	Moon time	408

197	Load of bricks	410
198	Wish list	412
199	Rights	414
200	Revolt	416
201	Shame	418
202	Keep close	420
203	A thousand days	422
204	Fury and forgiveness	424
205	Two-way loyalty	426
206	Down and up	428
207	Unique	430
208	Devotion	432
209	Just like mother	434
210	Citizenship	436
211	Feeling like death	438
212	Darkness	440
213	Heaven sings	442
214	Your world	444
215	Kindness	446
216	Promises, promises	448
217	Non-stop love	450
218	More promises	452
219	Rejection	454
220	Deliverance	456
221	One-day weeds in God's home	458
222	Short life	460
223	Future generations	462
224	Whoever	464
225	Angelic protection	466
226	Long life	468
227	Deep thoughts	470
228	Flourishing	472
229	Immovable	474
230	Eyes and ears	476

231	Corruption and constancy	478
232	Bow down	480
233	Good news	482
234	All creation	484
235	Gladness	486
236	A new song	488
237	Supreme	490
238	Cloud-speak	492
239	Enter	494
240	Loyalty	496
241	A lonely bird	498
242	Ashes and tears	500
243	Write it down	502
244	Healing	504
245	A father's love	506
246	Seed sown	508
247	Living creation	510
248	Order	512
249	New life	514
250	Volcanic power	516
251	Remember	518
252	I am only one, but I am one	520
253	Proved right	522
254	Horrible history	524
255	A new land	526
256	Poor memory	528
257	I want	530
258	Swap	532
259	Grumbling	534
260	Think before you speak	536
261	Adoption and abandonment	538
262	Distress	540
263	Wandering	542
264	Gloom	544

265	Reprieve	546
266	Raging storm	548
267	Be wise	550
268	Greatness of the sky	552
269	Worthless help	554
270	Opposition	556
271	Ouch!	558
272	Scorned	560
273	Loud	562
274	Drink for strength	564
275	Wonderful actions	566
276	Dependable	568
277	A good person	570
278	East to west	572
279	Trembling	574
280	No sense	576
281	Triple trust	578
282	World of the living	580
283	What can I give him?	582
284	Triple praise	584
285	Eternal dependability	586
286	On the victory side	588
287	Stones and branches	590
288	Pleasure in obedience	592
289	Open eyes	594
290	Wrong way	596
291	Explain	598
292	Meditate	600
293	Compose songs	602
294	Conduct	604
295	More than money	606
296	Understanding	608
297	Tired eyes	610
298	Through all ages	612

299	Sweet as honey	614
300	Light the way	616
301	Hold me	618
302	Watching	620
303	Tears of sorrow	622
304	Just instructions	624
305	Non-stop learning	626
306	Perfect security	628
307	Lost sheep	630
308	War and peace	632
309	Wide-awake God	634
310	Let's go!	636
311	Pray for peace	638
312	Look up	640
313	What if . . .?	642
314	Shaken, not moved	644
315	Laughter	646
316	Building	648
317	Children	650
318	Fruitfulness	652
319	Bless you!	654
320	Eager	656
321	Given up	658
322	Contentment	660
323	A place for the Lord	662
324	Priests	664
325	Flourish	666
326	Harmony	668
327	Raise your hand	670
328	Whatever he wishes	672
329	All generations	674
330	Idols	676
331	He alone	678
332	Eternal love	680

333	Greatest joy	682
334	Supremacy	684
335	Too deep	686
336	Darkness and light	688
337	Baby talk	690
338	Grains of sand	692
339	Examination	694
340	Living with God	696
341	Keep me	698
342	Keep trusting	700
343	Ready to give up	702
344	All I want	704
345	Bring to mind	706
346	Morning reminder	708
347	Pay attention	710
348	Puff of wind	712
349	Reach down	714
350	Happiness	716
351	Beyond understanding	718
352	Good to everyone	720
353	Royal power	722
354	Look hopeful	724
355	Near	726
356	Dust	728
357	Sight	730
358	Star-naming	732
359	Message	734
360	All together now	736
361	Honours for the humble	738
362	Music-making	740
363	Subject matters	742
364	Favourites	744
365	Love songs	746

Dedication

In memory of my parents,
Robert and Eileen Hunt,
who knew and loved the psalms.

About the Author

Pam is a writer, speaker and photographer whose work reflects her observations of the natural world and its human inhabitants.

Why Didn't God Create Me With Green Hair? was Pam's first book, published in 1999. She has written a number of other books, plus many magazine articles on subjects as diverse as sleeping on the pavement in the Wimbledon queue, the work of hospital chaplains, and the merit of cows. She has contributed columns to local and national newspapers, broadcast morning thoughts for local radio, written an RE syllabus and teaching outlines, and writes meditations for an international magazine.

Pam is married with three daughters, three sons-in-law and six grandchildren. She enjoys being a homemaker, walking in the countryside, watching period drama on TV, blogging on her website: https://pampointer.wordpress.com/, and listening to 1960s rock music, Classic FM and Test Match Special. Pam is passionate about God, and Jesus is the solid rock on which her life is built.

Introduction

The Psalms are heartfelt comments on life, in the words of poets who lived in Old Testament times. Many are written by David, the shepherd lad who became king. He, and the other poets, wrote candidly about fear, joy, despair, nature, music, dancing, sleeplessness, anxiety, elation, bitterness, wonder, birth, ageing – the whole spectrum of life. The Psalms have been read and sung for centuries. What makes them so appealing is something that is true of the Bible as a whole: honesty.

Strive and Thrive with the Psalms is not a theological tome but a contemporary look at how the Psalms resonate with us in today's twenty-first century culture. Methods of communication three thousand years ago were different to the technological media of today, but human nature doesn't change. The poetry of the Psalms covers the same broad topics that continue to impact life and are still written about by poets today.

If you expect worthy words and deep study, then you might be disappointed by, or even disapprove of, the 365 bite-sized pieces – one to chew on every day for a year. I've sometimes taken verses out of context or majored on one or two words in a verse. Occasionally I've commented on the historic background to help us understand why the psalmist feels as he does. But my main aim is to give us all something from God's word that can help us through the day. We strive in the situations that cause us concern, along with the writers who struggled with their situations. We thrive on the goodness of God and his created world just as the writers did when life was going well for them.

What we read in the Psalms reflects our experiences – harm, qualms, calm. The overriding message of the Psalms seems to be that, whatever our situation, whatever our circumstances, God is still good, he is still faithful, he still cares for us and we can trust the Almighty God who knows the bigger picture when sometimes we just see one little piece of life's jigsaw.

I've mostly used the Good News Translation of the Bible, but please use whichever version you can be friends with. Each day's piece contains:

Title
Question time
Read Psalm . . .
Comment
Challenge or Be encouraged
Pray

I hope you enjoy your year of striving, thriving – and surviving – with the Psalms.

1

Growth

Question time

🍃 Are you a rebel?

🍃 Do you question authority?

🍃 Do you like to buck the trend or flout the rules?

Read Psalm 1:1-3

Comment

The book of Psalms starts with the startling statement that joy comes from obedience, that delight is in the law of the Lord. If you're a rebel that may be an uncomfortable thought. It's *who* we're to obey that is key to this psalm. There's no joy in rejecting God. Rather, the joy comes from obeying . . . *him*. Are you prepared to obey his word? The fact that you're reading this suggests that you might be! Though, so often, there's a tendency to do what is right only on our terms or when we feel like it. When we immerse ourselves in God's word, we will grow and produce fruit in our lives. What a lovely picture we have of a tree planted by a stream.

The water helps to nourish the tree which, in turn, helps it to produce fruit. Joyous indeed.

Challenge

'Since you have accepted Christ Jesus as Lord, live in union with him. Keep your roots deep in him, build your lives on him, and become stronger in your faith.'

Colossians 2:6, 7

'The Spirit produces love, joy, peace, patience, kindness, goodness, faithfulness, humility and self-control.'

Galatians 5:22, 23

Pray

Use the verses above as the basis for your prayer.

2

Contrasts

Question time

🍃 How does religious art help your understanding of God?

Read Psalm 1:4-6

Comment

In medieval times artists decorated churches with paintings, often depicting Bible stories – for the benefit of non-readers and in the absence of Bibles – thereby bringing, in graphic detail, an illustrated guide to biblical teaching, with images of people, places and situations. In some churches, such as St Thomas's in Salisbury, there is a doom painting. It shows Christ in glory, his disciples, angels, and two groups of people: those whom the artist depicts as condemned-to-hell evil people and those whom he depicts as heaven-bound righteous people.

These three verses in our meditation make that contrast. On one side we see people who are condemned and, on the other, people who follow

God's ways. But, you might ask, won't God save everyone if he's a God of love? Maybe it's not that simple. We all have free will to make choices about life. We're not robots, nor puppets on God's strings. Some people deliberately turn their backs on God and would be horrified at the thought of being in heaven in the presence of God and his believers. Whether they would prefer the alternative option is questionable. Fortunately it's not up to us to say who's 'in' and who's 'out'. We leave that to the fair-minded judge of all the earth – God himself.

Challenge

Choose to be guided and protected by God, or to be separated from him.

Pray

You might like to use a religious painting to help shape your prayer.

3
Plots

Question time
🌿 Why do you make plans?

Read Psalm 2:1-3

Comment

News bulletins focus on the gloom of war and crime so we can echo the psalmist's questioning in verse 1 of our reading. Plans and plots. Some plans are good, positive, beneficial and helpful. Plans for a birthday celebration, a holiday or to phone a friend in need. All good stuff. And plots – well the allotment plot can be beneficial! But too often plans and plots stir up unrest and hatred which lead to factions and end up as fights. These can happen in the home, in a community, in a nation or globally.

Here, it seems to be God under attack – for his plans for the benefit of nations. His choice of a king began with Saul, continued with David and Solomon, and a host of other goodies and baddies who aimed for peace – or waged war. Ultimately

God's choice of king was Jesus himself who wasn't the sort of king people expected – no white horse, no powerful army. He was a person of goodness, humility and service, but with power and authority, the like of which had never been seen before or since. As verse 3 hints at, Jesus himself was rejected.

Challenge

Are you a plotter, seeking freedom from control? Or do you willingly participate in God's kingdom?

Pray

For wise choices when making plans.

4
Warning

Question time

🍃 **How good are you at obeying the rules of the road?**

🍃 **Do you know the difference between circular and triangular UK road signs?** The circles depict mandatory rules, the triangles depict warnings. So 'Stop' is on a circle, 'Give Way' is on a triangle.

Read Psalm 2:4-12

Comment

In these somewhat alarming verses, God is posting triangle signs. But take a look at his emotions: laughter, mocking, anger, fury . . . How much notice do you take of God and his reactions to the people he's created? How well do you know his rules for living? Have you ever read the Ten Commandments? Maybe you once memorised them. I remember teaching Year 6 children the Commandments in an RE lesson. We chatted together about what each one meant. Jesus summarised the Old Testament laws when he said we should love God with our whole being – heart, soul and mind – and love other people as we love ourselves. How can we apply these commands in our daily lives – with our family, friends, neighbours, workmates, anyone on our front line? If we all took those commands seriously, might the world be a more harmonious place?

Challenge and Encouragement

The words here are not just warning. There is a bright side too. Be wise. Put God first. Serve him. Respect him for who he is. And be blessed.

Pray

That you may be an obedient follower of God.

5
Night and day

Question time

🍃 **Are you a morning or an evening person, a lark or an owl?** I'm a lark. I like to be up early, go out for a walk, and get my brain in gear for the day ahead. I seem to have my most lucid thoughts first thing and certainly work better in the morning than in the afternoon and evening.

Read Psalm 3:1-8

Comment

How do you begin each day? A Christian friend told me that he wakes each morning and thanks God for the gift of a new day. Is that something you do? Or could start doing from today? None of us knows how each new day will pan out, but in the morning we can say thank you and commit the day's activities to God.

Here, the psalmist has woken up feeling people are against him and gossiping about him. How do you deal with that kind of unease? You can arm yourself with the metaphorical shield of God's protection. It is he who gives courage when we ask for it and he who will see us through the tests of the day as we trust him for each moment.

Challenge

What danger or 'enemy fire' might you be facing today? How will you deal with it?

Pray

Thank you, God, for the gift of today. May I use it wisely and courageously.

6
Worth

Question time

- How do you rate your self-worth?
- Do you brim with confidence, or lack self-esteem?

Read Psalm 4:1-5

Comment

Each of us is different. I can speak to a big audience but find it extremely difficult to enter a room with an unknown group of people and join in a discussion. You might be a brilliant mother, giving your children love and care and guiding them in the adventure of their lives, but be more reticent when in the presence of other adults. You may be brash and bold and a party animal, or you may be quiet and reflective and prefer to listen and observe. Whoever you are and whatever you may think of yourself, God values you. He thinks you're worth his Son dying for you to give you life – a full, abundant, hope-filled life. So, as in this psalm, remember God's presence and power in your life in the past, and ask for his help and peace in the present. Whatever your circumstances, whoever loves or loathes you, God is the constant one who is by your side at all times, rooting for you and cheering you on your way through the obstacle course of life.

Challenge

When you feel worthless, try telling yourself that you're worthwhile. Verse 3 reminds us that God has chosen you; he hears your outward cries and inward sighs. Lie in silence on your bed, ponder – and put your trust in God.

Pray

Thank you, Father God, that you value me.

7

Bedtime peace

Question time

🍃 **Do you find it hard to keep awake for your bedtime prayers?** I start off with good intentions but drift off into sleep in a silent mid-sentence.

Read Psalm 4:6-8

Comment

Maybe you come to God at the end of the day with a shopping list of hopeful blessings for the next day. Do you long for riches, for good health, for the money to pay a deposit on a house, for good weather, for plenty of food and drink? God may bless you with those things, or he may not. The psalmist says that however much 'stuff' we have, it's nothing compared with the joy that God gives us through knowing him. How often and how much time do you spend getting to know God better? How much do you trust God with your life?

It is joy that makes the psalmist lie down to go to sleep in peace. When our trust is wholeheartedly in God, we can rest in his presence – free from fear, and with the light of his face shining on us.

Challenge
To rest in peace.

Pray
For those who find rest and peace elusive.

Sunrise

Question time

How often have you woken with a sigh or a cry?

Read Psalm 5:1-6

Comment

The roller coaster of emotions continues. How relevant the psalms are and what a contemporary feel they have! Here we see that, even in the midst of feeling down, the psalmist knows that his voice is heard by God. Just as the sun rises, so our prayers rise to the throne of God's grace. The book of Lamentations is just that: a series of laments. But there is a glimmer of hope, as it says in Lamentations 3:22, 23:

> The Lord's unfailing love and mercy still continue, fresh as the morning, as sure as the sunrise. The Lord is all I have, and so in him I put my hope.

I love a winter sunrise. For a start, I don't have to get up quite so early to witness it as I do in the summer. If you have an opportunity, go outside on a crisp and clear winter morning and watch the sun rise. Before you see the sun, the sky in the east lightens, and then slowly the golden orb rises until eventually the light from the whole sphere dazzles you with its majesty. It's a glorious sight and a reminder of the Creator of the universe who, for all his power and authority, still cares for little old you!

Challenge

Get up early to see the dawn.

Pray

Praise God for the sun in all its beauty.

9

Reverence

Question time

🍃 Have you ever met a Very Important Person?

Read Psalm 5:7, 8

Comment

One January morning some years ago, I went with my brother and my parents to Windsor Castle. Our taxi took us up the Long Walk and we were greeted at the door and treated by the Queen's staff with utmost courtesy, as if we were royalty ourselves. The occasion was to witness my father receive an OBE from Her Majesty the Queen. He was told what to do, where to walk, how to stand and when to bow. He showed reverence to the Queen. She, in turn, smiled, gave him his award, spoke a few words to him and shook his hand. It was an impressive occasion.

Any reverence we might have for a fellow human being is as nothing compared to the reverence we have – or should have – for God. When you go to church, how do you show reverence to the King of kings? Different places of worship have different traditions. Some worshippers bow as they face the altar, others make the sign of the cross, some sit in silence to contemplate the presence of God, and in other places of worship there is informality and no outward sign of reverence.

Challenge

Ultimately, it's not the outward gestures that are important but the inner attitude. We are honoured to be the recipients of God's love and we show him our gratitude and respect.

Pray

For a right attitude when meeting God in prayer and worship.

10
Safety

Question time

- How good is your balance?
- Have you ever walked a tightrope?

Read Psalm 5:9-12

Comment

When I was a child, I was taken to the circus. I hated the clowns – was terrified of them – but I found the tightrope walker fascinating. How could she balance on that thin wire so high above the arena? Was she never afraid? What happened when she wobbled? Fortunately there was a safety net down below and if she were to fall, though she might suffer a few minor hurts, she would be saved from serious damage by the net.

Sometimes life can seem like walking a tightrope. If you're a Christian believer, life can be a bit lonely up there on the metaphorical tightrope where you're the only believer in your place of work or in your class at school or in your family. If you wobble on the rope or fall off, God is there as your safety net. And what does that mean? It means you rejoice, you sing for joy, you know you're loved and you know God's protection. It doesn't mean life will be easy all the time, but it means that, in those testing times, God will be right there with you.

Challenge

What tightrope are you having to walk at the moment? How much do you trust God when you wobble?

Pray

Thank God for his safety net.

11

Exhaustion

Question time

How often do you hear someone say they're exhausted? 'I'm exhausted; the baby was awake all night!' 'I'm exhausted; the boss is a slave-driver!' 'I'm exhausted; that shopping weighed a ton!' 'I'm exhausted; we had to play extra-time and then a penalty shoot-out!'

Read Psalm 6:1-3

Comment

The book of Psalms is a collection of poetry that expresses every conceivable emotion that human beings go through and is a great source of comfort and encouragement. Here we find the psalmist feeling faint and in anguish, worn out, troubled, and wondering whether God will ever answer his prayers. This is whole-being melt-down. Body, mind and soul are affected. Can you identify with that?

And do you question God: How long do I have to wait, Lord, for you to answer me? Are you really there? Come on, what are you waiting for . . . ?

God knows all that each of us goes through in the adventure of life. He understands our exhaustion. I can recall, as a young mother, feeling utterly spent, exhausted beyond words. I can understand the psalmist yelling at God, 'Have pity on me!' 'Give me strength!' 'How long?'

Challenge

Be honest with God and tell him how you feel.

Pray

Use some of the words in these three verses as your prayer.

12

Weeping

Question time

- What makes you cry?
- A sad movie?
- Grief from the death of a loved one?
- Seeing images of starving children?
- Pain caused by injury?
- Have you howled in despair, made your pillow soaking wet with silent tears or loud sobs?
- Or maybe you're a stiff-upper-lip sort who keeps such emotion in check?

Read Psalm 6:4-10

Comment

'Big boys don't cry.' No? Well, the big boy in this psalm certainly did. What a graphic description we're given of his soaked pillow, his swollen eyes and the grief that's worn him out. He is overwhelmed, drowning in the spilt tears. Have you known such weeping yourself? The psalmist finds respite in the Lord who hears his weeping and listens to his 'Help!' yelp. When a small child sobs with pain or grief it may take the loving parent time to calm the child, to reach a point where the child lies quietly and peacefully with the parent's arms around him, comforting him. That's the kind of love and care God has for each of his hurting children.

Challenge

Is there something you need to share with God now? Be real with him. Cry and shout if you need to.

Pray

That God will hear your cries and respond with his peace.

13

Torn to bits

Question time

🍃 Have there been times when you've felt pursued and torn apart?

Read Psalm 7:1-5

Comment

Lions can kill humans, as news stories confirm from time to time. In this psalm David compares his human pursuers to a lion who will carry him off and tear him to bits. Not a pretty picture.

Peter tells us in one of his letters in the New Testament that, 'the Devil roams around like a roaring lion, looking for someone to devour' (1 Peter 5:8) and that believers should be on their guard, watching out and resisting the evil intentions of the lion-like Devil.

Paradoxically, Jesus is described in Revelation 5:5 as a lion: 'The Lion from Judah's tribe, the great descendant of David, has won the victory.' Jesus is the ultimate and everlasting king. A lion conveys strength, beauty, majesty and royalty. It is often symbolised on coats of arms. The difference between the Devil and Jesus is that the first 'lion' is a deceptive predator whose aim is to harm and kill, whereas the second 'Lion' is the victorious, just and righteous King.

Be encouraged

Whatever the nature of the lion that pursues us, we need not fear it, for the Lion of the tribe of Judah outwits, outweighs and ousts forever the deceptive one.

Pray

Ask God for the protection you need today.

14
Judgement

Question time

What attracts you to a particular book?

Read Psalm 7:6-9

Comment

I'm a great fan of the public library and like to browse and choose books to take home. What's the first thing you look at? The cover. If I don't like the cover, I tend to put the book back on the shelf. But the saying goes, 'Never judge a book by its cover.'

We have a tendency to make judgements – on events, on politicians, on the state of the roads or railways, on someone's cooking and, yes, on book covers. Is our judgement right? As far as people are concerned, God makes it clear that he doesn't judge people by their outward appearance. When God sent Samuel to choose a successor to King Saul, the whole line-up of Jesse's sons was brought, one by one, to be inspected by Samuel. None was found suitable. Samuel was puzzled until he discovered there was the youngest son working out in the fields. In a hierarchical society, it was unthinkable that the youngest child would be appointed king! David became king; he wasn't perfect, but he was God's choice and his heart was in the right place. It's reassuring to know that God, the creator, is the judge of human beings. He knows our thoughts and desires and knows whether or not we're innocent.

Challenge

Are you content to let God be the judge of you and of others?

Pray

For a non-judgemental attitude.

15

Justice

Question time

🍃 **Do you get indignant if you think an injustice has been done?**

Read Psalm 7:10-17

Comment

Judgement and justice – or righteousness – are both mentioned in this psalm. We like fair play and although, as children, we were told by our parents that 'life isn't fair', we still want justice to prevail. God had a go at his people through Amos the prophet in Amos 5: 21, 23, 24:

> I hate your religious festivals; I cannot stand them! . . . Stop your noisy songs; I do not want to listen to your harps. Instead, let justice flow like a stream, and righteousness like a river that never goes dry.

God is a God of justice. When we feel indignant let's relax and remember that God said, in Genesis

18:25, 'The judge of all the earth has to act justly.' One day all will be well and justice will prevail forever. Meanwhile we can play our part in working for fairness in a world that isn't fair – in family life, locally, nationally and globally.

Challenge

What cause might you be able to speak up for? How might you be used by God as an agent of his justice in a world that largely ignores his ways?

Pray

For those who work for justice in the world.

16
Baby praise

Question time
🍃 How do children help you appreciate nature?

Read Psalm 8:1, 2

Comment

The wonder in a child's eyes and voice at seeing, for the first time, a ladybird with its distinctive red coat and black spots, or a wiggly worm, or a furry caterpillar, is a tonic to any adult who has come to take such wonders for granted.

My grandchildren take great delight in collecting sticks. No walk is complete without finding, using, and bringing home, a length of stick. They also love finding horse chestnut shells, crushing the spikes and fishing out the shiny conker inside. Or jumping over rippling waves on a sandy beach, or spotting trout in a stream.

It must thrill the heart of God to watch little people enjoying his creation. Jesus was in the Temple one day when he heard children shouting in praise to

God. Temple officials were affronted. Jesus quoted this psalm to them.

When a child brings indoors yet another twig or leaf, or snaps off your prize rose to show you, isn't he, unknowingly, showing you the Lord's greatness and praising him? Jesus encouraged his listeners to become like little children in order to understand more of God. Childish? No. Childlike? Yes – with the innocence and joy and unclutteredness that children have. Let's be thrilled when a child's joy wafts its way up to heaven.

Challenge

Let's encourage children to discover God through creation.

Pray

For the children you have contact with.

17
Sky at night

Question time

When a toddler sings, 'Twinkle, twinkle, little star' is he praising God for the wonder of the night sky? Not consciously maybe.

Read Psalm 8:3, 4

Comment

Take a group of small children into the garden on a clear dark night to look at the stars and you'll hear the wonder in their voices and their excitement as they try to count the stars and even name some of the visible star groups: the Plough, Orion . . . and planets: Mars, Jupiter, Venus . . .

Each year, it seems, the universe expands as scientists discover its further reaches. Each new discovery just adds to the mind-boggling incomprehension of the size, diversity and awesomeness of the universe.

David, the shepherd, may have written this psalm when he was out at night watching his sheep

– and watching the night sky at the same time. The awesome sight of a small part of the universe on display prompts him to ponder whether and, if so, how the Creator can spot an individual human being amongst the vastness of the universe – and care for that person.

Challenge

Take the opportunity when it arises to go out at night, away from the light pollution of our cities and towns, just to gaze at the stars and think about your relationship with creation and the Creator.

Pray

A favourite hymn about creation.

18

Man's dignity

Question time

🍃 What are human beings, that God thinks of them?

Read Psalm 8:5-9

Comment

I love the Bible's little connecting words: yet, but, so, if... Here we have, in some translations, a 'yet'. In verse 4 David has posed the question, 'What are human beings, that you think of them; mere mortals, that you care for them?' YET... And here's something even more amazing than the universe itself: you made them inferior only to yourself; you crowned them... you appointed them... you placed them... What value God puts on each individual person! And not just on people. He knows the number of hairs on our head, the number of stars in the universe, the number of grains of sand on the seashore, the number of cattle, worms, ants, spiders (too many?)... You name it, he knows it, and he cares for it. Wow. No wonder David concludes that God's greatness is seen in all the world. As Paul put it in Romans 1:20, 'Ever since God created the world, his invisible qualities, both his eternal power and his divine nature, have been clearly seen; they are perceived in the things that God has made.'

Challenge

Can you comprehend what it means to be the pinnacle of God's creation? To be inferior only to him? To be crowned? Appointed? Placed precisely where you are at this moment?

Pray

To your Creator and Carer.

19
Wonder

Question time
How often do you tell other people about the wonderful things God has done?

Read Psalm 9:1-6

Comment
Three walkers were in high spirits, their boots laced and shiny, ready for the off. The walk took them high into the mountains through heather-covered rocks, across open scree, up slippery, crumbling zigzag paths. They paused every now and again for breath, and to take photos. Joy filled their hearts; what fun it was to be in the open air, how exhilarating the climb was, and as for the views? Stunning. Praiseworthy. Wonderful.

Think of what God has done in the created universe, what he did through Jesus, and what he has done and is doing in your life. If you have a sense of wonder about the stars in the sky or mountain views, how much more of a sense of wonder do you have about God's actions with human beings? I'll chat to anyone who'll listen about my love of, and wonder for, the stars and moon, but how much do I share with other people my wonder for God himself?

Challenge

Let's be challenged to praise God wholeheartedly; to show and tell; to sing with joy. And not just at church on Sunday.

Pray

Lord God Almighty, help me to enjoy the wonders of your creativity, love, grace, and mercy, and to share your attributes with others.

20
In charge

Question time

- Are you a control freak?
- Do you like to be in charge?

Read Psalm 9:7, 8

Comment

Sometimes control is a power thing, sometimes it's a security thing, sometimes it's just plain selfish. There are lists of the world's most powerful men and women in the world. Why are human beings so obsessed with power and status? Take another look at Jesus who, despite being God, humbled himself to become a man and had a servant attitude towards people. Paul describes Jesus in such words when he writes a letter to the church in Philippi. He says the Christians there should have the same attitude as Jesus. Do you have a servant attitude? Can you emulate Jesus? We're told in Acts that Jesus went about doing good. He didn't strut his stuff or lord it over other people. So what should we do? Think of others in a kindly manner, treat people as we would like them to treat us? Eat a good helping of humble pie?

When it comes to thinking of the world, how often do we talk about 'our world' when we'd do well to remember that it's actually God's world that we inhabit? He is the one who is in charge of the universe as these verses indicate.

Be encouraged
God is king. Forever. He rules the world. He is just. He is in charge.

Pray
That you may be willing to submit to God's control.

21
Refuge

Question time

🍃 Have you ever been on a mountain when the weather takes a turn for the worse?

Read Psalm 9:9-12

Comment

Mountains can be treacherous if the weather changes. The wind gets up, clouds rush across the sky and, without too much warning, misty rain falls on you. You and your companions become disorientated, unable to see landmarks. Using compass and map, you plod on until, eventually through the mist, you see the solid outline of a mountain hut. You go inside and sit out the rainstorm, thankful for a roof over your head and a place of safety.

The mishmash of life includes high and low points, joie de vivre and fearful situations. Your misty 'mountain' experience may, in reality, be a period of illness, redundancy, homelessness, ostracism, addiction or imprisonment.

Be encouraged

God is a refuge, a place of shelter and safety. God never turns away anyone who comes to him. What a comfort that is! He never abandons his beloved child. He has a good strong hold on us. All we have to do is push open the door of that refuge and go in.

Pray

For humility and wisdom to turn to God as our place of refuge.

22

Testimony

Question time

- Have you ever had to write about yourself?
- Was it easy?

Read Psalm 9:13, 14

Comment

Publishers like to have a biographical paragraph about the author whose book they're going to publish. I find it really tricky to write about myself. I don't want to sound boastful. Any short biographical piece may read like a concise CV, an expanded version of what you might send when applying for a job, or a Personal Statement such as young people have to write when at school.

In these verses, David is quite prepared to stand up in front of people and talk. But look at how he phrases it. He's not actually talking about himself but about God and how God impacts his life. And that seems less narcissistic than talking just about yourself!

Have you ever stood up in your church or in a home group and told people all the things for which you praise God? If you're a parent, you might ask your child at bedtime what he can say thank you to God for at the end of the day. If you're a teenager, have you had the courage to share with your friends that God is with you? Whoever we are, whoever we share God with, the emphasis is on God, not on me, me, me.

Challenge

Does your face, voice, attitude and behaviour demonstrate the honour you're giving to God?

Pray

May I honour you, God, in what I think, say and do.

23
Hope

Question time

🍃 **What is your attitude to beggars on the street?**

Read Psalm 9:15-20

Comment

This morning I walked past a lady sitting on the pavement. She asked for money. I didn't quite walk by on the other side, but I didn't engage with her at all. Was I guilty of neglecting her need, as in verse 18 of this passage? When I worked in a run-down area of London, I met many people whose lives were blighted by poverty. The hospital where I worked gave them health care and, on discharge from hospital, clothes and food – but never money.

Jesus said there would always be poor people in society. It was true in the time of the psalmist, in the time of Jesus, and is still the case today in the UK and in many parts of the world. Is it true that the rich get richer and the poor get poorer?

Poverty is crushing. But verse 18 offers hope. The lives of the needy will not always be neglected, nor the hope of the poor crushed for ever. It is up to those of us who have plenty, or even just enough, to share what we have, thereby offering a glimpse of the hope that is to come when God's kingdom of justice and peace is here forever.

Challenge

What role can you play in sharing what you have and bringing hope?

Pray

For all those who are homeless or impoverished.

24

Questions

Question time

Would you like to sit God down in your living room and ask him questions face to face?

Read Psalm 10:1

Comment

How much easier it must have been for Jesus' disciples to be with him and ask their questions – even though they didn't always understand the answers.

Although God came down to earth – the Word made flesh – he is still Almighty God, the divine, and there is mystery about God. There are some things that are incomprehensible to us. As Paul said in 1 Corinthians 13:12:

> What we see now is like a dim image in a mirror; then we shall see face-to-face. What I know now is only partial; then it will be complete – as complete as God's knowledge of me.

Just because we don't get answers (in both senses of the word 'get') it doesn't mean we shouldn't ask the questions. God wants us to communicate with him. A child asks questions of its parents, as on the occasion when I asked my dad why cows are brown, eat green grass and produce white milk! So we, as children of our heavenly Father, are to ask God any questions that come to mind.

Be encouraged

Communication is two-way. We speak to God through prayer and he speaks to us through the scriptures, through other people, through nature, through the cross, through circumstances. Keep asking the questions!

Pray

Thank you, Father, that you always have time to listen to our questions.

25
Pride

Question time

🍃 Do you have a high opinion of yourself?

Read Psalm 10:2-9

Comment

You might hear someone say, 'He's as proud as a peacock.' A male peacock isn't actually displaying its plumage as an act of vanity; it is part of a courtship ritual to attract a mate. But the idiom makes the point about pride. People who have excessive self-esteem could be guilty of pride. They might be so self-reliant, so confident that they rely on their own abilities and circumstances to guide them through life.

Conceit, arrogance, pride, boasting . . . Not attractive attributes! Martin Luther reckoned that 'the god of this world is riches, pleasure and pride'. Pride, according to Henry IV of England, defeats its own end, by bringing the man who seeks esteem and reverence into contempt.

'Pride comes before a fall', says the proverb. So in verse 6 we have the smug person saying that nothing will shake him, that he'll always be happy and never have trouble. More chilling, perhaps, is the end of verse 4. The proud man has no room for God. God doesn't matter.

Challenge

How much do you rely on yourself and how much on God?

Pray

O Lord, when my pride rears its head, please bash it down and help me to walk humbly with you.

26

Unseen?

Question time

🍃 **Have you ever played hide and seek with a toddler?** She lies on the floor, head down and eyes closed, then says, 'I'm hiding! Come and find me!' And you pretend to search elsewhere while the child is in full view for all to see!

Read Psalm 10:10-13

Comment

In verse 11 we have someone who thinks God doesn't see them. This wasn't unusual in Bible times. Throughout the Old Testament we read of the waywardness of people: sometimes close to God, other times far away from him. In the prophecies we read about people carrying on as if God didn't exist or turns a blind eye to what they're up to. This is pride rearing its ugly puffed-up head again! By contrast, in Proverbs 3, verse 5 we're told to trust in the Lord and not rely on our own unreliable understanding. Elsewhere in the psalms we're told that God sees us all the time, so we can't pretend otherwise.

Challenge

Does the fact that God is all-seeing affect what you think, say and do?

Pray

Make me more mindful, Lord, of your good eyesight and help me to live honourably in your sight.

27
Commitment

Question time

- How many different types of native newt are there in the UK?
- Where is it snowing in the world right at this moment?
- Who was the first person to make a phone call?
- Why do we shed tears when we're sad?
- When did Socrates live?

Read Psalm 10:14-18

Comment

Well, there are three different types of native newt. As for the other questions, you could try consulting the internet. The internet is a wonderful resource but an inanimate one. A friend said to me, 'The internet can inform but it can't listen and what many of us need is someone to listen.'

Sometimes we feel that nobody really listens. Even close family members or friends can't seem to see our needs and even if we try and express them, they don't always listen! That's not the case with God.

Living in the social media age of computer-generated communication can actually make us feel alone or lonely because there is less personal contact with other people. But however alone or lonely we may be – and for whatever reasons – God's promise is that he is always there to listen.

Challenge

How much face-to-face communication do I have with people?

Pray

Lord, may I be committed to other people, in person as well as via social media.

28
Confidence

Question time

🍃 Do you know what it is like to be persecuted for your faith?

Read Psalm 11:1-7

Comment

I wonder whether this psalm is a comfort to Christians who are persecuted for their faith? In the UK there is little overt persecution because many people are indifferent to God and wouldn't bother to make trouble for believers. In some parts of the world, however, persecution is rife and Christians pay dearly for standing up for God. There is much mention here of 'The Lord'. It is in the Lord that the persecuted may trust, in him they can take refuge. We live in God's world and though there is much wickedness – and the Bible doesn't try and hide the ghastliness of evil and the human behaviour that comes from it – it is still God who is in control.

'The Lord is in his holy temple . . . he has his throne in heaven . . . He watches . . . He examines . . . The Lord is righteous.'

Be encouraged

Whatever arrows are fired at us, and even if we are wounded or die because of our faith, God is still on the throne and his own are safe for eternity in his care.

Pray

For Christians around the world who are persecuted for their faith.

29
Flattery

Question time
- Do you like receiving compliments?
- Are you good at giving them?

Read Psalm 12:1-4

Comment

Giving compliments is good but flattery takes it a step further and may be a way of ingratiating oneself with somebody else. It is then self-indulgent and deceptive. Praise is one thing and can be beneficial; flattery is something else and can be malicious.

David, it seems, is surrounded by flatterers and he sees through them for who they really are. He can't seem to find a genuinely good person at all. No wonder he says, 'Help!' It must have been lonely for David to feel that godly people were conspicuous by their absence and that the faithful, honest people couldn't be found.

Centuries later, Paul also came across flatterers. At the end of his letter to the Christians in Rome, having mentioned many by name, he warns:

Watch out for those who cause divisions and put obstacles in your way that are contrary to the teaching you have learned. Keep away from them. For such people are not serving our Lord Christ, but their own appetites. By smooth talk and flattery they deceive the minds of naive people.

Romans 16;17, 18, NIV

Challenge

It's disheartening for David to have to listen to these 'boastful tongues' and if we are surrounded by similar flatterers, we have to watch out and keep looking and listening to God.

Pray

Help me, Lord, to be able to distinguish between considerate compliments and flash flattery.

30
Help me!

Question time

🍃 How often do you call for help?

Read Psalm 12:5-8

Comment

My car started making a horrendous noise when I was out driving through moorland on a lonely road. I stopped, got out of the car and found one of the back tyres was flat; it had been punctured and gone down like a pin-stabbed balloon. What could I do? It was back in the early days of mobile phones and I had my phone with me – but had never used it! I managed to phone for assistance and waited for someone to come and help me. It seemed a very long wait but when the mechanic came, he reassured me, changed the wheel, and set me on my way again.

Help was at hand for David. God heard the cry for help and sprang into action to protect his faithful servant. Unlike the malicious flatterers, God's words to David were flawless and his promises could be trusted. Like a beautiful piece of silver or a precious diamond, the words of God are without blemish. What a wonderful thought and what a comfort to David in his hour of need.

Be encouraged
The Lord can be trusted.

Pray
Thank you, Lord, for the security and help that you give.

How long?

Question time

How often do you ask a question beginning with 'How'?

Read Psalm 13:1-6

Comment

There used to be a children's television programme called 'How?' The presenters answered all manner of questions that started with the word, 'How?' Much of the content of the programme was scientific and included demonstrations of how things worked, fuelling the children's imaginations, encouraging enquiring minds, and informing them of some useful facts.

The psalmist puts the question 'How?' several times over!

Factual questions can be easier to answer than philosophical or psychological ones. I can tell a child that gravity causes her to stay on the ground rather than float about in the air. It's not so easy to tell her that she has to go to school for the next thirteen years when she's come home on the first day and asked, 'How long do I have to go to school for?'

How was God to answer the pain-filled questions of the psalmist? Well, the writer, it seems, answers his own questions. He gives God an earful, which is quite acceptable; God wants us to communicate with him. He shares his woes, begs God to listen to him and answer him.

Be encouraged

Remembering, perhaps, moments from his past, the psalmist says, 'I rely on your constant love; I will be glad, because you will rescue me. I will sing to you, O Lord, because you have been good to me.'

Pray

Lord, help me to rely on you because of your constancy and your love.

32
All bad

Question time

Have you ever said to yourself, 'There is no God.'?

Read Psalm 14:1-3

Comment

When I was a child my father used to go out into the garden every morning in autumn to pick an apple to have on his cornflakes. He'd chop it up, and put it in the bowl, along with the golden cream from the top of the milk. Sometimes apples fell to the ground before they were picked. When cut open, we might find the inside of the apple was brown and inedible, sometimes crawling with earwigs that contaminated the fruit. If you store apples you have to ensure they don't touch each other because one bad apple can spread its nastiness to others, perpetuating the loss of the whole lot.

These sobering verses tell us that fools are like those apples: corrupt, vile, all bad. There are plenty of people today who say there's no God, and that opinion spreads to others. The ten-yearly census in the UK reveals a decline in belief in God.

The good news is that nobody has to stay being a fool! The Bible tells us that everyone has sinned so we can't have a holier-than-thou attitude and think we're OK. There is a way back to God but it's not of our doing, but of Christ's doing – through the cross.

Challenge

Do you need to turn around to face God?

Pray

Deliver me from foolishness, Lord, and make me turn away from evil.

33
Humility

Question time

🍃 **Have you ever eaten the innards of a deer?** That is what humble pie was made from in medieval times. These days the expression 'to eat humble pie' refers to admitting you were wrong about something.

🍃 **Do you like admitting you were wrong?** It's not an easy thing to do!

Read Psalm 14:4-7

Comment

Am I prepared to turn my back on pride and self-aggrandisement and acknowledge that God does exist and that he cares for me so much that he gave his only Son to be my Saviour? It takes humility to say, yep, I was wrong about God and about myself and about a whole host of other things.

Jesus is the supreme example of humility. He left the glory of heaven to come to earth and live as a human being, acting as a servant while being the Prince of Peace and Saviour of the world.

Challenge

In these verses, God challenges people to return to him in humility. Are you, am I, ready to pray, to obey, to be humble? When we do, we are assured by God of his presence and his protection and of restoration to a relationship with him.

Pray

For humility.

34
Sincerity

Question time

🍃 How often do you go through the motions of worship at a church service, without really engaging in true worship?

🍃 And do you think worship is just for Sundays?

Read Psalm 15:1-5

Comment

In these few verses we learn that sincere worship is whole-life worship. Look at verses 2-5. Rephrase them into questions to yourself: Do I obey God in everything? Do I always do what is right? Do I always speak truthfully and sincerely . . . ?

Our allegiance to the Lord and our worship of him should show itself in our everyday behaviour, not just our Sunday-best appearance at church. Think of Christian believers whom you could truly look upon as sincere and who have a worshipful lifestyle worthy of the Lord. What can you learn from them and from this psalm about your own approach to worship?

Challenge

What shall I bring to the Lord, the God of heaven, when I come to worship him? . . . The Lord has told us what is good. What he requires of us is this: to do what is just, to show constant love, and to live in humble fellowship with our God.

Micah 6:6-8

Pray

For a sense of justice, love and constancy – in your own life and in the lives of fellow God-followers.

35
Pleasure

Question time

Who is your favourite companion?

You might say your dog because he's faithful and doesn't answer back. It might be your brother, your dad, your best friend or your pastor.

Read Psalm 16:1-3

Comment

In these few verses the psalmist describes God's people as excellent and, for him, his greatest pleasure is to be with them.

Is that your experience? Do you find God's people, followers of Jesus, lovers of God, to be excellent? Do they give you great pleasure? What is it about true Christians that gives such pleasure? Perhaps it has something to do with yesterday's reading – whole-life worship of the living God. Do we look for the image of God in our fellow-believers? Do we see God's excellence in our Christian friends? Are we ready to forgive their failures, as we acknowledge our own shortcomings and wish for forgiveness from them?

Verse 2 reminds us that all good things come from God. That includes the pleasure derived from the flawed but faithful people of God.

Challenge

Paul, in his letter to the Christians at Philippi where there was a bit of argy-bargy, urges, 'Fill your minds with those things that are good and that deserve praise: things that are true, noble, right, pure, lovely, and honourable' (Philippians 4:8).

Pray

For a mind full of the right stuff.

36
Security

Question time
 How obsessed are you with being safe and your property secure?

Read Psalm 16:4-8

Comment

Be in the moment. Live the now. This mindfulness advice is nothing new. Jesus told people not to worry about tomorrow. Here the psalmist is content and secure in his knowledge of God's presence with him, day and night, today, tomorrow, forever. From the pleasurable companionship of God's people in Psalm 15, the psalmist expresses his contentment in God alone: 'You, Lord, are all I have, and you give me all I need; my future is in your hands.'

I've just unbolted the side gate to the garden. Two bolts, actually, plus other security measures, in order to keep the unwanted out and, in this case, to let two workmen in to repair a roof. Whatever measures I may take to be secure, whether in my home, or through careful management of money, or in making sure I look before crossing the road, there are no guarantees of a secure life. Burglars could still break into my house, I could lose my money through scams or a banking collapse, and motorists go through red lights and make my crossing of the road a potentially life-threatening walk.

It behoves us to place our security in something more substantial, long-lasting and reliable.

Challenge

Look at verse 8. Does this apply in your own life?

Pray

Help me to put my life in the most secure place of all: with you.

37

Delight

Question time

🍃 **What delights you?**
Blossom in spring time . . . the night sky . . . a baby's first smile . . . baking a cake . . . ?
There is much in life to delight and fill us with contentment.

Read Psalm 16:9-11

Comment

Joy, pleasure, thankfulness, gladness. Add them together to bring delight. This is a psalm of confidence in God. David is well aware of God's presence and he's brimming over with the delight of God being with him. Can you share his delight? Does God's presence have that effect on you?

The troubles of the world can overwhelm us such that our minds are filled with the What Ifs and Hows and Whys and Whens. If that happens there isn't much space for God. He's still there but until we push aside the concerns that burden us with their heavy weight, he can't get in very comfortably. Delight comes when it is God's presence that fills our whole being: body, mind and soul. That isn't to say that with God everything will always be hunky dory. We know that's unrealistic. But it means that God is with us in all circumstances and so we can delight in that – even when life is tough.

Be encouraged
By God's presence in all circumstances.

Pray
Show me, Lord God, how I might bring delight to others because of my delight in you.

38

Innocence

Question time

🍃 **Are you real with yourself and with God?**

Read Psalm 17:1-7

Comment

Like Peter in the New Testament, David in the Old Testament doesn't attempt to pussyfoot around. He says what he thinks, shows his feelings, and you feel you're seeing the real person, not someone who's pretending to be something he's not.

From the confidence of Psalm 16, David's tone changes in Psalm 17 to an honest prayer for justice. How often do you say, 'It's not fair!'? Have you ever been accused of doing something that you didn't do?

David was frequently in a spot of difficulty, sometimes because of his own errors, often because of other people. Here he pleads his innocence. His first few phrases are an appeal to God's fairness and knowledge of the individual: 'You will judge in my favour . . . You know what is right . . . You know my heart . . . You have come to me at night . . . You have examined me completely . . . You have found no evil desire in me.'

The Fall meant that all humans fell from grace; everyone in all time has fallen short of God's standards.

Be encouraged

Thanks to Jesus' work on the cross, those who put their trust in him have had their sins forgiven and are declared 'Not guilty!' Do you know that to be true in your life?

Pray

For those who suffer miscarriages of justice.

39
Shadows

Question time

Do you wear sunglasses or a visor in bright sunlight? The sun's rays, welcome though they are, are so powerful that we need to protect our eyes. Factory workers or builders will wear goggles to stop bits of metal or rock from entering their eyes. We need to look after these precious organs.

Read Psalm 17:8-15

Comment

David asks God to protect him and uses a picture of eye-protection to illustrate his point. He moves on to the image of a bird protecting its young in the shadow of its wings, an analogy that is used elsewhere in the Bible for God's personal familial care.

David's description of his enemies is sparse but graphic in verses 9-12. No wonder he needs protection. The cool comfort in the shadow of God's

'wings' is very different from the shadow of fear or death, and it is enough for him to conclude that, after a good night's sleep, God's continuing presence will fill him with joy.

Challenge

Do you turn to God for protection? Do you feel his presence enveloping you when you face attack? Be still in his presence now and know that he is there.

Pray

Look kindly on those who need your protection today, Lord God, for whatever reason and whatever their age or stage in life.

40

Fortress

Question time

Do you have a favourite castle or fortress, one that you enjoy visiting or one that is awe-inspiring?

Read Psalm 18:1-6

Comment

Around the coastline of Wales, down the north-east coast of England, and elsewhere in the British Isles, are fortresses. Immense blocks of stone were built up in strategic places to form impregnable castles. Many, though hundreds of years old, still stand – some as ruins, others in remarkably good condition. Tall towers once saw soldiers clanking up spiral staircases in their suits of armour, ready to look out for, and fend off, unwelcome intruders. You probably have a favourite castle. Mine would be any of the Welsh castles but especially Criccieth Castle on its rocky mound overlooking Cardigan Bay, or Caernarfon Castle on the Menai Strait. Each castle has its own characteristics but each is a powerful symbol of protection of people and place.

David's song of victory that is Psalm 18 uses the imagery of a fortress. He describes God, his Lord, as 'my defender', 'my protector', 'my strong fortress', 'my protection', 'a shield'. With him, David says, 'I am safe.'

In verses 4-6 David talks about death and destruction. What does he do? He calls to God for help.

Challenge

How do you view God? Is he your fortress in times of trouble? Do you recognise his protection of you? Do you find safety in his presence?

Pray

Thank God for his protection and pray for the protection of vulnerable people.

41

Thunder and lightning

Question time

🍃 Do you ever look out at night for the International Space Station?

🍃 What feelings cross your mind when you spot it?

Read Psalm 18:7-15

Comment

From the International Space Station astronauts get astonishing pictures of Planet Earth. One of the striking features, captured on camera by Tim Peake when he was on the ISS, is the number of lightning strikes that occur on Earth all the time. There can be as many as 100 lightning bolts striking the Earth's surface every second. That's about 8 million per day and 3 billion per year. Earth is a living globe of constant and violent activity. Thunder, lightning, volcanic eruptions, earthquakes and tsunamis bombard and shake the planet constantly.

David uses these verses to describe God in earth-quaking terminology. David lived and worked in one small part of the globe long before technology gave us colour images of Earth's wonders. He saw the stars and used his limited knowledge of the cosmos to describe what we now see on satellite images and through telescopes.

God's power is equal to all the power of the universe and David sees God using his divine authority to repel David's enemies and ensure David's safety.

Challenge and Encouragement

While we may marvel at the splendour and power of Earth and the cosmos, maybe we should take time to marvel, too, at the God of creation who, while overseeing and sustaining the universe, also has time to be concerned for individual human beings who recognise and are thankful for his care.

Pray

Thank you, Lord, for the universe, and for those explorers who show us more of your creation.

42

Rescued

Question time

🍃 Why are so many people drawn to the sea?

🍃 If you're one of them, what is it that you like so much about the sea?

Read Psalm 18:16-19

Comment

I have great admiration for the Royal National Lifeboat Institution. Their volunteers are ready to rush down to the local lifeboat and to put out to sea in order to rescue those who are in trouble. The RNLI has more than 350 lifeboats covering thousands of miles of coastline around the British Isles. The crews are available to protect and save, and are on call 24 hours a day all year round.

Similarly, God is there to protect and save his creation. His love and care for people is such that he is on call 24 hours a day, always there for us. (See verse 16.)

What deep waters do you find yourself in? We're in it up to our necks, as the saying goes, as a result of us all having sinned and fallen short of God's glory. And it was for this reason that Jesus came as the great rescuer, the Saviour. But even though we may have been saved from our sins by admitting our sins, believing in Jesus and committing our lives to him, we still find ourselves in deep waters from time to time, and in need of rescue.

Be encouraged

Next time you find yourself in deep waters, remember to call out for rescue. And the God of all time will be there for you.

Pray

For those in peril on the sea, and for rescuers.

43
Faithful

Question time

🍃 **Are you one of the following: a beaver, a gibbon, a wolf, a French angelfish, a swan, an albatross or a penguin?** If so, congratulations. It seems that you set up a partnership with your mate that lasts for life. Unfortunately, the likelihood of you being one of those creatures is nil if you're reading this.

Read Psalm 18:20-27

Comment

If you are married, what are your chances of being together for life? Statistics concerning divorce vary, but there may be up to 50 per cent of marriages that end in divorce. Good intentions on the wedding day, it seems, are not enough to guarantee a life-long partnership.

What about your relationship with God? God is faithful. His faithfulness to us doesn't waver. He isn't fickle. He isn't moody. He isn't unreliable.

He isn't devious. Indeed, in Lamentations 3:22, 23 we read that, 'The Lord's unfailing love and mercy still continue, fresh as the morning, as sure as the sunrise.' In Hebrews 13:8 we read that, 'Jesus Christ is the same yesterday, today, and forever.'

Challenge

In verse 25 of this psalm we read, 'O Lord, you are faithful to those who are faithful to you.' While you may have trouble being faithful in your human relationships, how are you at being faithful to God?

Pray

Faithful God, help me to keep faith with you and to be faithful to those to whom I'm committed.

44
Sure-footed

Question time

🍃 How sure-footed are you?

🍃 Do you easily trip up or overbalance?

Read Psalm 18:28-34

Comment

David, the shepherd, draws on his experiences of being out in nature's varied terrain, as he continues to describe his relationship with God. In verses 32 and 33 he writes about safe pathways and being as sure-footed as a deer. The Nubian ibex are some of the most sure-footed creatures in the world. They live safely in what, to most other creatures including humans, are some of the most inaccessible mountain habitats imaginable.

On three occasions I've climbed to the summit of Snowdon, the highest mountain in Wales. The first time, as a teenager, I was ill-prepared, more concerned about looking 'with it' as it was termed in those far-off days, than in wearing sensible boots and waterproofs. It's a miracle that I made it to the top and back down in safety. Subsequent summit bids were undertaken wearing good boots but I was still well aware of the care that needed to be taken. On those steep rocky mountainsides, you can spot mountain goats that negotiate with ease what humans find tricky.

Perfect and dependable is how David describes God. It isn't David's natural ability that keeps him sure-footed in his pilgrim journey on the rocky mountain path of life. It is God who keeps him upright and steadies his feet from slipping on the rocks.

Challenge

Will you let God help you to be sure-footed in your walk with him?

Pray

However challenging my path may be, Lord, please keep my feet firmly planted on your foundation so that I can walk safely.

45
Rebellion

Question time
- How turbulent has your life been?
- Were you a rebel teenager?
- Or a rebel adult?

Read Psalm 18:35-45

Comment

David had a turbulent life. He was the youngest son, worked as a shepherd, was chosen to be king – against all human odds – and had to deal with a rebellious family, rebellious people and his own errors of judgement. But he was ready to admit when he was wrong and to return and keep close to the God whom he always recognised as his Lord.

It's not easy for leaders in any situation to deal with rebellion. Political unrest, warring tribes, feuding families . . . What wisdom is needed! What tact and diplomacy! What dependence on God! And David, as king, did depend on God for help, encouragement, wisdom and guidance.

Challenge

Are you a rebel today? Do you need to learn humility – with God's help? We could all do with a good dose of grace.

Pray

For leaders: in nations, in government, in the church, in the family. And if you're a leader yourself, pray that you'll draw on God's wisdom.

46
Victorious

Question time

- Do you follow the fortunes (or otherwise) of your local football team or your favourite tennis star?
- Do you wave the appropriate flag, wear the T-shirt, go to matches?
- Is your voice the loudest when there's victory?
- Do you cheer on the terraces or from your armchair?

Read Psalm 18:46-50

Comment

We all love it when we win a game. It may not be sport; it could be a board game at home with your children: Scrabble; Snakes and Ladders; Trivial Pursuit; Snap. Or maybe you've been battling an addiction to alcohol or smoking, and a small achievement – a day without a drink or a cigarette – can seem a victory.

David had been battling with his enemies. The former king Saul was jealous of David's popularity and hounded him. David eventually won the battles. But this long psalm focuses a great deal on God. Verse 46 shows us that David recognised God as the saviour. It was God who'd won the victory. The result is praise. Not praise for David or by David for himself, but praise of God. David was in a privileged position as king but never took it for granted.

Challenge

How much do we acknowledge God as our saviour in the little battles of life as well as the big battles?

Pray

For those who use bullying tactics to win victories – whether at home, at work or in the church.

47

Heaven's glory

Question time

- Do you walk along, looking at the pavement?
- How often do you look up at the sky?

Read Psalm 19:1-6

Comment

I was in the choir at secondary school. To say the choir was mediocre is to be kind. But on one occasion we sang, 'The Heavens Are Telling' from Haydn's *Creation*. As choral music goes, it's a relatively easy four-part harmony to sing. And we made a reasonable fist of it. It gave me great pleasure, not just to be capable of reading and singing the alto part, but because of its joyous melody and grand words.

In this psalm we have one of the great declarations of the bright goodness of the created universe. This morning I was out early with my camera for the sunrise. The sky was shot through with aircraft trails, pink with the, as yet unseen, shining sun that was still below the horizon. As I stood on the frosted grass with chilly fingers waiting to press the shutter, the orb of the sun began to appear. The heavens do, indeed, tell the glory of God. Let's never ever take the wonder of the sky for granted.

Be encouraged

If it's sunny with you today, spend a bit of time just marvelling at the light, warmth and glory of the sun. And if it's a grey, miserable day, remember that behind that greyness, the sun still declares God's glory to someone, somewhere in the world. And soon it will declare itself to you once more.

Pray

With your eyes open as you look at the sky. Use the sky as a visual aid for praise.

48
Words

Question time

🍃 Which words would you use to describe God's word – and words?

Read Psalm 19:7-14

Comment

Words are my work. My first English lesson at secondary school was a surprise. The teacher swept into the classroom and said, 'I'd like you to write down everything that has happened since you came in here.' Well nothing had happened. But I ended up writing my first piece of truly creative writing. It was a revelation to me and the start of the pleasurable pursuit of putting pencil to paper.

David's outburst of sunburst has given way to talking about words: God's words and his own words. He describes God's guidelines for living as: perfect, strengthening, trustworthy, full of wisdom, just, mind-blowing, desirable, and enlightening.

That's some list. And then he talks about himself, confessing his shortcomings and asking for release from sinfulness.

Challenge

The last two verses are used by preachers before sermons. But they are equally important for each of us who claims to belong to God. 'May *my* words and *my* thoughts be acceptable to you, O Lord . . .' As a writer, it's a prayer I need to pray each time my fingers curl over the keyboard, but also to pray them for my everyday life as I speak to others, whether in conversation or in preaching and teaching. Look again at the descriptive list David has for God's words and apply them to *your* words.

Pray

The words of verse 14 for yourself and then pray them for Christian writers.

Blessings

49

Question time

🍃 **What do you want in life?**

Read Psalm 20:1-5

Comment

'I want . . .' a child might say to an adult. And the adult, if she's trying to teach her child, will say, 'Now ask properly.' And the child will say, 'Can I have . . . ?' And the parent will say, 'You *can*, but that's still not the proper way to ask!' 'Please may I . . . ?' Ah, that's better.

Each phrase in these verses starts with, 'May. . .' And what a delightful psalm of blessing it is. Wouldn't you like to say this to a friend or a relative? It's a wonderful thing when we realise that someone else is blessing us with God-wishes. There may be little we can do to help someone, other than to be a listener, sitting quietly with that person, offering companionship rather than advice. And that's often enough. We might be able to offer a prayer or blessing, such as this, or the wonderful priestly prayer found in the book of Numbers 6:24-26:

> May the Lord bless you and take care of you;
> may the Lord be kind and gracious to you;
> may the Lord look on you with favour and
> give you peace.

Challenge

Is there someone you could bless today with God's word?

Pray

God's blessing on someone you might not choose to bless!

50

Trust

Question time

In what, or whom, do you put your trust?

Read Psalm 20:6-9

Comment

Horses were used in war for centuries. David mentions them here. Since then they were used frequently in medieval times and, more recently, in World War 1. Today's war-chariots are tanks and other armoured vehicles that can travel swiftly and have deadly powers to be unleashed by operators on the enemy.

Nearer to home, perhaps, are the weapons used by individuals, gangs and terrorists: guns and knives. Crimes using these weapons are on the increase and many people, including children, carry the weapons as trusted 'war-chariots' and 'horses' to use in attack and in defence.

Maybe you carry a knife or a gun – just in case. My cousin was killed accidentally by a gun going off in his workplace. What we think we can trust is not always the case.

David, the shepherd with a sling, the king with sovereign power, the soldier with armour, puts his trust in none of these human things, but in the power of 'the Lord our God'.

Ironically, perhaps, the United States of America's motto is 'In God We Trust'. How many Americans truly believe that, I wonder? And what about you and me?

Challenge

Do you trust God rather than human inventions and powers?

Pray

For local, national and world leaders.

51
Royal humility

Question time
How important is status?

Read Psalm 21:1-6

Comment

Wealth, status, fame, are put aside here by David. He gladly acknowledges all that he has: strength, victory, his heart's desire, answered prayer, blessings, a crown, life, glory, fame, majesty, joy . . . BUT he doesn't say, 'Aren't I the clever one, who's achieved all this!' No. The focus is on God the giver. Notice how many times David addresses God directly: 'O Lord', 'You gave . . .', 'You made . . .', 'You have given . . .', 'You have answered . . .', 'You came . . .', 'You set . . .', 'You gave . . .', 'Your help . . .', 'You have given . . .', 'Your blessings . . .', 'Your presence . . .'.

Another sovereign, Queen Elizabeth II, is known for her faith in God. She lives in a palace, has great wealth, and is known the world over. And yet her humility is Christ-like; indeed she talks of following Jesus' example of servanthood. How does she manage that? Through her faith in the steadfast love and steadfast faithfulness of God.

The Queen is, arguably, the most famous woman in the world, but she is not one who seeks personal glory but God's glory. The chosen king, David, recognises from where his blessings come.

Challenge

Consider where your blessings come from. Think of incidents that you could preface with some of David's words to God. 'You gave me a roof over my head . . .', 'You made me the person I am . . .' and so on.

Pray

For those who have been given royal authority on earth.

52
Royal praise

Question time

🍃 On a scale of 1 to 10, how much do you trust God to help you overcome difficulties?

Read Psalm 21:7-13

Comment

Sometimes we face almost impossibly difficult tasks. For me as a child, it was solving sums. I found maths very hard and, however much I tried, my brain didn't seem to be wired to cope with numbers.

For this reason I was sceptical about the verse in Philippians 4:13 which, in the King James Version reads, 'I can do all things through Christ which strengtheneth me.' I thought, oh no I can't. I can't do sums and there are plenty of others things I can't do, with or without Christ.

Paul was writing about various hardships he'd been through on his missionary travels. The difficulties hadn't always gone away but he'd learned to live with whatever situation he found himself in. The Good News Translation reads, 'I have the strength to face all conditions by the power that Christ gives me.' I didn't necessarily have to get my sums right; indeed, more often than not, I got them wrong! With hindsight I see that God has given me strength to face all sorts of situations that I would otherwise have thought impossible to get through.

Challenge

David faced battles – physical, mental and spiritual – at different stages of his life. But in verse 13 he's able to praise God for God's strength and power, when his own has not been so evident. Can you do the same?

Pray

That God's strength and power will prevail in the world and in your life.

53
Abandoned

Question time

- Have you ever felt abandoned?
- What were the circumstances?

Read Psalm 22:1-5

Comment

The little girl didn't understand. Why had Daddy gone away? Why wasn't he coming back? Was he cross with her? Was that why he'd left? Who would help her with her maths homework? Who would mend her bike? Who would take her to the theme park? Who would give her a piggy-back? Would she ever see Daddy again?

Can there be anything more chilling, more upsetting, more frightening, than when the person who means most to you leaves you? David cries out in anguish to God (verse 1).

Jesus quoted this verse when he was on the cross. He'd been tortured, then crucified. It took hours for him to die, during which time he was in agony.

Even the natural elements shared his darkness. Darkness fell on Jerusalem from noon till three o'clock in the afternoon. At three o'clock Jesus shouted, 'My God, my God, why have you abandoned me?' (Matthew 27:46). Shortly afterwards he died. Yet, in a poignant moment immediately before death came, Jesus called out again, 'Father! In your hands I place my spirit' (Luke 23:46). The father/son relationship hadn't been severed. When we cry out, fearing that God has abandoned us, has turned deaf, has turned his back on us, we must hold on. Those last words of Jesus give us hope.

Be encouraged

There are times when God seems to have gone for good, but he hasn't. He doesn't leave us.

Pray

Be still and listen for God's peace and presence then pray for those who feel abandoned by God.

54
Bullied

Question time
Have you ever been bullied, or has your child?
Think how it made you feel.

Read Psalm 22:6-8

Comment
'Nobody loves me, everybody hates me; think I'll go and eat worms. Big fat juicy ones, long thin skinny ones, see how they wriggle and squirm.' Did you learn that rhyme as a child? Children love funny rhymes, many of which are nonsensical, but some touch on truth.

Is there an element of self-pity in today's verses, worms and all? If so, it's understandable. David is feeling down. *Everyone* has abandoned him. That's what it can feel like when even a few people are rotten to you. Think of situations where you have felt alone and abandoned, when everyone seems to turn their backs on you, where bullying has replaced kindness, mockery has replaced compassion and you feel you're slogging on without help.

In verse 8 we might spot elements of the Devil's tempting of Jesus in the wilderness. The wilderness or desert is bleak and stark, a place of drought with burning sun during the day and the chill of dark nights.

Challenge

Whatever your desert place might be, whoever has forsaken you, whatever your circumstances of aloneness, how can you deal with it without slumping into self-pity?

Tomorrow's reading may help . . .

Pray

For bullies and those who are bullied.

55
Dependence

Question time

How might the 'long view' help when you feel abandoned?

Read Psalm 22:9-11

Comment

There's a robust bit in Handel's *Messiah* where members of the chorus sing, 'He trusted in God that he would deliver him.' It comes in Part 2, the sober section where Jesus' purpose in entering our world as a human being is fulfilled. It doesn't make for pretty reading or joyful singing. Rather it reminds us of how much Jesus went through on behalf of us. We hear that he was despised, that he bore our griefs, that all who saw him laughed him to scorn. And then we have this chorus, 'He trusted in God.' But did God let him down? Does God let us down?

From the misery of yesterday's section, David moves on in verses 9 and 10. He starts with a cry of anguish and changes tack to praise God.

Glance back to verses 4 and 5: 'Our ancestors put their trust in you . . . They trusted you, and were not disappointed.'

Be encouraged

Hang on in there in the face of opposition and bullying. Depend on the dependable God.

Pray

For adults in abusive relationships and for children who are bullied at school.

56
Bulls, lions and dogs

Question time

What animals do you find menacing? Why?

Read Psalm 22:12-21

Comment

Bullying bulls, lip-licking lions, destructive dogs. What an unhappy picture of attack on a desperate man.

A favourite Saturday afternoon pastime when I was a child was a walk to the local farm. Dairy cows grazed quietly in the fields, pigs squealed in their sties, and the ring-nosed bull stood behind secure metal fencing, and stared belligerently. A sign read, 'Beware of the bull'. Bulls are potential killers and need to be treated with caution. They are heavy but quick – faster than a human – and can be unpredictable. Best avoided.

It's courting trouble to get too near a lion too. Hilaire Belloc's cautionary tale, *Jim, who ran away from his nurse, and was eaten by a lion,* says it all! And, sadly, we hear too often about dangerous dogs whose destructive jaws have killed children.

David's vivid animal pictures describe his physical, mental and spiritual state. His whole being was affected by those who had turned against him. Here is a picture too of Jesus and his aloneness as he took on the sins of the world. Verse 18 reminds us of the soldiers who gambled for Jesus' clothes.

Challenge

Spend a bit of time thinking about how these words might apply to David, to Jesus and to yourself, and ask God for his presence in times of trouble.

Pray

For the livelihood and well-being of farmers in uncertain times.

57
The bigger picture

Question time

How easy do you find it to face the bigger picture of life when troubles come your way?

Read Psalm 22:22-26

Comment

I made the mistake of eating a Mars bar on my way to a visit to the midwife, shortly before my daughter was born. When the midwife did the routine tests my blood sugar level had shot up and she was concerned. I had to confess my energy-boosting snack.

Blood sugar levels are best when they're level rather than resembling a sine wave of monstrous proportions that would alarm a sailor on a stormy sea. My blood sugar settled down after a few hours. Did I learn from the experience? Temporarily. My lifestyle and life sometimes resemble ocean waves rather than a mill pond. What about our spiritual life? Do we depend on quick bursts of spiritual intake, or do we have a steady absorption of God's food through study of his word each day?

This psalm is a wave of severe ups and downs, a mixture of alarm and despondency followed by peace and hope. David is back on course here, his troubles set aside, as he announces to God – with determination – how he will share God's goodness with people. Look at the words he uses of God: praise, honour, worship.

Challenge

When troubles smack you in the face, are you able to turn your cries of worry into cries of worship? Is there a way of keeping the stormy sea more tranquil, the levels more stable – and level?

Pray

For steadiness when alarmed or in adversity, and praise God for his goodness.

58
Global testimony

Question time

- Do you want to save the world – from issues concerning climate change, use of plastic, deforestation, poverty, injustice, war . . . ?

- We can feel pretty helpless. What can one person do?

Read Psalm 22:27-31

Comment

God wants us to be good stewards of his world and he has placed each of us where we live to do our small part in helping to manage our environment more effectively.

Nobody but Jesus the Saviour can save the world from its greatest evil: sin. His death and resurrection enable us to have a restored relationship with God. But what should be our part in enabling 'the whole world' to turn to God? Modern technology means that more people can hear the good news of Jesus than ever before, but there are still many millions who have not yet heard the name of Jesus. How can you be God's ambassador where you are?

David speaks in verse 31 of the whole world turning to the Lord. Part 2 of *Messiah* starts with, 'Behold the Lamb of God that taketh away the sin of the world', goes on with the sober facts of how that happened, but ends with the mighty, triumphant 'Hallelujah!' chorus.

Be encouraged

God is the one who is in control of his world and one day all people will recognise him for who he is.

Pray

That the word of God may spread to all people.

59
Shepherd's goodness

Question time

What qualities and skills do shepherds have today and how are they the same or different from David's time?

Read Psalm 23:1-6

Comment

Imagine you're a sheep . . . You have a quiet life in the fields with plenty of grass to munch and a stream from which to drink. In summer months you venture further afield, up mountains to wander more freely, picking your way along narrow paths, sometimes encountering people – around whom you're a bit nervous. Occasionally you find yourself stuck – on a ledge, or in a ditch, or caught up in a spiky bush. The shepherd comes with his helpers: a couple of black and white collies. He has his shepherd's stick with him too. He speaks to you, gently. You don't panic.

You know him. You know he has your best interests at heart. He provides for you, he protects you, he patches you up when you're hurting. You feel safe in his care.

A soldier, about to go on his first tour to Afghanistan, asked a senior officer for advice: 'Carry the twenty-third psalm with you.' The soldier wrote it out on a tiny piece of paper, covered it with plastic to protect it, and kept it in his pocket throughout his six months' tour.

When my father was dying, he frequently asked me to read this psalm to him. He faced the deepest darkness, the valley of the shadow of death, with courage and at peace because he knew that God's goodness and love would be with him and that God's house would be his home forever.

Be encouraged

Reread the psalm and see how each phrase is a positive affirmation of God's presence with you.

Pray

For shepherds and thank God for Jesus' role as the good shepherd.

60
Foundations

Question time

🍃 What foundations have you laid down for your life?

Read Psalm 24:1, 2

Comment

My parents once bought a new house. Their first viewing of it was simply a piece of paper with a scale plan of its layout. They had to use their imagination to work out what it might look like when the builders had actually constructed it as a 3D dwelling. The plot of land was a sea of mud and looked totally unpromising as a suitable place to build. But trenches were scooped out of the gloop, and concrete poured in to lay good foundations. From the foundations a house was built and my parents turned the house into a home.

David, in Psalm 24, describes in a couple of sentences, the building of the world by God. It is God's world, not ours. We, as God's creation, belong to him. It is he who lays the foundation for life and, if we're wise, we build our lives on the foundation that is Jesus Christ. Remember the story Jesus told of the wise man and the foolish man and their house-building?

In Colossians 2:7 Paul urges Christian believers to: 'Keep your roots deep in him (Jesus Christ), build your lives on him and become stronger in your faith.'

Challenge

Do you acknowledge God as the builder of the universe and do you build your life on his Son, Jesus Christ?

Pray

For housing developers, builders, home owners and landlords.

61

Purity

Question time

🍃 Ask yourself the questions in verse 3.

Read Psalm 24:3-6

Comment

Once David has acknowledged the greatness of the God of the universe and God's ownership of the world, he asks two questions (see verse 3). The psalm was probably sung as King David and the people ascended the hill on which Jerusalem was built, taking the ark of the covenant with them. You can read the story in 2 Samuel 6:12-15, 17.

Imagine the joy and excitement as David and his people approached Jerusalem. Imagine them singing this psalm as they got closer to the holy place. It was important that they remembered the Almighty God whom they would worship and they needed to prepare their hearts and minds.

At a Sunday school anniversary, I once had to recite verse 4 in the King James Version of this psalm. I was about 8 years old and, when it came to my turn to stand on the platform, I trotted out the words parrot-fashion: 'He that hath clean hands, and a pure heart; who hath not lifted up his soul unto vanity, nor sworn deceitfully.' I hadn't a clue what it meant, apart from the washing hands bit. It was years before I realised the importance of preparing my heart for worship of the Almighty God. One of the strengths of the Anglican communion liturgy is the opportunity for confession at the start of the service.

Challenge

How might you prepare for church this Sunday?

Pray

When I approach your table, merciful Lord, may I be mindful of my own shortcomings, but also mindful of your grace and mercy.

62
Triumphal entry

Question time
Which sporting events do you enjoy watching?

Read Psalm 24:7-10

Comment

When you watch a great sporting event, the chances are that there'll be some sort of fanfare or the playing of national anthems, pyrotechnic displays and a lot of razzamatazz to celebrate the occasion. At the ATP World Tour Finals in London in recent years, the lights are dimmed and a thumping heartbeat is broadcast around the arena as the tennis players enter.

Here in Jerusalem the excitement is mounting as the people ascend still further. David and the people believed God was with them and that he, the great and everlasting King, needed space to enter. So, fling wide the gates, open the ancient doors. Let the King in.

The God of the universe! The King of glory! We can put sporting celebrities on a pedestal but their prowess doesn't last for ever. They are mere mortals and their careers as sportsmen and women are often over in their late twenties or thirties. Not so with God who is from everlasting to everlasting.

Challenge

Think of the way you cheer a sports team or an individual sportsperson. Do you show the same enthusiasm for God? Do you sing at the top of your voice to him? Do you worship him with a pure heart and wholeheartedly?

Pray

Spend time worshipping God now.

63

Teach me!

Question time

- What have you been taught to do?
- Read, write, tie your shoelaces, play a musical instrument, spin a cricket ball, spot the stars in the night sky . . . ?

Read Psalm 25:1-7

Comment

We need people to teach us skills, to give us knowledge and to enable us to live full and useful lives. I've been taught basic skills on a computer but my grandchildren have been taught more – and are much less scared and far more capable than I am!

The king of Israel asks the King of the universe to teach him. David knew more about shepherding than I shall ever know; he knew how to play the harp which is something I don't know how to do. He knew how to lead people. But he wanted God to teach him . . . what? In verses 4 and 5 he puts it clearly. 'Teach me your ways . . .', 'Teach me to live according to your truth . . .'

When Jesus was with his disciples he told them, 'I am the way, the truth and the life' (John 14:6).

Challenge

Do you ask God to teach you his ways, to teach you about Jesus? Do you ask God to show you Jesus the Truth? Are you teachable or do you think you know it all? We all need to be taught God's ways, to know Jesus better. Who is your teacher of God's ways? Your church leader? A good Christian friend? God's word, the Bible?

Pray

Lord, make me teachable. Help me to want to learn. May those who teach me about you be filled with your wisdom and clarity to convey your truths to me.

64
Friendship

Question time

🍃 Think of your closest friends. What attracts you to them?

Read Psalm 25:8-14

Comment

I've seen the Queen at Windsor Castle, I've seen her on television, I've been to her house: Buckingham Palace, I've written letters to her, but I couldn't honestly say that she's my friend. Yet here we are, in this lovely psalm, finding that the Lord 'is the friend of those who obey him and he affirms his covenant with them'. The King of glory wants to be my friend and, thanks to my faith in his Son, Jesus, is my friend.

Pause. Take that in!

Why would God want to teach us and be our friend? Because he is righteous and good, faithful and loving. He longs for a close relationship with his created people, each one. He teaches us the way we should go, he teaches us his will.

In John 14:23, 24, Jesus told his disciples, 'Whoever loves me will obey my teaching . . . The teaching you have heard is not mine, but comes from the Father, who sent me.' He continued in the following chapter, verses 14 and 15, by saying, 'You are my friends if you do what I command you . . . I call you friends, because I have told you everything I have heard from my Father.' And as he was about to go to the cross when he said these words, he went on to assure his concerned disciples that the Holy Spirit would come to be their guide, companion, friend and teacher.

Be encouraged

That the Lord is the friend of those who obey him.

Pray

For your friends and ask God that you'll reflect his friendship as you befriend others.

Your ways

Question time

Who do you trust? Why?

Read Psalm 25:15-22

Comment

David has another wobble. Despite looking to God 'at all times' he admits he feels lonely and weak. He seeks God's ways but reminds God that he's not always very confident.

Jesus said that God's way is a narrow path but one that leads to life. That's what David aimed for and he continued to trust God to lead him in the right way, whatever the circumstances. Horace, the Roman poet who lived from 65–8BC said, 'When things are steep, remember to stay level-headed.' How do we do that?

In Hebrews 12:2 we read, 'Let us keep our eyes fixed on Jesus, on whom our faith depends from beginning to end.' Determination and perseverance in the face of adversity are needed.

Be encouraged

By God's continuing presence and that we can go to him for safety when we're worried or in danger or are fearful.

Pray

Bring your concerns to God now in prayer. Meditate on his word and rest in his presence. Then thank God for his continuing faithfulness to you.

66

Desires

Question time

- Do you have a bucket list – things you want to do, places you want to see, stuff you want to acquire – while you have breath in your body to enjoy them?
- Perhaps you want to meet your favourite broadcaster, actor, football hero?
- Maybe you fancy going to the Grand Canyon, Antarctica, the Moon?
- Or perhaps you'd just like more money, or a baby, or a partner, or an original work of art?

Read Psalm 26:1-5

Comment

While Jesus said he came so that we could have a full life, I'm not sure he meant for us to necessarily have all that we desire in the way of stuff! His was a life of servanthood – of thinking of others, of total selflessness.

So in this psalm David invites God to test his motives, to examine his desires and thoughts. David's aim is to please God, to acknowledge God's love and faithfulness – and then to live accordingly.

You may be fortunate to have many of the things and to have visited many of the places that other people long to do but haven't had the chance to do. You may be someone who has always had enough money to live a prosperous life.

Challenge

Whatever your circumstances, think how you will balance living for God and living a full life.

Pray

That God will help you to discern which of your desires are honouring to him.

67
Glory

Question time

🍃 **How many hymns could you name that have the word 'glory' in them?** To God be the glory; Glorious things of thee are spoken; Glory, glory, hallelujah; Glory to the King of kings . . . And in the Anglican church the 'Gloria' is sung or said at every Communion service as part of the worship of Almighty God who is worthy to receive honour, glory and praise.

Read Psalm 26:6-12

Comment

In these verses we see David actively worshipping. This is no passive eyes front, stand rigid, mumble a whispery hymn, sit down, look bored, worshipper. David washes his hands, marches in worship, sings a hymn of thanksgiving, tells of God's wonderful deeds. He's thrilled to be in God's house; he loves going to church! Why? Because he is aware of God's glorious presence in that place of worship.

I sometimes visit my nearest cathedral very early in the morning when nobody else is there. It's a peaceful place for silent prayer and a place to meditate on the glory of God. But in verse 12 David shows us that it's good to worship God with other people. Corporate worship when all can sing praises to God, when everyone together can unite in enjoying the awesome glory of God.

Challenge

How might you need to change your attitude to worship and to seeing the glory of God?

Pray

For places of worship and for those who maintain the buildings for worship.

68

Light and salvation

Question time

> Who or what is the light of your life?

Read Psalm 27:1-6

Comment

David's theme of glory continues in this psalm. The Lord is described as light and salvation. It's a personal recognition. The Lord is *my* light and *my* salvation. It's a wonderful thing to be able to say that of the creator of the universe. The words are a foretaste of Christ himself who came as the Light of the world and as the Saviour.

This morning's sunrise was a surprise. The sky had been cloudy overnight but a little break in the cloud revealed Venus and then the sky cleared in the east and the most glorious dawn was revealed. We enjoy the light of the sun rising to shine on us.

How much more do we enjoy the Light of the world shining on us?

If you're stuck and injured on a mountainside, there's no greater joy than hearing the whirr of the rescue helicopter's blades or the reassuring voice of the person who's come to save you. How much more do you welcome the Lord as your Saviour?

Challenge

Can you truly say, as David did, 'The Lord is my light and my salvation'?

Pray

For those who are going through dark times, that they may see the light of Christ and know his saving presence.

69

Parental care

Question time

- If you have parents, what do they mean to you?
- If you no longer have parents, can you remember any of their special qualities?

Read Psalm 27:7-10

Comment

When my father was dying, he asked for this psalm to be read to him. The words of Psalm 27, along with those of Psalm 23, were a great comfort to him as he got closer to his heavenly home where he would 'live in the Lord's house all my life' (verse 4). It was something of an irony, therefore, for me to read verse 10: 'My father and mother may abandon me, but the Lord will take care of me.'

There was a role reversal between parent and child. The parent who had imparted love and wisdom on me, was now in a position of helplessness where I was being the adult and he the child. And I felt a sense of abandonment when he died and went to be at home with the Lord.

David's emphasis is on praise. Whatever our circumstances or the circumstances of our loved ones, we can be assured of God's continuing care. Ultimately it is the all-loving, totally reliable, ever-present God the Father who is our parent.

Be encouraged

Jesus and his Father were one. They communicated with each other and the care for each other spilled over into their care for every human being who's ever lived. If, like me, you no longer have an earthly father, be assured of your heavenly Father's care for you.

Pray

For those who have been bereaved of a parent.

70

This present life

Question time

🍃 Can you think of an example of God's goodness to you in recent days?

Read Psalm 27:11-14

Comment

Ellie had been ill for months. She had just turned thirty and wasn't expected to see her thirty-first birthday. Knowing that she was soon to die, she took time and effort – and it was a huge effort as she was very weak – to plan her funeral service. Plenty of uplifting music, hymns of praise to God for the life she'd been given, prayers of thankfulness and prayers for those who would grieve for her, and . . . Psalm 27 with its expression of confidence in God, a delight in the presence of God, and trust that God would take care of her.

When Ellie died, many people turned up for the funeral and marvelled when this psalm was read out. Ellie's had been a short life, but a life lived with God and for God.

'I know that I will live to see the Lord's goodness in this present life. Trust in the Lord. Have faith, do not despair. Trust in the Lord' (verses 13 and 14).

Ellie had been realistic about pain and discomfort but knew that God was there with her in it, helping her to live through it and then to live on with him in eternity for ever.

Be encouraged
See verse 13 and say it aloud.

Pray
Father God, my light and my salvation, my shelter, my parent and my Lord, help me to trust you today and each day that you give me.

71

Deception

Question time

- Do you ever speak ill of someone behind their back?
- Do you have a friendly conversation with a person but harbour unkind thoughts about them in your heart?

Read Psalm 28:1-5

Comment

In yet another call for help on David's part, he asks God not to condemn him for his frustration and fear. He is particularly concerned about the deceptive nature of some of his enemies: those who appear and sound friendly, but have hatred for him – and perhaps, also, hatred for God – in their hearts.

It's not David's place to judge other people. Samuel, God's agent in choosing David as future king, had to be reminded that God doesn't judge by outward appearances or spoken words but on what someone is like on the inside: their thoughts, their true feelings, their real character. David was chosen to be king against all human odds; he was the youngest boy in the family and a mere shepherd. David pleads with God to bring judgement on those who persecute him so much. He vents his feelings vociferously. But then allows the Almighty to do his work in dealing with people with justice.

Challenge

When people treat you badly, how do you react? How could you turn your frustration and fear into something positive?

Pray

Help me, Lord, to be honest in my words and actions with other people.

72
Shepherd's care

Question time

🍃 How much do you depend on another human being – your parent, spouse, friend?

🍃 And how much do you depend on God?

Read Psalm 28:6-9

Comment

After the stormy outburst comes a sense of calm. David praises God for listening to him, he trusts God, acknowledges God's presence and help in his life – and is glad. So glad that he sings for joy!

In the last sentence of this psalm David recalls his days as a shepherd. He is aware of all that he did in his youth to look after his sheep. He protected them day and night, he gave them shelter, he dealt with predators that would harm the sheep, he led them to streams of water, to grass on which to feed. He looked after his sheep. And he can think of no better analogy than to consider the Lord as his shepherd.

Jesus came as the Good Shepherd who was willing to die for his sheep. He knows his sheep, as David knew his sheep. But Jesus' sheep are you and me.

Be encouraged

Spend some time thinking about Jesus as your shepherd and the ways in which he cares for you.

Pray

That those who don't yet know God may be drawn to him because of his loving care.

73
God's voice

Question time

- What 'voices' are the loudest in your daily life?
- Traffic noise, 'music' in shops, arguments on TV soaps, raised voices in your own family, the constant whirr of computers?

Read Psalm 29:1-11

Comment

3000 years ago the psalmist had none of those noises – apart, perhaps from brotherly tiffs in his family when he was growing up. And the sounds of battle. How do we hear the voice of God above the noise of twenty-first century daily living? David describes some of the ways in which the God of creation uses his voice in nature: thunder, the sound of the sea, the wind through the trees, earthquakes, lightning, the movement of desert sand, the autumn fall of leaves from the trees, and so on. And we do well to 'hear' the voice of God through nature.

Above the clamour of today, let's ensure that we take time to listen to the still, small voice as Elijah had to do. Elijah had had a horrendous time with opposition from King Ahab and Queen Jezebel. He had periods of depression and fear. On one occasion he'd gone to sleep in a cave when God woke him up and demonstrated who was in charge of the world and had all things in his control. The Lord himself. The Lord sent a furious wind, an earthquake, a fire. And then came the voice of God that Elijah needed to hear: the soft whisper of a voice. God's voice.

Challenge

Make time today to listen for the soft whisper of God.

Pray

That God will make you more aware of his presence in the world of nature.

74

Sadness and gladness

Question time

🍃 Do you know someone who is going through a period of deep sadness at the moment?

Read Psalm 30:1-5

Comment

10-year-old Charlie deliberately scratched a line along the side of his dad's car, with his penknife. Dad was furious when he saw the damaged car. Charlie knew he'd done wrong and that he deserved to be on the receiving end of Dad's anger. And he was. He said he was sorry and spent the next few months owing his pocket money to Dad for repairs to the car. Dad's anger abated long before those months were up. Indeed, the anger was put aside at bedtime, Dad not wanting to take his anger into the night and another day.

Have a look at verse 5. The Lord's anger. It only lasts for a moment! The Lord's goodness lasts for a lifetime. How wonderful that is. And how much we need to remember that when tears flow in the night.

God has every reason to be angry with human beings who flout his rules for living, rules that were given to enhance rather than restrict life. We read of his anger but it is momentary; his goodness is constant and forever. God is gracious, merciful and loving.

Be encouraged

Are you feeling fragile at the moment? God knows our personalities; he knows our future. Whatever the reason for your tearful night, be encouraged that, thanks to God, joy comes in the morning.

Pray

For friends whose tears are flowing at night.

75
Fear and favour

Question time

🍃 Do you fear being cut off from God?

🍃 Are you afraid of death?

Read Psalm 30:6–10

Comment

Judges have a tough job, particularly if there has been a lot of publicity surrounding the arrest and impending trial of a well-known person. They have to be without fear or favour, not influenced by any consideration of the people involved in a situation or any external influence.

It is reassuring to know that God is the righteous judge of all the earth. David, having expressed praise in the first few verses of the psalm, had a moment of self-belief followed by self-doubt, of trust followed by fear (see verses 6 and 7). In fairness to David, in verse 7 he admits that it is God who has protected him in the past rather than his own prowess. But, like cloud cover hiding the sun, David felt cut off from God and became afraid. He calls out for help and begs God to look on him with favour and be merciful to him.

Are there times when you are afraid? Do you try and soldier on in your own strength or do you rest in God – even when he seems to be hidden?

Be encouraged

God is fair and, though we may have trials in this world, he will ensure that all things will be well.

Pray

For police officers, magistrates, judges and all who work to uphold justice and alleviate fear.

76

Dance for joy

Question time

🍃 How are your dancing skills?

Read Psalm 30:11, 12

Comment

When my granddaughter was 3 she was the innkeeper's wife in her preschool Nativity. My daughter captured the event in a video on her phone. The little girl was singing at the top of her voice and swaying and moving her whole body in time to the music. Perhaps it was because she'd watched her dad take part in a local Strictly Come Dancing competition and it had inspired her to sing and dance for joy. She had no inhibitions and was completely rapt by the occasion.

In 2 Samuel 6 we read how David danced before the altar of the Lord, much to his wife's disgust. David's explanation was simple: 'I was dancing to honour the Lord' (verse 21). God appreciates true worship, however it's expressed.

The tears expressed in verse 5 of Psalm 30 have stopped flowing and David is filled once again with joy. Morning has dawned. And David's joy is expressed in dance and song. However long our 'night' may be, there will come a time when the light of day floods your soul again. Will you relax and say, 'Phew! Thank God that ghastly darkness is over!' or will you take it further and express your heartfelt thanks to God in exuberant praise and thanksgiving, maybe even doing a little dance?

Be encouraged
Play some dance music and bop for God.

Pray
For your inhibitions to disappear as you praise God wholeheartedly and whole-bodily.

77
Shelter

Question time

- Which charities do you support?
- Do any of them work for providing shelter for homeless people?

Read Psalm 31:1-8

Comment

I grew up in a typical suburban semi-detached house; nothing special in itself but a safe and secure family home that gave shelter from the elements and was a happy haven to which to return after a day out in the world.

Later I worked in London where homelessness was an issue. It still is. Agencies like Shelter and London City Mission provide a roof over homeless heads, hot meals, showers, clothing, support and care.

David asks God for shelter and places himself in God's care. Most of us live in communities where we can look out for one another's interests.

All of us, at different times, need shelter from danger, a refuge of protection, safety from traps. Needs vary. Loneliness, addiction, disability . . . Let's each play our part in showing godly compassion and care.

Challenge

Are there ways in which you can act in a godly way to offer shelter to those who have none? Maybe there's a charity in your town that works to offer shelter and food. Could you be a volunteer on God's behalf?

Pray

For charity workers who provide for those who need shelter.

78
Weak bones

Question time

How does tiredness affect you physically and mentally?

Read Psalm 31:9, 10

Comment

Osteoporosis is a debilitating and wasting disease of the bones. Instead of solid-looking bones, scans may reveal bones to look more like a randomly patterned piece of lace. Today there are medications that can be taken to improve bone structure but sometimes it's too late and pain and immobility may result from the disease.

David's troubles are such that his whole being is wearing out. His eyes are tired; he feels worn out and exhausted and believes his life to be shortening because of his problems. The weakness has seeped right through his body to his bones that are wasting away.

As someone diagnosed with osteoporosis, I have much sympathy with David. Whether his bone disease was real isn't clear but if it was, then there was little that could be done three thousand years ago to alleviate the disease. Maybe he was so down that his whole body ached in sympathy to his mental and spiritual state. Either way, he does the right thing; he calls out to God for mercy.

Challenge

How might focusing on God help us in our physical and mental anguish?

Pray

For doctors making diagnoses, and for patients receiving treatment for osteoporosis.

Whispers

Question time

- Have you ever been on the receiving end of whispers?
- Or have you initiated whispers?

Read Psalm 31:11-18

Comment

When you feel low, you feel the whole world is against you. Nothing is right. Everyone has the appearance of being an enemy. And when you know people are whispering about you, it can be very isolating and you can become paranoid. Have you ever known such isolation? It smacks of playground bullying, of workplace ostracism, even of church 'cliquiness'.

David was king. You might think he would be treated with respect and honour. But the kingdom was surrounded by incursions from neighbouring tribes and there were continual battles that David had to face. Sadly, the Middle East today is also a place of unrest, division and hatred.

Despite the wearisome cycle of battles, David shares his feelings with the God who put him on the throne. In verse 16 he refers to himself as 'your servant' which reminds us of the servant king who was to come a thousand years later and would face the ultimate battle of the sins of the world.

Be encouraged

'Hail to the Lord's Anointed, great David's greater Son! Hail in the time appointed, his reign on earth begun! He comes to break oppression, to set the captive free; to take away transgression, and rule in equity.'

Pray

Thank God for this hymn by James Montgomery (1771-1854) and for Jesus, the servant king and saviour.

80

Courage

Question time

- Is there a time when you have needed to show courage?
- What helped you in that situation?

Read Psalm 31:19-24

Comment

The psalm ends in praise of God. Look at some of the words that describe God: good, secure, loving, faithful. The last verse echoes words of Joshua who led the people from the wilderness into the Promised Land. The book of Joshua tells the history of the Israelites' conquest of the land and includes many descriptions of battles. It was no easy era. But Joshua believed that it was God who was in charge and that it is God who, ultimately, decides history. So he urges his people to be strong and courageous, determined and confident – not in their own abilities but in God's purpose and fulfilment of those purposes. It was a matter of trust because they couldn't know – as we know – what would happen in the ensuing decades and centuries before the coming of Christ. In Joshua 24:14-28 Joshua made a farewell speech to the people before he died. He said, 'Decide today whom you will serve . . . As for my family and me, we will serve the Lord' (verse 15). David, in verses 23 and 24 of Psalm 31, throws out a similar challenge: 'Love the Lord, all his faithful people . . . Be strong, be courageous, all you that hope in the Lord.'

Be encouraged

Whether we live in a peaceful land or a lack wracked with troubles, we can do no better than to put our trust in God, pledging to serve him faithfully, and to be strong and courageous. Our hope is in the Lord.

Pray

For courage for those who struggle to be brave, and praise God for his constant goodness.

81

Defiance

Question time

- Have you ever kept quiet about a wrong that you've done?
- How did it make you feel?

Read Psalm 32:1-4

Comment

'Who's going to own up?' Silence. Nobody raised their hand. 'All right, class detention!' barked the teacher.

'I didn't do it,' said the child to her mother. 'I'll ask you again. Did you do it?' The child looked down. And shook his head. 'No.'

Do either of these scenarios sound familiar? It's not just children, of course, who fail to own up to something they've done wrong. Adults are just as guilty. The thing is, that you often feel worse for *not* confessing your wrongdoing. If you confess, you may have to accept some discipline, but in the end it might make you feel better than the misery of having defied and deceived.

In verse 3 David's misery, from the defiance of not confessing, is exhausting and prolonged. Better to keep short accounts with people – and with God.

Challenge

Is there something you need to confess to God now? Or do you need to put something right with someone else?

Pray

For the humility to own up to wrongs, and praise God that he forgives.

82

Open and hidden

Question time

🍃 **Is there a place for confessing to other people as well as to God?** Think of an example in your own life when you've had to admit your shortcomings to someone else.

Read Psalm 32:5-7

Comment

David brings his wrongdoing into the open and shares it with God. He's stopped concealing stuff from his Lord. There's no point in hiding things from God when he knows us through and through!

In the New Testament we're encouraged to confess our sins. In 1 John 1:8-10 we read:

> If we say we have no sin, we deceive ourselves, and there is no truth in us. But if we confess our sins to God, he will keep his promise and

do what is right: he will forgive us our sins and purify us from all our wrongdoing. If we say that we have not sinned, we make God out to be a liar, and his word is not in us.

It couldn't be clearer, could it? And yet we still fail to bring our sins out into the light, preferring instead to hide them in the dark. 'If we live in the light,' writes John, 'just as he is in the light – then we have fellowship with one another, and the blood of Jesus, his Son, purifies us from every sin' (verse 7).

Be encouraged
The only place to hide is in God. We can't hide from him; we hide *in* him.

Pray
Hold your hands out and open, as a gesture of bringing your entire self into the open with God, then close your hands slowly as you allow God into yourself.

83
Unbridled

Question time

Have you ever had to be restrained from doing something rash, saying something inappropriate, or lashing out physically or verbally at someone?

Read Psalm 32:8-11

Comment

I used to help with the local Riding for the Disabled. The only animal I had ever ridden on was a donkey on the beach when I was a child. The horses and ponies at the riding school, docile though they were because of the nature of their role, filled me with some trepidation. I did ride my favourite pony round the school once or twice, but I preferred to be walking at the side, looking out for the well-being of the child who was perched, unafraid, in the saddle.

The pony was controlled by his bit and bridle and by the calm presence of the expert horseman or woman who led him. Each pony had been selected and trained and was under control.

God uses the image of a horse or mule to indicate the way we should live. 'I will teach you', he says, 'I will instruct you and advise you.' The pony that has a good working relationship with its master will do well.

Challenge

How much are you prepared to submit to God's training and leading of you?

Pray

Help me to submit to you willingly, Lord, and allow you to instruct and advise me.

84

Skill with strings

Question time

- What is your favourite musical instrument?
- Do you play something?
- Or do you like going to concerts or listening to CDs?

Read Psalm 33:1-3

Comment

My husband never learnt to play an instrument when a child but claims he is an expert at playing CDs. We can all get enjoyment from music, even if early efforts to learn an instrument can be something of an endurance test for player and listener.

David played the harp. We know he was a poet from the many psalms he wrote. But he played and sang – and he played the harp with skill. Maybe he took the harp with him when shepherding, to play in moments when he could sit and watch his sheep and enjoy the countryside and the gentle murmur of harp strings. He later played for King Saul to soothe Saul's mood. Here, David wants everyone who is in a right relationship with God to shout for joy for what the Lord has done and to play stringed instruments with skill. When you play with skill, it is true *play* – sheer enjoyment because you can concentrate on melodies and harmonies rather than on trying to get the right sound and rhythm. After years of practice it comes more naturally.

Be encouraged

Whether you play an instrument or not, learn how to praise God in a really enjoyable way, and thank God for those who *are* skilled and enhance your enjoyment of music.

Pray

For composers and musicians who write, arrange and play music.

85
Full earth

Question time

> What or who gives you fullness of joy?

Read Psalm 33:4-9

Comment

It's easy to see how a human being changes from being a baby to being an adult and we can monitor the different stages of growth. It's not so easy to see nor to comprehend that each human being changes on a daily basis as cells die – as many as 300 million every minute! It's estimated that the body replaces itself every 7 to 15 years. Some bits are never renewed while others are renewed frequently.

It was Heraclitus, a philosopher in ancient Greece, who said that, 'Change is the only constant in life.' And it seems he was right! Humans change and the earth itself is changing all the time too. How amazing it is, then, to read about the one constant that brings reassuring hope and stability into life: God's constant love (verse 5). Moreover, his constant love fills the earth.

We see changes through the cycle of the seasons, in the ebb and flow of tides, in the time of dawn and dusk, but all the time God's love filling the earth remains constant.

Be encouraged
Think about the changes in your own body over the years and thank God for the fullness and constancy of his love.

Pray
That the earth may be filled with the love and glory of God. Every part of it, including you.

Endurance

Question time

- What makes a great leader?
- Which leaders have stood the test of time?

Read Psalm 33:10-22

Comment

From the natural world of creation, David turns his attention to the world of politics and power. Kingdoms come and go, governments rise and fall, civilisations soar and crumble. Think of the history of your own nation. Is it enjoying a time of peace or is it at war? Is there contentment or unease? Is there unity or division?

Verse 11 shows us the enduring quality of God and his plans. Amidst all the muddle and mayhem created by humans in their attempts to rule the world, the nation, the town, the home, any endurance is very short-lived.

It's important for all of us to have an understanding of the whole of the Bible, not just the New

Testament. God's plan is revealed and his purposes gradually fulfilled from the Garden of Eden, through the patriarchs, the judges, the kings, the prophets, through Jesus and then through the church, with the promised hope of completion by God at the end of time.

Be encouraged

That God's love endures forever.

Pray

If your country is in turmoil, pray for its leaders, and thank God that we live in his world where his reign is supreme and everlasting.

87
Freedom from fear

Question time

- Are you scared of walking alone in the dark on a country lane or a city street?
- What are your fears?

Read Psalm 34:1-7

Comment

When our daughters were teenagers we lived at the top of a hill. The walking route from town to home took us up a quiet road bordered by open woodland. On winter mornings and evenings the road – or even the path through the woods – had to be negotiated in the dark, and it was a bit creepy. One of the girls spoke of feeling she had a guardian angel watching out for her as she walked up the hill. In verse 7 David writes of God's angel guarding those who obey him.

Does God always free us from our fears? In other psalms we've already seen that David was frequently afraid and told God so! Very often, after bringing his fears to the Lord, he felt better. If you feel panicky, it's sometimes a good idea to take some deep breaths. Breathe in for a count of 4, breathe out for a count of 4. If you're puffing your way up a steep hill, that's not always an easy option. It sometimes helps to breathe in God, by which I mean that as you take a deep breath in, you imagine that the breath is God's presence flowing into you and filling you with his peace.

Challenge

Practise the art of breathing in God.

Pray

For anyone you know who has a hazardous walk home from school or work.

88
Find out

Question time

🍃 Do you sometimes need to be encouraged or chivvied into trying something new – new food, a new pastime, a new book or a new idea?

Read Psalm 34:8-10

Comment

I was once persuaded to try honey. It actually made me feel nauseous; I thought it was horrible and it would take a lot of persuading to make me try it again. Children are sometimes reluctant to try a new food and vegetables are disguised into soup or grated into a mince mixture for burgers or meat balls – just to try and get them to eat it. I once took my young grandchildren to the fruit farm to pick strawberries. 'I don't like them,' one of them said. 'Have you ever tried a strawberry?' 'No.' 'Well, why not give it a go?' She did, and after that it was difficult to persuade her to put the strawberries she picked into the basket and not into her mouth!

The New International Version, for verse 8, reads, 'Taste and see that the Lord is good.' If you don't try him, you won't find out if God is good!

How do we find out whether God is good? David's testimony in the psalms so far may already have persuaded you. By reading his word, the Bible, you are discovering God – the God of the universe and the God who loves you and cares for you.

Be encouraged

To keep finding out more about God because his goodness and wholesomeness never run out.

Pray

Lord, give me the desire and courage to taste new things about you.

89
Goals for the young

Question time

- **What is the secret of happiness?**

- **What do you want from life?**

- **What are your goals?**
  The internet comes up with all sorts of ideas. Here are a few: marriage; family harmony; work/life balance; make money; success; travel the world.

Read Psalm 34:11-14

Comment

David addresses young people in this section. He offers to teach them to honour the Lord. Hmm. Was that on their ambition list? He goes on to pose the questions: 'Would you like to enjoy life?' Er . . . yes. 'Do you want long life and happiness?' Yes . . . as long as I'm fit and healthy.

And David comes up with the solution: 'Turn away from evil and do good; strive for peace.'

God's values, as spoken here by David, are not those of the world where, on the whole, we tend to be thinking of ourselves and our own wish list rather than of God and his ways.

Jesus said, 'Seek first God's kingdom . . .' Is that what you do, whether you're young or not so young?

Challenge

Think how you could change your mind-set to put God first and discover his plans for your life. How might you accomplish his desire for your life?

Pray

That young people may have opportunities to hear about God and to learn to honour him in their lives.

90

Preservation

Question time

What is your favourite preserve? Think how the fruit of that jam or chutney has been transformed into something that will last for months, long after the tree has stopped fruiting or the vegetables have stopped growing.

Read Psalm 34:15-22

Comment

The 1662 Book of Common Prayer has in it 'A General Thanksgiving' which isn't used as often now in church worship as it once was. Its words may be old-fashioned but its sentiments are beautiful and we do well to say it from time to time and take in the meaning of the words as we express them to God. Look it up in your prayer book – or on the internet.

Did you notice the word, 'preservation' in the prayer? In verse 20 of the psalm David says that, despite all the troubles that people suffer, the

Lord saves and preserves that righteous person completely.

Challenge
What is my relationship with God like today, this very minute? Do I trust his promise that I will be preserved by him for as long as he wants me on Planet Earth?

Pray
The words of the General Thanksgiving.

91
Deep hole

Question time

🍃 Have you ever dug a proverbial hole for yourself? The more you say, the more inappropriate your words are and the deeper the hole becomes!

Read Psalm 35:1-16

Comment

One of my favourite characters is Winnie-the-Pooh who features in the books by A A Milne. In one story, Piglet and Pooh dig a Very Deep Pit to catch a Heffalump. Piglet ends up being terrified by the 'Heffalump' who turns out to be Pooh who had got into the hole to retrieve a pot of honey put down as bait for the Heffalump. Christopher Robin came to the rescue and all ended well.

In reality, the deep holes of life can be places of fear and uncertainty. Jeremiah tells of his experience of being put in a well. There was no water in the well but Jeremiah sank into the mud and was left to die of starvation. God had further plans for Jeremiah, however, and he was rescued and continued his work for the Lord after his terrifying ordeal. (See Jeremiah chapter 38.)

David says that those who dishonour God by treating his people badly will be 'caught in their own trap and fall to their destruction'. Hatred, cruelty, evil will be dealt with by God – forever. And the rescuer would be Jesus, his Son.

Be encouraged

However deep our hole, God can rescue us if we call on him.

Pray

For Christians who are reviled and tortured for their faith.

92
Lies and leers

Question time
Has anyone ever told lies about you?

Read Psalm 35:17-21

Comment
It's awful to be wrongfully accused. Sometimes lies sound like truth and we may be hoodwinked into believing falsehoods. It happens in law courts and lawyers have a tussle trying to get at the truth. Can you think of people who have been falsely accused of something? If it's someone famous, the media get hold of the story and people gossip on social media about it and the posts may be seen all around the world. Everyone has an opinion and many want to voice it.

If David were alive today, I wonder whether he would be the subject of vitriol on social media? Read verses 19-21. Think how you might feel if you were in that sort of situation.

Challenge
Think how we can use social media responsibly.

Pray
For those who are falsely accused, that they may know God's presence with them.

Rouse yourself, Lord!

Question time

- Do you sometimes think God is asleep?
- That he's forgotten about you, that he's got tired of your cries for help, that he's lost interest?

Read Psalm 35:22-28

Comment

David knows that the Lord sees everything that is going on in the world and knows of David's own woes. So he's bold and says, 'Rouse yourself, O Lord!' Wake up. David gives God a proverbial shake. Think of the storm on the lake in the Gospels. Jesus was asleep in the boat. A storm blew up and the disciples were petrified. What did they do and say? The same as David did: 'Wake up!' Jesus was asleep because he knew there was no need to panic.

He woke and dealt with this part of the created world that was causing havoc and panic among his friends.

David wants God to defend him against his human enemies that were causing havoc and panic, pain and fear.

Be encouraged

Don't be afraid to ask God to wake up if he seems to be asleep.

Pray

Like David, you'll be able to say: 'Then I will proclaim your righteousness, and I will praise you all day long' (verse 28).

94
Wickedness

Question time

- What sort of opinion do you have of yourself?
- Do you see yourself as capable, competent, confident, self-sufficient?
- Or are you full of self-doubt and low self-esteem? Or somewhere in between?

Read Psalm 36:1-4

Comment

In verse 2 David describes a wicked person as thinking so highly of himself that he thinks God won't discover and condemn his sin. I remember being told, as a child, 'Be sure your sin will find you out.' This terrified me so much that, following an appeal at a gospel meeting, I thought I'd better put my trust in God and confess my sin otherwise I'd end up in hell in a place of torment and never-ending fire. This wasn't the best way to commit my life to God and, as an 8-year-old, it was many years before I understood more clearly that God loved the world and he loved me and he came to give me new life.

In reality, I don't think that my 8-year-old self was particularly wicked. I didn't always do what I was told and I wrangled with my siblings, but I didn't do anything really bad! The Bible does say, however, that all have sinned. So I wasn't completely innocent. And neither was David though he recognised his wrongs and his need of God and put his trust in him. And that's what we can all do.

Challenge
Beware of thinking too highly of yourself (verse 2).

Pray
For wisdom and goodness (verse 3).

95
Goodness

Question time

🍃 Who protects you when you're in a dangerous situation?

Read Psalm 36:5-12

Comment

I was perched on the dizzying cliff-top of one of the Farne Islands off the north-east coast of England. Within a few centimetres of my foot a young cormorant sat on a scruffy nest, in the shadow of its mother's wings. Mother stood by her precious offspring, wings outstretched, keeping a watchful eye on baby and a wary eye on me.

It wasn't hard to imagine the dangers that might befall that young bird without its mother's protection. Larger predatory birds might take the chick, gale-force winds buffeting the cliffs could jeopardise its life, and the clumsy boots of humans might have crushed the little one.

Look at verse 7. The Bible frequently uses such imagery. God is there for his faithful people. In an impassioned exclamation of love and exasperation, Jesus said:

> Jerusalem, Jerusalem! You kill the prophets and stone the messengers God has sent you! How many times have I wanted to put my arms round all your people, just as a hen gathers her chicks under her wings, but you would not let me!
>
> *Matthew 23:37*

Be encouraged

'How precious, O God, is your constant love! We find protection under the shadow of your wings' (verse 7).

Pray

That you won't resist God's maternal care, that you may find protection 'under her wings'.

96

Don't worry

Question time

- Are you a worrier?
- And how often when you say thank you to someone, do you hear the response, 'No worries', a phrase that has popped into the English language in recent years? Well, I'm glad that the speaker has no worries – if that is the true case.

Read Psalm 37:1-4

Comment

The country in which I live is going through a bit of a crisis at the moment. That's an understatement. There are unresolved issues that threaten the nation's future security. Around the world we see similar unrest and the wickedness that results from God being booted out of people's lives.

'Don't be worried,' says David. Often we feel helpless. There seems nothing practical that we can do or say that will change the ways of the world; all that's left is for us to worry. Not so!

Our concentration needs to be on God. Trust in the Lord. Do good. Seek your happiness in the Lord. In the New Testament we read that Jesus went about doing good. He didn't just go about. He did good. And if we want to be Jesus' ambassadors, we can do the same. We don't just sit at home watching the television news and getting increasingly worried. Yes, we can be informed of what's going on in the world and should take an active interest in it, because we have dual citizenship – of this world and of God's kingdom.

Challenge

While we may feel helpless, we are called to trust God and to do good. So let's get cracking on both and by doing so, help to extend God's kingdom.

Pray

For the countries of the world, for fair government and wise words and action.

97

Waiting

Question time

- What makes you impatient?
- What would you like to happen right now rather than at some point in the unknown future?
- How good are you at waiting?

Read Psalm 37:5-11

Comment

'Are we nearly there yet?' It's often the plaintive cry of a child going on a car journey. It's not great if the child poses the question after 10 miles when you have 200 still to go.

'Be patient and wait for the Lord to act.' We live in a world of time. We have clocks that show us 60 seconds in a minute, the 60 minutes in an hour, the 24 hours of the day, and calendars and diaries that reveal the 365 days of the year. I visited a house the other day where every clock showed a different time

– and none of them was correct. One had stopped completely, another was about an hour fast, another was twenty minutes slow. I don't wear a watch but rely on my Smartphone's clock to tell me the time.

God lives outside time as we know it. He is eternal and we can't really get our minds round that. Our brains are complex and clever but limited in their capacity for understanding. Once again we're told to trust God.

Be encouraged

We don't have to fret; God is in control. Be patient and trust him.

Pray

Give me patience, Lord, to wait on you and be calm as I wait.

98

Little and good

Question time

- How much stuff do you have?
- Do you live in a cluttered home?
- What have you got stashed in your loft apart, perhaps, from Christmas decorations?
- Are you a hoarder or do you live minimally?

Read Psalm 37:12-22

Comment

I recently had to clear someone else's home. I couldn't believe how much was there, and a lot of it hadn't been touched in years.

In this section of Psalm 37 David contrasts wicked men with good men. Verse 16 gives a godly perspective on possessions: 'The little that a good man owns is worth more than the wealth of all the wicked.' Elsewhere in the Bible we're told not to store up for ourselves treasure on earth. The more simply we live, the less clutter there is in our homes

– and the less clutter probably in our brains and therefore more space for God.

God is the great provider. We can play our part in his provision by sharing what we have with those who don't have enough. Could you give a lift in your car to someone who doesn't have access to a vehicle? Could you make a meal for someone who's coming home from hospital? Could you send a gift of money to a charity to provide for someone in need?

Challenge

Let's hold lightly not tightly to what God gives us and share what we do have – and not be jealous of those who have more.

Pray

For contentment with what you have.

99
Old age

Question time

How do you cope with the prospect, or reality, of old age?

Read Psalm 37:23-26

Comment

What a wonderful testimony comes from the words of the now old king David! Here is a reminder of the goodness of God as David looks back at his life. He has felt guided by God, protected by him, and when he's fallen God has helped him up. He witnesses to God's provision and to the blessings of life.

Whatever age you are, think how you would describe God's presence in your life. Think of when you were a child, a teenager, a young adult, an older adult. How has God been a part of each stage of your life? Or maybe you've only more recently known his presence and been in relationship with him.

Write down or think of what you might say if someone asked you how God has impacted your life. We're told to be ready to give an answer to anyone who wants to know about God. It was Peter – who had a story and a half to relate – who wrote in 1 Peter 3:15:

> Have reverence for Christ in your hearts, and honour him as Lord. Be ready at all times to answer anyone who asks you to explain the hope you have in you, but do it with gentleness and respect.

Be encouraged

It doesn't matter how old we are. If we know God, then we have a story to tell.

Pray

For those who are facing challenges in old age.

100
Observe

Question time

- Do you like people-watching?
- Have you ever sat on a train and discreetly observed your fellow-passengers?
- Or sat in a cafe and watched couples as they communicate with loving, or frosty, looks over their coffee cups?

Read Psalm 37:27-40

Comment

There are so many opportunities to observe! Go to a football match and see how your fellow spectators behave. Watch a film and analyse the characters and see how they interact. One of my friends, a fellow-writer, gleefully observes people, as it gives her plenty of material for her works of fiction.

A wicked man, according to David, watches a good man and tries to kill him (verse 32) but in verse 37 we're urged to notice 'good people, observe the righteous'.

There are 'goodies' and 'baddies' in many stories. Think of Little Red Riding Hood and the Big Bad Wolf; Harry Potter and Lord Voldemort; Princess Leia and Darth Vader in Star Wars; Oliver and Bill Sikes in Oliver Twist. As we read or watch the story, we observe the characters and can distinguish between good and bad, virtuous and vile, victorious and vanquished.

Challenge

Consider, from these verses, the fate of the wicked. And of the righteous.

Pray

Thank God for the peace he gives to those who honour him.

101
Struck down

Question time

Have you ever seen an object on the road and wrenched the steering wheel round to avoid it? 'Always hit a pheasant rather than cause an accident by swerving to avoid it', a farmer friend advised me. Driving is instinctive. Sometimes we can't avoid hitting things. A baby rabbit shot out of the hedge in front of me into the lane. There was nothing I could do other than feel a pang of sorrow as I looked in the rear view mirror and saw its motionless body on the road behind me.

Read Psalm 38:1-8

Comment

All manner of things can hit us and damage us, some of them of our own making, some unavoidable.

David is struck down by his own foolishness, his sins, the burden he bears. 'I am bowed down, I am crushed; I mourn all day long. I am burning with fever and I am near to death. I am worn out and utterly crushed; my heart is troubled, and I groan with pain' (verses 6-8).

When things go wrong we feel everything is against us. Will things ever go right again? This is a psalm of lament. David knows that he feels the way he does because of his own folly.

Challenge

Do you need to do as David did and talk to God, expressing how wretched you feel?

Pray

Thank God for his readiness to listen when we turn to him.

102
Suffering

Question time

> Do you know what it's like to be shunned by a close friend or by members of your family?

Read Psalm 38:9-22

Comment

No wonder David feels so alone in his suffering. Imagine you're in hospital; you long for the comfort of your mother or brother or wife or a friend, but nobody comes to see you. Or imagine being in a care home with relatives at a distance. You can feel lonely even when among other people. When in distress, for whatever reason, it's those nearest and dearest to you that you want to have by your side.

Be encouraged

For David the turning point comes in verse 15 with that wonderful little link word, 'But'. 'But I trust in you, O Lord; and you, O Lord my God, will answer me.' He asks for God's presence and help. When all else is failing, to whom can we go but to the Lord?

Pray

Thank God that you can be honest with him. Ask him to hear you in your own need and to stay with you in your distress.

103
Head below parapet

Question time

🌿 Do you put your head above the proverbial parapet or do you like to keep a low profile?

Read Psalm 39:1-4

Comment

If you stuck your head above the parapet of a castle in medieval times you were likely to be hit by an arrow. Today we talk about keeping our head below the parapet if we want to avoid being targeted for an undesirable task or for an opinion on a divisive issue. Avoid conflict by keeping hidden.

David decides it's easier to keep quiet and not say anything when his enemies are near him. He wants to keep a low profile. He wasn't even prepared to say anything good! But his docile demeanour didn't help the inner turmoil he felt. His suffering grew worse and he was overcome with anxiety.

He was over-thinking things and, as a result, became more troubled.

Perhaps this is your experience. You try to do and say what is right, you try to be sensible, you don't get involved in stuff that might have undesirable repercussions, but it doesn't work. You just feel worse.

Challenge

What do you do when you're at your wits' end, as David was?

Pray

Be honest with God in your prayers now. If you question how long your life might last, tell God how you feel. He alone knows our comings and goings, the end from the beginning and he understands our problems. Didn't his own Son question *his* suffering?

104

Anxiety

Question time

🍃 Have you suffered from depression or anxiety or do you know someone who has?

Read Psalm 39:5-13

Comment

It's said that depression occurs when you dwell on the past, and anxiety occurs when you look to the future. Both are debilitating conditions that affect not only the mind but the whole being: body, mind and soul.

David, in his suffering, wonders about the significance of life (verses 5 and 6). His words resonate with the gloom of Ecclesiastes where the writer feels that life is meaningless, futile, a waste of space. God never promised an easy journey. With him in the picture, life – though difficult and testing – is a gift and an opportunity for adventure with its mix of vales of tears and mountain-top views.

Be encouraged

David recognises that, despite his anxiety, he can put his hope in the Lord (verse 7). We don't have long on Planet Earth; we're like a puff of wind, here for a season, then above. So it's sensible to live each moment of each day the Lord gives us. Live it with him and for him, knowing that he is the creator of life, the sustainer of life, and your personal carer.

Pray

For your own needs or the needs of someone else who struggles to manage anxiety or depression.

Patience and loyalty

Question time

- Do you have a supermarket loyalty card?
- How loyal are you to that supermarket?
- And is it loyal to you, its valued customer?

Read Psalm 40:1-11

Comment

I have a supermarket loyalty card but I have a far greater loyalty to my husband and to my family who mean much more to me than does the supermarket!

From the despair of Psalms 38 and 39 we move into the more optimistic Psalm 40. The psalmist had waited patiently for the Lord's help – and it had come. So this is a song of thankfulness and praise. It's so much easier to be thankful and to praise God when he has answered prayer and when life is on a more even keel. The irony is that, so often, when times are good, we fail to acknowledge God. We're more likely to cry out to him when life is troublesome. Human beings are fickle. God, by contrast, is not. He *never* stops being merciful, his love and loyalty are *always* there. I hope that my relationship with God is less fickle than my relationship with the supermarket. If they don't have what I want, if their staff are less than helpful, if I get bored, I go elsewhere. It would be foolish to turn my back on God, however, and go elsewhere, when he is constantly loyal, merciful and loving.

Be encouraged

Patience is rewarded as we wait for God. He is ever loyal to us.

Pray

Why not use verse 11 as a prayer right now?

106
Aid

Question time
Who is the greatest giver of aid?

Read Psalm 40:12-17

Comment
I had a clear-out and discovered several pairs of glasses that I no longer wear because the prescription changes every year. So I took the discarded glasses to the optician who was glad to receive them to send to a relevant charity. Thousands of pairs of glasses found their way to new homes in the last year. There are many aid charities that give specialised and general aid where it is needed.

The Lord himself is the greatest giver of aid. After David's prayer for help in these verses, he praises God and is thankful that God has not forgotten him. And he asks him to hurry to provide aid.

Jesus told a wonderful story about giving aid. And said that when any of us does something for somebody else in the way of aid, it's as if we are

doing it for the Lord himself. The aid we give is a reflection of the aid we receive from the Lord.

Challenge

Why not do a bit of research on aid charities and see whether there is some way in which you can offer aid in thankfulness to the aid God gives you?

Pray

For a charity that you support.

107
Illness

Question time

- Can you think of a time when somebody has come to your aid?
- Or when you have given aid to someone else?

Read Psalm 41:1-13

Comment

A young boy fell off his bike near my home. Immediately neighbours were there to help, followed by paramedics, then the crew of the air ambulance, and finally by a large ambulance whose crew took the lad to hospital. We are made for relationship – with God and with each other. We're not called to be independent but interdependent. How grateful I am for those who show me care and concern when I'm ill. Paramedics, nurses, doctors, surgeons, physiotherapists, and those who keep an eye on my eyesight (pardon the pun), my hearing, my blood pressure, my general well-being.

The Lord helps those who help others and his help is demonstrated in the help that we all give to each other in times of need.

Be encouraged

Sometimes it's the most unexpected person who gives help and encouragement – when others have turned away. Read verses 6-8. Nobody wants a pessimist to minister to us when we're ill! At our local hospital there are trained volunteers to engage with elderly patients. They visit individuals in the wards, listen to them, chat to them, encourage them and aim to leave the patient feeling uplifted rather than downcast. This is a picture of our Lord who comes alongside us to help us and minister to us.

Pray

Thank God for the people who have come to your aid when you've needed healing or help. Thank God for paramedics and air ambulance crews and pray for *their* well-being too!

108

Heartbreak

Question time

🍃 **An old question: Apart from people, what would you rescue from a fire in your house? Photos?**

Read Psalm 42:1-5

Comment

I have old-fashioned photograph albums with pictures of our family in their growing years. Curiously, these happy pictures can make me feel melancholy, so I understand what the writers of this psalm mean in verse 4. Heartbreak and happiness in the same verse. They question why their hearts break at happy memories and why they feel sad and troubled.

Today I looked at the computer folders of pictures I've taken on my digital camera. To my dismay I found that a number of folders, covering two years in particular, had vanished. The computer is a mysterious beast at the best of times, but I don't understand where the pictures have gone and why I can't retrieve them. My heart was breaking as I read the name of the empty folders and the lost pictures: 'Tenby holiday', 'Half term with the family', 'Christmas' . . .

There *will* be heartache in the less than perfect world that we inhabit. What is the antidote to heartbreak? A refocus on God. The psalmists have to keep refocusing on God through the ups and downs of life.

Be encouraged

The refrain of verse 5 is repeated in verse 11 with the same result: hope and praise.

Pray

For those who are going through particular heartbreak today, maybe someone known to you, maybe someone you hear about on the news.

109

Longing

Question time

What do you long for?

Read Psalm 42:6-11

Comment

At the beginning of Psalm 42 there is thirst for God. In today's verses we have water imagery but, rather than quenching thirst, the waters here are hostile: 'waves of sorrow', 'chaos . . . like a flood', 'waterfalls thundering'.

Watery weather is helpful for the garden, but can do immense damage if it is rampaging through villages and towns and across fields. Riverbanks burst, homes are flooded and people stranded. Tsunamis are truly waves of sorrow, causing death and destruction.

Just when the writers were longing for God's presence like a deer pants for water, they find themselves being overwhelmed by the waters that engulf them. God spoke via Isaiah in words of great comfort: 'When you pass through deep waters, I will be with you; your troubles will not overwhelm you.' Why? 'For I am the Lord your God' (Isaiah 43:2, 3).

And that is the conclusion that is reached as, for the third time, we read the refrain of verse 11 and, once more, hope is put in God.

Challenge

Can you put your hope in God when the waters threaten to overwhelm you?

Pray

For anyone you know for whom life is overwhelming at the moment.

110
Exile

Question time

What do the following people have in common: Napoleon Bonaparte, Albert Einstein, Aleksandr Solzhenitsyn, Charles II? They were all exiled at some point in their life.

Read Psalm 43:1-5

Comment

In the 1970s we lived near Heathrow Airport in London. It was the time when many Asians were expelled from Uganda when Idi Amin was in charge of that country. Our community received many people who came to live in the area, far from their own homes. The neighbourhood was slightly hostile but the church held welcome parties and gradually the exiles felt welcome. In the early 1990s another group of displaced people arrived – Kurds who had been uprooted as a result of the Gulf War. One family, none of whom spoke English, came to live in a house opposite ours. My youngest daughter befriended the little girl in that family when she was put in my daughter's class at school.

The writers of this psalm – which is a continuation of Psalm 42 – long to return to where they belong. Meanwhile they feel lonely and abandoned. The cry rises to God in verse 5 and is a repeat of the refrain of the previous psalm. 'Why?', 'Why?' And then the mental turmoil calms down as, once again, trust and hope is put in God.

Challenge

Are there people in your community who need a friendly face of welcome? What role could you play in that?

Pray

For people who are struggling to settle in a new country amidst hostility and prejudice.

111

Assurance

Question time

🍃 What assurance can you pass on to younger people about God's faithfulness?

Read Psalm 44:1-8

Comment

Back in the days of Moses the people were urged to pass on the story of God's activities and commands to the younger generations. Such oral history was very important as the Israelites left the wilderness and progressed into the promised land where they would face many challenges:

> Never forget these commands that I am giving you today,' said the Lord, 'Teach them to your children. Repeat them when you are at home and when you are away, when you are resting and when you are working (Deuteronomy 6:6, 7).

The psalmist or psalmists – because the authorship of this psalm (and the previous two) is attributed to the sons of Korah – here recall how God was at work in the history of the people. They acknowledge that it was God's power and strength, not that of humans, which conquered the promised land. And at the end of verse 3 we read of the assurance of God's presence which showed the people that God loved them.

Be encouraged

Fanny J Crosby (1820-1915) wrote the hymn, *Blessed Assurance*. Despite her own disability – she'd been blind since she was six weeks old – she had an unwavering faith in God's goodness and was assured of the blessing of being in relationship with him through Jesus. She saw this assurance as a 'foretaste of glory divine' and praised God for it.

Pray

Meditate on the words, 'foretaste of glory divine'.

112

Accusation

Question time

Have you ever accused someone – and kept on accusing?

Read Psalm 44:9-19

Comment

What a sudden change of sentiment! From praise to accusation. 'You have rejected us!; 'You made us run . . .'; 'You allowed us to be slaughtered . . .'; 'You scattered us . . .'; 'You sold your own people . . .'; 'You have made us an object of contempt . . .'; 'You left us helpless . . .'; 'You abandoned us . . .'.

How could there be such a swift change of mood? The Korahites (descendants of Levi) became leaders of music in the tabernacle during David's reign. Eleven of the psalms are attributed to the sons of Korah. Mostly they're beautiful psalms that express gratitude to God but, like many a piece of music, they can switch from major to minor key, from joy to melancholy, from loud to quiet, from fast to slow.

I imagine their music-composition and music-making were inspirational to the people and reflected their own thoughts of life and of God.

Someone recently said to me that there isn't enough opportunity in worship for lament. And maybe we think it rude to question God with our 'Why?' questions. If we're to be honest with God – and we have to remember he knows what we think anyway – there's no reason to withhold the 'Why?'

Challenge

Do you truly believe that God knows your accusations – against him and against other people?

Pray

For those who feel abandoned by God.

113

Low notes and high notes

Question time

🍃 **What, specifically, do you find hard to understand about the ways of God?**

Read Psalm 44:20-26

Comment

William Young Fullerton (1857-1932) wrote a hymn, 'I cannot tell . . .' It has an eight-line pattern, the first line of each verse begins with the words, 'I cannot tell . . .', and the fifth line of each verse begins, 'But this I know . . .' It's sung to the Irish folk tune, Londonderry Air. Although the music is in a major key, the first four lines are quiet and low and then with the positive words of lines 5-8, the music soars to great heights.

This is how it is with many of the psalms. We have the low notes of not understanding the ways of the world and – often – the ways of God, and then the assurance of what we *do* know of God's ways and of his sovereignty. Look at the psalm as a whole and work out which are the *I cannot tell* bits and which are the *But this I know* parts.

Challenge

When you're tested by the trials of life, are you able to conclude, as the psalm does, that God will come to your aid and that he will save you – because of his constant love?

Pray

Thank God that, although there is much we don't understand about him, he reveals as much as we need to know.

Euphoria

Question time

🍃 **Do you have days of unbridled joy? Days when you just want to sing and dance and shout your delight?** Maybe after the birth of a child, or at a wedding or when you've received good news . . .

Read Psalm 45:1-7

Comment

The sons of Korah are overwhelmed with delight and put quill to parchment to express their joy. It's a song of affirmation of the king. Look at all the positive words: beautiful, handsome, eloquent, blessed, glorious, majestic, strength, justice, right, happiness . . .

I recently came across a box of love letters between my mother and father, written when they were an 'item' but several years before their marriage. They were written during World War 2 when they were in different places and life was very uncertain. They had no idea whether either or both of them would survive the war. I haven't read the letters but they evidently meant a great deal as they'd been kept in a cardboard box in their envelopes for more than 70 years. They represent a celebration of each other, of their mutual love, and of life itself.

We're fortunate to have the psalms, written thousands of years ago but which resonate today with us. This is a kind of love letter to the king and also a foretaste of the King of kings who rode into Jerusalem a thousand years after the psalm was written.

Challenge

Could you write a love letter to God?

Pray

Use as many appropriate adjectives as you can think of in a prayer that expresses your love for God.

Royalty

Question time

Who is your heart's desire?

Read Psalm 45:8-17

Comment

The love poem continues with descriptions of the king's bride and her joy at entering the king's palace.

In the New Testament, Jesus the King of kings is described as the bridegroom and, amazingly, we the church, as his bride. As such, how might we be described? Imagine this poem is about Jesus and us. We listen to him, we are his heart's desire, he is our master, we obey him, we're clothed in beauty, we come to him with joy and gladness, we become his family, our testimony will keep his name and his fame alive for ever, everyone will praise him for all time to come.

Have a look at Revelation 19:5-9, which is a description of the future when the wedding feast between Jesus and his church will take place and we will forever be united with him.

Challenge

Think about this picture of Jesus the King and of you as part of the church, the bride. How might it affect the way you think, speak and behave?

Pray

For your love relationship with Jesus and for your love relationship with all those he loves.

116
Shelter and strength

Question time

> Where have you found shelter when you've been in trouble?

Read Psalm 46:1-11

Comment

Salisbury Plain is a vast area. Some of the land is for livestock, much of it is a golden carpet of ripening grain in late summer, but there is also a hidden, more sinister aspect of the Plain.

It is the home and training ground for soldiers. Armoured vehicles move across the undulating landscape; more often you hear rather than see the activity. The local newspaper publishes a weekly list of troop activity: which guns will be firing on which days. The sound of ammunition can be heard from miles away. It's loud and unsettling, more so for those who live close by when the house shakes if the big guns are in action.

God is our shelter and strength, always ready to help in times of trouble. So we will not be afraid, even if the earth is shaken . . .

Earthquakes, volcanic eruptions, tsunamis . . . and warfare. Soldiers train for battle and are put into places of immense danger. How many lives have been damaged or lost because of people's inability to live at peace with one another?

Be encouraged

It's easy to panic when natural or human-instigated events threaten us. But we can draw on the promises of God.

Pray

Thank God that he is there with his people in whatever circumstances they encounter.

117
Applause

Question time

🍃 Have you ever given God a 'clap-offering'?

Read Psalm 47:1-9

Comment

In this exuberant psalm, everyone is encouraged to clap – for joy! And to sing LOUDLY – which reminds me of when Nehemiah, after the exile and the return to Jerusalem, got everyone celebrating God's deliverance. The walls of Jerusalem had been rebuilt, the city was reoccupied, God's laws had been read, sins had been confessed and now it was celebration time. Trumpets were blasted, voices were raised, people marched and, 'the noise they all made could be heard for miles' (Nehemiah 12:43). The sons of Korah would have been proud.

These insights, plus the perhaps more staid but musically perfect worship of cathedral choirs today, and the happy-clappiness of exuberant worshippers in Pentecostal churches, give us a glimpse of what heavenly worship might be like:

I heard every creature in heaven, on earth, in the world below, and in the sea – all living beings in the universe – and they were singing: 'To him who sits on the throne and to the Lamb, be praise and honour, glory and might, for ever and ever!' (Revelation 5:13).

Handel's mighty work, *Messiah,* ends with 'Worthy Is the Lamb' and 'Amen', choruses of immense joy and the culmination of God's great plan of salvation.

Be encouraged

To applaud God loud and long for he is, indeed, worthy to receive glory, honour and power.

Pray

For singers in choirs and thank God for the ability to sing.

118

Cityscape

Question time

- Do you have a favourite city? Shanghai? New York? Adelaide? Paris?
- Or perhaps one of the smaller ones: Wells in England, Vatican City in Rome, or Adamstown where all the people (less than a hundred) of the Pitcairn Islands live?
- What is it that makes your favourite city special?

Read Psalm 48:1-14

Comment

Jerusalem, to the Israelites, was *the* city, the city of God, the city where King David had his throne, the city where God was worshipped and where the people felt safe. In these few verses it is God who is central to life in the city.

Think again of your favourite city. What evidence is there, if any, that God is present there? Verse 10 says that people everywhere will praise God – including people in your favourite city.

Challenge

Is God central to the place where you live? Is he in your city, your town, your village, your hamlet, your house, your flat, your caravan, your tent, your heart?

Pray

Spend time praying for your favourite city and its people, that God may be known and worshipped there.

119
Priceless

Question time

🍃 If you had a limitless supply of money what would you buy?

Read Psalm 49:1-9

Comment

Some of the most costly single man-made objects in the world include the International Space Station, the Large Hadron Collider, and the Alaska Pipeline. The most expensive gemstone in the world, a blue diamond, would cost nearly $4 million per carat. A Ferrari might set you back $50 million, a piece of fine art or sculpture could relieve you of millions of pounds, a swish yacht could be several billion pounds (very swish) and, more shockingly, a rhino horn might be bought for over $100 per gram.

This psalm is headed, 'The Foolishness of Trusting in Riches', and addresses rich and poor people. There's no point in trusting in the possessions you have. Verse 7 says it all: 'A person can never redeem himself; he cannot pay God the price for his life, because the payment for a human life is too great.'

Who paid the price to redeem us? Jesus, who said, 'The greatest love you can have for your friends is to give your life for them' (John 15:13). The price God paid for our salvation was costly: the sacrifice of his own Son.

Challenge

In the light of Jesus' action, what is your response to verses 7-9 of this psalm?

Pray

For those for whom wealth has become more important than God.

120

You can't take it with you

Question time

What is your favourite possession?

Read Psalm 49:10-20

Comment

At the end of international tennis matches, the players may fling parts of their clothing or their towel into the crowd. At one tournament television pictures showed two spectators having a tug of war (which ended in fisticuffs) over which of them should have the headband that had been hurled towards them. They both claimed it as theirs. In the end security officials were called in to deal with the situation, and neither claimant received the headband!

Jesus was approached by a man who said, 'Teacher, tell my brother to divide with me the property our father left us' (Luke 12:13). Jesus told a story which you can read in Luke 12:14-20, in which he warned about riches. They won't make you rich in God's sight!

None of us can take any of our possessions with us when we die. However rich, however great you think you are or others may see you to be, it makes no difference in the end.

Challenge

Are there things in your life that you could share, or relinquish now?

Pray

Use these words of Peter for your prayer:

> Let us give thanks to the God and Father of our Lord Jesus Christ! Because of his great mercy he gave us new life by raising Jesus Christ from death. This fills us with a living hope, and so we look forward to possessing the rich blessings that God keeps for his people. He keeps them for you in heaven . . .
>
> *1 Peter 1:3, 4*

121

Mine!

Question time

 Who are your local landowners?

Read Psalm 50:1-11

Comment

David was a musician and music was very important in the community life of the Israelites. In 1 Chronicles 16 we read that David appointed some of the Levites to lead the worship of the Lord – and that Asaph was appointed leader. Psalm 50 is by Asaph and there are others later in the collection.

A local walk takes me up a hill to a viewpoint. To the right there is open countryside, mostly agricultural land, and on a far hill there is always a herd of cows. Whenever I see them I think of verse 10 of this psalm. The cows are a reminder that everything in the world, including each animal, is owned by God. How often humans talk about 'our world'. It isn't ours, it's God's! When I see a flock of chattering long-tailed tits, gathered together in community, I imagine them to be praising God; likewise the early morning song of a robin, or the evening praise of a blackbird perched on a chimney pot.

Swiss artist, Annie Vallotton, drew pictures for the Good News Bible. Her drawing for verse 10 shows an owl in the cleft of a tree, rabbits nibbling the grass, a deer tiptoeing through the trees, a squirrel and birds on branches, toadstools and flowers on the ground and butterflies in the air. The Almighty God, the Lord, speaks through creation.

Be encouraged

That the earth and everything in it belongs to God.

Pray

For local farmers, estate managers and property developers.

122

Reprimand

Question time

🍃 **How genuine is our worship of God?** Outward displays of piety aren't good enough. God knows our hearts. However good the music is, however holy the looks on our faces, however long we stay on our knees, all that is nothing unless the worship is genuine.

Read Psalm 50:2-23

Comment

God is frustrated with false worship. He doesn't want gestures, he wants true thankfulness (verse 14). Many parish churches have the Ten Commandments in a prominent place behind the altar, etched in stone or carved in wood. As you kneel at the altar, your head may be bowed and you may not notice the words above you. God throws out a challenge in verse 16: 'Why should you recite my commandments? Why should you talk about my covenant?' It seems that the people were not letting God correct them, they were ignoring his commands, and living life how *they* chose to – and still coming to worship! God sees right through them and gives them a stern reprimand.

Challenge and Encouragement
Read verse 23. Let it be a challenge and an encouragement to you.

Pray
That you will be willing to be corrected by God and learn to worship him sincerely.

123
Wash day

Question time

🍃 Think of an item of clothing or furniture from which you've tried to remove stains. How did you go about it and were you successful?

Read Psalm 51:1-5

Comment

In the 1970s I used towelling nappies for my babies. When they were soiled I plunged the nappies in a stain-remover solution, which disinfected them before they were washed in the washing machine. The stain remover contained powerful ingredients: Peracetic acid generated from Tetra-Acetylethylenediamine and Sodium Percabonate. The stains would come out from the nappies and then they could be washed.

We're back to a psalm from David's pen now, and it's a sober psalm, written after his adultery with Bathsheba and his murder of Bathsheba's husband. God sent Nathan the prophet to talk to David and, as a result, David repents and confesses his sin to God.

David asks God to wash away his sins and make him clean. Before we point the finger at David, we have to ask ourselves what we are stained with. As 'all have sinned', we're in no position to judge David or anyone else. I find it slightly embarrassing to read this psalm; I'm not sure I'd want everyone to know about the stains in my life, but at the same time I'm grateful that the Bible is a book about real people in real situations with whom we can identify. And as a result we can see how God deals with the life issues that face us all.

Challenge

Is there something you need to confess to God?

Pray

For people whose relationships have broken down.

124

Snow white

Question time

Why do you wash yourself?

Read Psalm 51:6-9

Comment

It used to be the case that you washed nappies on a very hot setting. Now, in our eco-aware world, washing machine manufacturers claim that you can wash items on a much lower temperature and they'll still come out clean.

In David's case he asks God, 'Remove my sin, and I will be clean; wash me, and I will be whiter than snow.' In Titus 2:14 we read of Jesus: 'He gave himself for us, to rescue us from all wickedness and to make us a pure people who belong to him alone and are eager to do good.' And in Titus 3:4, 5: 'But when the kindness and love of God our Saviour was revealed, he saved us.' It was not because of any good deeds that we ourselves had done, but because of his own mercy that he saved us, through the Holy Spirit, who gives us new birth and new life by washing us.

David wanted a new start, like a nappy that's been through stain removal and washing and then blown dry in the wind and fresh air. Once that was done, he could move forward to live a sincere and truthful life with the joy of forgiveness and gladness in his songs and in his heart.

Be encouraged
That our sins can be washed away.

Pray
Thank God for his mercy.

125
Pure heart

Question time

🍃 Have you ever had a change of heart about something or somebody?

Read Psalm 51:10-15

Comment

David wishes for a change of heart: a pure heart. What does this mean?

The nappy has new life when its stains have been removed and it's been washed. The process, however, will need to be repeated time and again! A washing machine isn't used once a year, or even once a month; it's used frequently. And think how many times during the day you wash your hands to rid them of grime and germs... If we have confessed our sins to God and asked Jesus to be our Saviour, we will be cleansed from sin. We have been saved! But we continue to be saved on a daily basis as we continue to live in a fallen world. One day when our earthly life is over or when Jesus returns, we will be saved for ever. It's a process.

Be encouraged

A life lived with God means that we are being gradually changed into the likeness of Christ. We are new creatures being renewed.

Pray

Ask God to create in you a pure heart and to change you little by little, into a purer, more Christ-like person.

126
Proper worship

Question time

🍃 **What is the secret of proper worship?**

Read Psalm 51:16-19

Comment

The Old Testament prophets frequently reminded the people about honest, humble worship. Jesus had a fascinating conversation with a woman from Samaria. The circumstances were unusual in that he was talking to a woman; she was a foreigner, and their chat was not polite small talk but a genuine philosophical and religious discussion about God. The conversation got around to the subject of worship and Jesus said, 'The time is coming and is already here, when by the power of God's Spirit people will worship the Father as he really is, offering him the true worship that he wants. God is Spirit, and only by the power of his Spirit can people worship him as he really is' (John 4:23, 24).

As a result of this conversation, many of the Samaritans in the town where the lady lived, believed in Jesus! 'We know that he really is the Saviour of the world' (John 4:42).

Humility and repentance are the starting point for worship. How we worship – the ingredients of worship and how they're mixed together and presented as an offering of thanksgiving to God – should be the outcome of that humility and repentance.

Challenge

Think about how you worship God – at home on your own, and in the church where your community of believers gather together.

Pray

For the integrity of worshippers, including yourself.

127
Razor tongue

Question time

Have you ever said something spiteful or harsh about someone else – to them, or to others?

Read Psalm 52:1-4

Comment

'Sticks and stones may break my bones, but words will never hurt me.' True or false? If you've ever had a broken wrist or broken leg, you'll know the pain that results. And we may teach our children not to be concerned by cruel words in the playground, but in reality we all know that words can be very harmful. Another saying that was directed at me after I'd been spiteful was, 'Is it kind, is it true, is it necessary?' Often my words were unkind. Sometimes the nasty comments I made to other people may have been true, but they certainly weren't necessary! James, in his New Testament letter, warns us to be careful what we say:

No one has ever been able to tame the tongue. It is evil and uncontrollable, full of deadly poison. We use it to give thanks to our Lord and Father and also to curse other people, who are created in the likeness of God. Words of thanksgiving and cursing pour out from the same mouth. My friends, this should not happen! (James 3:8-10).

David was speaking of those who would put him down: his enemies. James is speaking to his fellow-Christians.

Challenge
Whoever we are, and whatever the circumstances, we need to beware of having a razor tongue.

Pray
That the way in which you speak, and the words you say, may be positive and helpful rather than negative and critical.

128
Wicked!

Question time

🍃 How would you define the word 'wicked'?

Read Psalm 52:5-9

Comment

Those who ignore God or deliberately flout his ways are doomed. They may appear to flourish and be in control but it is short-lived. In Proverbs 10:30 we read, 'Righteous people will always have security, but the wicked will not survive in the land.' Sometimes, it seems that the wicked are thriving and it's the righteous who suffer. Goodies and baddies again but God sees all that goes on. He's not a distant and disinterested deity. He has a relational purpose for his creation and that includes you and me.

David, by way of contrast, finds his security in the Lord. What analogy would you use to describe yourself as a member of God's kingdom? David uses that of the olive tree. What are some of the olive tree's characteristics? The trees were valued and useful in the Mediterranean lands and cultivation of them began early on in Canaan. They do well on rocky ground, are slow-growing but productive – eventually – when they bear fruit. The olive tree is a symbol of peace and is long-lived, undergoing renewal as it ages.

Challenge

David likens himself to an olive tree and if you apply some of the characteristics above to David, you can see why. Could your secure life in God be described in a similar way?

Pray

For wicked people, those who flout God's laws and the laws of the land.

129

Atheism

Question time

How do you respond to comments from atheist friends who say there is no God?

Read Psalm 53:1-6

Comment

Do you believe in God? The likelihood, if you're reading this, is that you do. And from the point of view of the believer, it's baffling how anyone could *not* believe in God. It's also puzzling that some people who claim there is no God, have a great deal to say about him!

In this psalm people who say there is no God are called fools. The dictionary defines a fool as someone who acts unwisely or imprudently; a silly person. One trait of a fool is that he has a great deal to say but doesn't listen to wisdom. In the book of Proverbs there are many references to fools: 'When fools speak, trouble is not far off' (Proverbs 10:14).

Proverbs 12:15 is blunt: 'Stupid people always think they are right.'

Hymn writer, Walter Chalmers Smith, writing in 1867, describes God as immortal, invisible and wise. If we deny God's existence, we miss out on his wisdom. When we live with God in relationship, we walk his way and live his wisdom. Proverbs 28:26 indicates that it is foolish to follow your own opinions.

Challenge

Don't judge others for their folly but, rather, make sure that you yourself are not a fool and that you're setting an example as someone who walks humbly with God.

Pray

For anyone you know who denies the existence of God.

130
Attack and Defence

Question time

Would you prefer to attack or defend in a sport? Why?

Read Psalm 54:1-7

Comment

Is it your instinct to hit back verbally at someone who has had a go at you? Or even physically? Is that the macho thing to do? Is it the wise thing to do?

David so often has problems with those who abuse him, verbally and physically. But he doesn't attack back. Instead, he talks to God, with whom he has a permanent and solid relationship.

'Save me . . .'; 'Set me free . . .'; 'Hear my prayer . . .'; 'Listen . . .'. When you're under attack, maybe from a member of your family, or someone at work, how do you react? What is your first instinct? To lash out, or to take it to the Lord in prayer?

David's trust in the God who chose him to be king is unwavering. 'God is my helper,' he says, 'The Lord is my defender.' David knows that God is faithful (verse 5) and he's had plenty of help in the past from God, so is reassured that God will continue to rescue him from his troubles.

Challenge
Do you have that same sort of faith in the faithful God?

Pray
For umpires and referees in sport, that they may administer fair play.

131

Escapism

Question time

> If you had the opportunity, where would you choose to escape to? Why?

Read Psalm 55:1-8

Comment

The psalms are all about the bond between God and people. They are also about the everyday life of his people – their concerns, their relationships, their illnesses, their grief. They're very honest and the writers are not afraid to express their weariness, sense of rejection, isolation, anger – and their dependence on, and relationship with God. If you can't tell your closest friend your joys and concerns, there is something missing in the friendship.

And so we find David pouring out his heart again at the terror and exhaustion he feels in the face of opposition. No wonder he wishes to fly away and escape from the turmoil. Life in this world will have periods of distress and fear as well as celebrations and joy. If we expect life as believers in God to be stress-free, we delude ourselves. The psalms alone teach us that life is tough and the Bible as a whole gives us plenty of examples of people who experience very testing times.

Challenge

Despite David's longing to escape, he is realistic enough to know that that is not the answer. The best way to deal with our life situations is to face them with God, so right at the beginning of this prayer, David engages with God. Can you do the same?

Pray

For anyone you know who is particularly distressed at the moment.

132
Betrayal

Question time

- **Have you ever let somebody down?**
- **Have you been let down yourself?**
  Think of the circumstances and how you felt in each case.

Read Psalm 55:9-15

Comment

We only have to watch our TV screens or see news bulletins on our Smartphones to know that there is violence in our cities, and crime and trouble are prevalent. David speaks of destruction, oppression and fraud. We've probably all come across people who've let us down. Fraudsters who've got into our computer system; or an authentic-sounding tradesman who dupes us into buying something that turns out to be dodgy. But it's somehow much worse if you've been let down by a close friend or work colleague. You feel betrayed. Maybe you've been the one to let down somebody else.

How must Jesus have felt when Peter denied knowing him, or when Judas received money for betraying him, or when James and John argued, or when Thomas expressed his doubts?

None of us can claim to be incapable of betrayal.

David is devastated that he's been let down by someone with whom he had 'intimate talks' and with whom he worshipped.

Be encouraged

To be an authentic and loyal friend, taking your example from God whose authenticity and loyalty to us is perfect.

Pray

For the people involved in marriages where there has been betrayal.

133
Let it go

Question time

> When someone lets you down, you can brush it off with a shrug, dwell on it incessantly and let it gnaw away at you, or you can put it all in God's capable hands. Which would you do?

Read Psalm 55:16-23

Comment

Jesus told people to lay down their burdens and rest in him. Easier said than done?

David starts this section of the psalm with a call to God for his help and the confident affirmation that God will save him. He then reminds himself and us and God that no part of the day or night is free from him moaning and groaning at God! He knows that God will hear his whingeing voice and he's not afraid to keep on at God. In verse 19 he acknowledges God as the one who has 'ruled from eternity' and that God is in control. But then he picks up the baggage again in verses 20 and 21, before relinquishing it to God again in verse 22.

Challenge

How prepared are you to 'leave your troubles with the Lord'? In Peter's first letter he urges his readers to, 'Leave all your worries with him, because he cares for you' (1 Peter 5:7).

Pray

Lord God, I may not have to fight the physical battles that David did as king. I have different battles, but a psalm like this reminds me that I don't have to fight my battles alone.

134
Mere humans

Question time

How do you react when things go wrong?

Read Psalm 56:1-4

Comment

When things go wrong, do you praise God? No, probably not. We don't praise God for *what* goes wrong; that would be illogical, and hypocritical when we're scared or angry inside. But can you praise God *in* the crisis or *in* the ongoing turmoil? That is a different matter. God is God in all circumstances. He is there in every situation. Common sense tells us that, because we live in the world, we will experience all the tests of daily life. God tells us that his hand is on us, that he has a purpose for us and that purpose will be fulfilled – whatever bricks are hurled our way.

David had been captured by the Philistines in Gath. Look at the words he uses: under attack; my enemies persecute me all the time; all day long

opponents attack; there are so many who fight against me . . . How does David deal with it? With a 'when'. He doesn't say, *If* I'm afraid, but *When* I am afraid . . He is a realist. He admits to God that he gets scared, he puts his trust in God and praises God for his promises. In the light of that, human attack comes from 'mere' humans.

Challenge

Think of circumstances where you've been afraid. How do you approach God – with reproach or praise?

Pray

Help me, God, to be authentic when I come to you. Thank you that you know me and understand my fears and are ever present with me.

135
The list of tears

Question time

🌿 What makes you cry? A poignant scene in a book; an emotional scene in a movie; a fall that breaks your leg; redundancy; the sight of starving people overseas; seeing your football team lose a vital match; the death of a precious loved one...?

Read Psalm 56:5-11

Comment

I heard today of the death of a lady of faith. She was the same age as me. Years of physical illness and pain, coupled with the mental anguish of depression, had taken their toll. So many tears had been shed. Now the tears flow from her loved ones who mourn their loss, made all the sadder because she had taken her own life.

David says he is 'troubled'. God knows how many tears David has shed. Even listed them in his book!

A number of God's books are mentioned in the Bible. This is a particularly comforting verse, showing just how much God notices and cares about our lives. We read elsewhere that he knows the number of hairs on our head; here he knows how many tears we've shed. Wherever the attacks on us come from – other people, circumstances, illness . . . we can be assured of God's understanding.

Be encouraged
To trust the God who knows you so well.

Pray
David repeats the refrain in verses 10 and 11 that he had used in verse 4, underlining his trust in God's promises. Can you do the same?

Companionship

Question time

🍃 Do you prefer to go for a walk on your own or with someone else? Why?

Read Psalm 56:12, 13

Comment

I stood in the Kop at Liverpool's football ground when I was a teenager. All around me was the sound of men (mostly) belting out, *You'll never walk alone.* It was stirring, if not always melodious, stuff.

In these beautiful verses at the end of the psalm, David responds to God's promise of companionship by committing himself to God. Companionship is a two-way thing. David is hugely appreciative of God's presence and help. He offers his deeply felt thanks to God. He doesn't just walk in the presence of God, wonderful though that is, but in the *light* of God too.

David walked in the light of God's presence. Christian believers have the privilege of walking in the light of Christ. Jesus said, 'I am the light of the world. Whoever follows me will have the light of life and will never walk in darkness' (John 8:12).

John H Sammis (1846-1919) wrote the hymn, 'When we walk with the Lord, in the light of his love, what a glory he sheds on our way.'

Challenge
Are you walking in that light?

Pray
Praise God that you need never walk alone.

137

Supply and demand

Question time

What would you do if – or what have you done when – there hasn't been enough money for your basic needs?

Read Psalm 57:1-4

Comment

I found Economics 'A' Level unutterably boring, as it seemed to consist of endless discussion and plotting of tables and graphs on the topic of supply and demand. Since then I've lived through times when there has been a shortage of various products. Supply has gone down, demand has gone up, and people have had to go without – or else pay inflated prices for the desired product.

Gladys Aylward, a parlourmaid at the beginning of the twentieth century, felt called by God to go to China and share the good news of Jesus. She had little in the way of financial resources and it seemed, humanly speaking, impossible for her to get there. She didn't have enough money for the voyage by ship but scraped together enough for the train fare to Vladivostok. Throughout her frugally lived life she depended on God's provision.

God is the great supplier, the great provider. David was on the run from Saul but basic needs of shelter and food were provided for him. The picture of God painted in these verses shows a God who protects, supplies, and is constant in his love and faithfulness – despite the ferocious 'teeth' and 'tongues' of opposition.

Be encouraged

'My God will supply all your needs' (Philippians 4:19).

Pray

For people who are dependent on food banks for basic meals.

138
Glory in the skies

Question time

What attracts you about your favourite time of day or season of the year? Why?

Read Psalm 57:5-11

Comment

There's something of a comic touch about the end of verse 6 though I don't imagine it was particularly comical for David at the time. But it's another reminder that God is sovereign, that his enemies will be defeated, and so David can say, in verse 7, that he has complete confidence in God. Trust in God evokes a response of obedience, and confidence in God leads to praise of him.

This section of the psalm begins and ends with a refrain of praise for God's magnificent majesty, exemplified in the glory of the sky and in the earth – all over the world. I always think that David would have been overcome with wonder to see the pictures we're privileged to see from space. How he would love the pictures of the blue planet which we inhabit, with its swirling cloud patterns, its brown deserts, green plains and vast oceans. Imagine what kind of psalm he might write!

Challenge

How could you respond in praise of God? Try writing a psalm, paint a picture of a sunset, go out and take photographs – taking time to really observe what you're witnessing in the sky and not just banging off umpteen digital pictures without thinking! Or simply take time to look up.

Pray

Pray with your eyes open in praise of God's creativity in the skies.

139
Slimy snails

Question time

- If someone harms you, what's your first instinct?
- To lash out physically or verbally?
- To curse them and wish them the worst?

Read Psalm 58:1-11

Comment

David speaks of snakes, lions, snails, dead babies, and weeds in this verbal onslaught on wicked people. His spoken curse is what theologians call imprecation. David calls on God to mete out punishment. David hands over to God, the judge of all the earth, the responsibility of judging fairly.

On top of the Old Bailey in London there is the Statue of Justice. In one hand Justice holds aloft the sword of retribution, in the other the scales of justice. These symbols represent fairness and impartiality in the carrying out of the law.

In David's time it seems that the rulers of the land were far from fair. They were godless, didn't listen to God and refused to obey God. Their judgements on the people were neither good nor fair.

An anagram of *imprecation* is Prime Action. We leave the Prime Action of judgement to God. He, and he alone, has ultimate authority to judge people. And he will be completely fair.

Be encouraged

We may mutter or utter imprecations about the wickedness we see and God knows how we feel, but in the end we can say, with David, 'There is indeed a God who judges the world.'

Pray

For magistrates, barristers and judges.

140
Snarling dogs

Question time

- What animals are you afraid of?
- Have you ever been attacked by an animal?

Read Psalm 59:1-7

Comment

Our family was on a beach when my 5-year-old was attacked by two dogs. They were giant poodles and far bigger than she was. In her terror she waved her arms about and the dogs thought it was a game and jumped on her. Her owners, higher up the beach, laughed. My daughter was traumatised and has been wary of dogs ever since.

David wrote this psalm after Saul had sent men to watch his house and find an opportunity to kill him. He likens these cruel prowlers to snarling dogs with tongues like swords. It's a terrifying picture. No wonder David calls on God to come to his aid.

Perhaps you could pray, as Reginald Heber (1783-1826) wrote, 'Brightest and best of the sons of the morning, dawn on our darkness, and lend us thine aid.' One darkness that Heber faced was the death of his infant daughter in the same year that he wrote this hymn.

Be encouraged

God is there in our dark places but we have the assurance of the light of Christ that dawns on our darkness.

Pray

Lord Jesus, you are the brightest and best of the sons of the morning. Please dawn on anyone who is in darkness today and give them your aid.

141

Growls and songs

Question time

> Other than cats and dogs, which animal species are prevalent where you live?

Read Psalm 59:8-17

Comment

So-called 'wild' animals are encroaching more and more on our urban areas in search of food. In the UK foxes are seen increasingly in towns. Leopards prowl round Mumbai, penguins waddle through Cape Town, sika deer tip-toe in Japan, mountain lions prowl in Los Angeles, black bears upend bins in Boulder, Colorado, and polar bears visit Churchill in Manitoba.

Such animal behaviour causes wary amusement, annoyance, and fear according to where you stand (literally and metaphorically). David's enemies were like snarling dogs invading his city and leaping at his door. Verse 14 is an action replay of verse 6. And yet David finishes this psalm with an outburst –

not of curses this time, but of praise for God. God's strength, his constant love, the fact that he is a refuge, shelter, and defender for David, are what prevails.

Martin Luther (1483-1546) wrote: 'A safe stronghold our God is still, a trusty shield and weapon; he'll keep us clear from all the ill that hath us now o'ertaken.' What was relevant in David's time and in Martin Luther's time, is relevant in our time. Our role is to trust God and obey him. We may growl at him sometimes in our fear and frustration but we also sing songs of praise to our faithful God.

Challenge

Think of a time when you have known God to be your refuge.

Pray

Praise God for his strength and constancy.

142

Earthquake

Question time

🍃 **Do you have a favourite psalm?** I bet it isn't Psalm 60! It isn't an easy one to understand but, like all of the Bible, it is there to help us understand God's history, his-story, and the way he deals with people in relationship with them.

Read Psalm 60:1-12

Comment

David feels rejected by God, thinks God is angry with his people, and has even abandoned them. He uses the image of an earthquake to express his thought that the land is falling apart and the people suffering. He cries out to God for deliverance.

Earthquakes occur all over the world. We tend to think of the world we inhabit as being solid and stable. But that's not the case. Earth is active, constantly on the move. Earthquakes tend to make the news because they happen suddenly and with devastating results. The bigger the quake the greater the damage.

Earth-shaking happenings are not just rumbles and splits in the ground beneath our feet. They can occur when we hear a life-threatening diagnosis, or when there is a sudden bereavement in the family, or when we're made redundant. The upside of this psalm is in verse 6 where we see God in his sanctuary and are reminded that he is holy.

Be encouraged
In the calm quiet of the sanctuary David can leave the turmoil outside and trust that God will prevail.

Pray
For people who are affected by the damage of earthquakes.

Despair

Question time

🍃 Think of a time when you've been far from home and felt homesick.

Read Psalm 61:1-8

Comment

Eruptions of the Icelandic volcano, Eyjafjallajökull, in 2010 caused an ash cloud that led to the unprecedented closure of much airspace. My husband was in Singapore at the time and ready to come back home to the UK.

In verse 2 we read, 'In despair and far from home I call to you!' My husband wasn't in despair but he did call to God and he called to me, via email, for news and for deliverance! His safe refuge was, in turn, the airport floor (2 nights), a hotel bed (2 nights), the ballroom floor of a hotel at Singapore airport (1 night), a seat in a plane to Barcelona, another plane seat to Santander, the floor of a ferry to Plymouth (1 night) and a seat on the train home. It was a prolonged journey home.

Be encouraged

It's not surprising that David, in his exile, longed for a permanent place in God's sanctuary and for protection under God's 'wings'. David didn't forget, despite his dire straits, that God's constant love and faithfulness continue whatever the circumstances of life.

Pray

I don't know your circumstances but can you, like David in verse 8, sing praises to God?

144
Broken fences

Question time

On a scale of 1 to 10, how patient are you?

Read Psalm 62:1-7

Comment

Our garden fence blew down in a ferocious gale one night. The fence's wobbliness had increased with each strong wind over a long period. Then came the gale that toppled it completely. Each section lay flattened.

David thinks of himself as a flattened fence, something that was once robust but unable to withstand the gales that come in the form of human opposition.

Count how many times the words *defend* and *defender* are used in these verses. David is full of trust in God's faithfulness and he has learnt to wait patiently for God to act. He has every confidence in God. Why? Because he can look back and see how God has provided for him in the past, how he has saved him and keeps on saving him, and how hope is found in God alone.

Be encouraged

Broken fences can be mended, re-erected, ready to do their job of protection. God wants to stand us up again and we can be confident that he will. Even when other gales come, as they surely will, he is there to prop us up.

Pray

For patience when you feel flattened by life's circumstances.

145

Weight

Question time

- How much do you weigh?
- Are you a lightweight or a heavyweight?
- Or somewhere in between?

Read Psalm 62:8-12

Comment

Much is made of people's weight. Some are too heavy, some are too light; some think they're too heavy, some think they're too light. Metaphorically, the seemingly heavyweights of the world: robbers, the violent, the wealthy... appear to have the upper hand, but it is short-lived. Jesus spoke about many people 'who now are first will be last, and many who now are last will be first' (Matthew 19:30).

For those of us who haven't been up into space, the nearest we come to weightlessness is probably when we're in the swimming pool, floating on our back and letting the water hold us up. David likens human beings to puffs of breath that weigh nothing, so light they're like a mere breath. By contrast, in verse 11 David acknowledges God's power.

The power of the heavyweight baddies will be dissipated into nothing compared with the good and holy heavyweight that is God. It makes sense to do as David does and 'trust in God at all times' (verse 8).

Be encouraged

To do as it says in Proverbs 3:5, 6, 'Trust in the Lord with all your heart. Never rely on what you think you know. Remember the Lord in everything you do, and he will show you the right way.'

Pray

For anyone who struggles with weight issues.

146

Feast

Question time

- What's the best meal you've ever had?
- What were the circumstances?

Read Psalm 63:1-5

Comment

My young grandson attended a large gathering where a buffet table was laden with food for afternoon tea. His eyes nearly popped out of his head. He was over-awed by the colours, textures, shapes, and variety of the food on offer: sandwiches, sausage rolls, mini pizzas, crisps, macaroons, fairy cakes, meringues, chocolate sponge, fruit cake . . . It wasn't long before his plate was filled and his taste buds could start enjoying the feast.

David was in the desert: a dry, worn-out and waterless land. He longed for a feast. Is that correct? No. In verse 1 he tells God, 'I long for you. My whole being desires you . . . my soul is thirsty for you.' Do you have the same desire for God as you do for the

food at a feast? Do you *feed on him with thanksgiving* as the words of the Communion service say? At the end of the Communion service we say, *We thank you for feeding us* . . . Jesus invited his friends to remember him through bread and wine representing his body and blood.

Challenge

Do you feast on God's bounty? It is not David's body that is filled with food, but his soul. 'My soul will feast and be satisfied, and I will sing glad songs of praise to you.'

Pray

Use these five verses as your personal prayer now.

147

Clinging

Question time

🍃 Are you a touchy-feely sort of person or do you prefer little physical contact with someone else?

Read Psalm 63:6-11

Comment

A baby koala starts life inside its mother's pouch. Once it's too big for the pouch it clings to its mother's belly for warmth and shelter but also rides on its mother's back, clinging tightly as they climb through the gum trees, looking for the best gum leaves. It's an endearing picture of relationship bonding.

David clings to God (verse 8). Do you cling to God? Or do you hold him at arm's length? Or are you detached from him completely? The clinging is that between a parent and child, in this case between God the heavenly Father and his adopted son, David.

In the New Testament Jesus talks about his own relationship with the Father. It's a close relationship of communication and interdependence. Jesus encourages his followers to have a relationship with God. We can be adopted into God's family and be his children. In John 1 we read that many people did not receive Jesus as God's Word made flesh, but 'Some, however, did receive him and believed in him, so he gave them the right to become God's children' (John 1:12).

Be encouraged
To cling to God. You are his child!

Pray
For families where hugs don't happen.

148
Mobs

Question time

- Have you taken part in demonstrations?
- Is there a place in society for people to gather for a cause?

Read Psalm 64:1-10

Comment

My husband took our two elder daughters on a birthday outing to London on 31 March 1990. I stayed at home with their little sister. The girls could have been forgiven for thinking all the world was out to celebrate the birthday as they approached Trafalgar Square where thousands of people were gathered. It was soon evident that this was no happy occasion but a protest for the unpopular Poll Tax introduced by the British government.

Paul, in the New Testament, was confronted by 'worthless loafers' who formed a mob in Thessalonica to oppose Paul and his message of good news about Jesus (Acts 17). In the Garden of Gethsemane Jesus was approached by Judas who arrived with a mob to arrest Jesus (Mark 14:43). Later, Pilate was shouted at by the raucous crowd – a mob – who wanted Jesus handed over for crucifixion.

God's people must expect opposition and sometimes it's one against many. Waiting at home for my family to return from London, I prayed for their protection. David prays for his own protection.

Challenge

Is there ever a time when it would be right, as a believer in God, to demonstrate?

Pray

Remember in your prayers believers who are isolated and under attack.

149
The whole world

Question time

🍃 Do you ever pray for Christians overseas?

🍃 If so, why? If not, why not?

Read Psalm 65:1-8

Comment

God's promises and purpose feature throughout the Bible. His great plan was outlined to Abraham when he told Abraham that he would have many descendants and that they would become a great nation (Genesis 12). Through the years of the patriarchs God multiplied the nation until a vast array of people moved towards the promised land in the time of Moses and Joshua. The judges followed, then the kings and prophets and God's people were growing numerically, despite their lapses from faith and obedience. Eventually Jesus arrived as the Saviour and in John 3:16 Jesus tells Nicodemus that, 'God loved the world so much that he gave his only

Son, so that everyone who believes in him may not die but have eternal life.'

Jesus' own disciples found it a hard concept to grasp that God loved the whole world and not just the chosen Jewish people. Peter learns the lesson when he visits Cornelius, a Gentile, and is told by God that the rescue plan of salvation is available for everyone.

David, in this psalm, has a clear vision of what is and what is to come. 'People everywhere will come to you on account of their sins' (verse 2); 'People all over the world and across the distant seas trust in you' (verse 5). And verse 8 summarises how God's message is absorbed by people everywhere.

Challenge

Choose a country and find out about the Christians in that place.

Pray

For Christian believers in your country of choice.

150

Harvest

Question time

🍃 What do you grow in your garden or allotment or window box or in a pot indoors?

Read Psalm 65:9-13

Comment

The first ripening cherry tomatoes in the hanging basket, the first courgette flower with the promise of its tasty fruit, the blackcurrant bush laden with fruit ... There is such joy in harvest, whether it's gathered from pots on a window ledge, an allotment, or vast fields.

David is full of the joys of harvest. He writes expansively about God's bounty and provision for us. We may pray, 'Give us today our daily bread . . .' as Jesus taught us. But do we make a habit of saying thank you to God for what he gives us each day? Jesus himself paused to give thanks for food before eating. Can we wait before picking up the knife and fork to take a moment to say grace?

Let's acknowledge God, the provider, and pass on the habit to our children as we recognise that we're not just consumers but receivers of God's gifts.

Challenge

When you sit down to eat, why not apply the 5, 10, 15, 20 programme: 5 deep breaths during which you look at and give thanks for the food, 10 seconds between each mouthful so you can savour the flavour and appreciate it, 15 minutes to eat the food, then 20 minutes to go for a walk and digest it. Don't take the harvest for granted. Be truly thankful.

Pray

For harvest workers in the UK, many of whom are migrant labour and far from home.

151

Come and see

Question time

How do you share news within your family or circle of friends?

Read Psalm 66:1-9

Comment

One of the joys of WhatsApp is that our family: my husband and I, our three daughters, their husbands and their children, can all share little snippets of what's going on in our different patches of the British Isles. Someone will post a picture of the sunrise; someone else will show a picture of their child with a completed jigsaw puzzle or Lego model; someone will share a joke, someone will share a Bible verse... Although we can't physically 'come and see', we can see through the modern methods of communication, enjoy each other's joys and commiserate with each other's woes.

David invites us to 'Come and see what God has done' (verse 5). He's bubbling over with joy and excitement for God. He doesn't hold back. He sings, he shouts, he worships, he rejoices. Can you do the same? And share it with others?

When the women arrived at the tomb where Jesus had been buried, they were invited by an angel to, 'Come and see' (Matthew 28:6). They saw that Jesus had been raised from death; he wasn't there! But that wasn't the end of the angel's message. He then told the women to, 'Go and tell' (Matthew 28:7).

Challenge

Are you as keen to share the good news of Jesus as you are to share news with family or friends?

Pray

Lord God, I've read and heard your good news. Help me to share it so that others may come and see too.

152
But now

Question time

🍃 **Have you ever been weighed down by a heavy rucksack or bags of shopping?** The burden may have become so intolerable that you felt unable to move forward.

Read Psalm 66:10-20

Comment

Imagine a set of old-fashioned scales. On one side you have the bowl; on the other the weights. You place a weight on one side and then measure out the required amount of flour into the bowl.

If you weigh up your life, there might be heavy weights on one side and not enough in the bowl to make it balance. Sometimes it may be the other way round. The bowl is laden with goodies and the weights are light. That's life.

David outlines, in verses 11 and 12, the burdens he has had weighing him down. And then he comes up with the two little words, 'but now'. Those two words redress the balance as he acknowledges God's goodness to him. Sin and troubles had weighed him down. Forgiveness and joys have replaced them.

Be encouraged

God does not reject our prayers – ever. And he never removes his love from us. Troubles come and go but God remains constant.

Pray

For peace and a lifting of burdens from those who are heavy-hearted.

Everyone praise God

Question time

🍃 Of all the blessings given in the Bible, do you have a favourite?

Read Psalm 67:1-7

Comment

This lovely psalm featured in the Book of Common prayer as part of the Anglican service of Evening Prayer. It was sung as an alternative to the Nunc Dimittis. Its Latin title is Deus Misereatur, which you might think sounds miserable but in fact translates as 'God is gracious', and is a song of thanksgiving, with the repeated chorus in verses 3 and 5.

It's a beautiful psalm to sing at any time of day but maybe particularly at evening time when we can come quietly before God and rejoice in the gift we've had of another day. We ponder God's mercy and kindness and ask him to bless us, not just for our benefit but for the benefit of everyone – so that the whole world may know God's will and his salvation.

Be encouraged

It's good to praise God when we're on our own and when we're with other people. This psalm uses the plural throughout so this is really a song for corporate worship. Maybe next time your family is together, or your home group, you could say it or sing it together.

Pray

The psalm at bedtime tonight.

154
Provision

Question time

In your neighbourhood, who provides practical help to those in need?

Read Psalm 68:1-10

Comment

While the world emphasises power and wealth, God focuses on the marginalised of society. The kingdom of God is open to anyone, irrespective of circumstances, but Jesus said it would be harder for a rich man to enter the kingdom of heaven. Orphans and widows, those imprisoned by addiction, mental health issues, loneliness or poverty, are looked upon with compassion by God, as are those who are persecuted and imprisoned for their faith.

Jesus, preaching in Nazareth, quoted Isaiah 61: 'The Spirit of the Lord is upon me, because he has chosen me to bring good news to the poor. He has sent me to proclaim liberty to the captives and recovery of sight to the blind; to set free the oppressed and announce that the time has come when the Lord will save his people' (Luke 4:18, 19). James, in his letter, reminded the believers to treat people with respect and courtesy – whatever their outward appearance and status. He wrote, 'What God the Father considers to be pure and genuine religion is this: to take care of orphans and widows in their suffering and to keep oneself from being corrupted by the world' (James 1:27).

Challenge

David recognises God's provision. Do we? How do we provide, in God's name, for those in need?

Pray

For orphans and widows, street pastors, refuge managers.

155
God our porter

Question time

🍃 What is burdening you today in your personal life, or in the life of the world?

Read Psalm 68:11-20

Comment

The Sherpas of Nepal are famous for their support of mountaineers. The logistics of getting climbers up Everest are complicated and have to be organised with military precision. A lot of equipment has to be carried, plus food and medical supplies, and it is the Sherpas who are hired to help out in the movement of people and baggage up the mountains. Pictures of the porters show them climbing slowly and steadily, taking the burden from the climbers.

God is our porter, according to David in verse 19 of this psalm. He carries our burdens day after day. Some days the burden may be light; other times it can be very heavy and would weigh us down. Is there something that is getting you down, something that makes you feel unable to put one foot in front of the other? Maybe it's bad news, or illness or a dilemma for which there seems to be no answer.

Be encouraged
Thank God for his constant willingness to carry our burdens, not just once but whenever we need help in that way.

Pray
For men and women who risk their own lives in their service to adventurers.

156

Procession

Question time

🍃 Think of a time when you have taken part in a procession. What was the occasion?

Read Psalm 68:21-27

Comment

When my grandson was seven years old, he was a Beaver in the Scout movement and walked in procession on 11 November as part of the Remembrance Day commemorations in the village where he lives. How proud he was to be taking part in this important occasion which culminated in a service of thanksgiving for those who'd given their lives to ensure peace in our country.

David describes a procession in these verses. The focus of the procession is God himself. Many people take part: singers, tambourine girls, musicians and the people themselves. In our cathedrals and churches, now as in centuries past, there are processions that mark special occasions: Advent, Christmas, Easter, when believers want everyone who witnesses the procession to know that it is God who is being celebrated.

Every Good Friday in my home town there is a procession of witness through the town. Hot cross buns are given out to passers-by. Brightly coloured balloons are given to children. The message is that Jesus died for our sins and rose to new life.

Challenge

Think about the relevance, or not, of Christian processions today. What do they 'say' to people who witness them?

Pray

For Christians taking part in religious processions, that their witness may be noted by onlookers and that those who watch may want to know more of Christ.

157
Majesty

Question time

🍃 **Can you define the word 'majesty'?**

Read Psalm 68:28-35

Comment

Have you ever been to tea with Her Majesty the Queen? It's probably something many people would like to do, but only a few have that privilege. Some are fortunate enough to be received by the Queen in different places and for various reasons. She meets people from all over the world – very important people and 'ordinary' mortals. Crowds flock to peer through the railings of Buckingham Palace, hoping for a glimpse of Her Majesty. People line the streets as she rides by.

The magnificence of Her Majesty pales into insignificance against the magnificence of the King of kings. And I dare say Her Majesty the Queen would be the first to acknowledge that. In this section of the psalm David talks about people coming from afar to acknowledge God and how all the kingdoms of the world praise the Lord. His might and majesty are not confined to one small place or building but are universal. No wonder David ends this psalm with the simple but profound acclamation, 'Praise God!'

Challenge

How do you praise God? What lengths would you go to encounter God?

Pray

For heads of state.

158
Mud

Question time

- Have you ever walked through a bog or in quicksand?
- What were the issues that arose from such an experience?

Read Psalm 69:1-3

Comment

There's a beach in Wales which has 'podgy' sand. When you walk on the sand your feet sink into it and each step is labour-intensive as you try and lift your foot from all that is trying to draw it further down – when you want to go upwards and onwards. The problem is compounded when the tide comes in.

In a different part of Wales I was walking with my husband and daughter across a peat area of heather, rock and bog. We'd struck off, away from the path and the going was hard. Petulance arose when our daughter put her trainer-shod foot into an invisible patch of bog. 'This is a miserable walk,' she exclaimed as we hauled her out of the mire and sympathised with her blackened, sodden shoe and wet foot. Years on we can smile, even laugh, at the experience but it wasn't funny at the time. Life is harsh at times. And deals us unexpected blows that pull us down. But while there's life – and God – all is not lost. So we walk on, with hope in our hearts.

Be encouraged

David begs God to save him from deep mud. Are you experiencing being bogged down in deep mud at the moment? Don't be afraid to call on God to save you.

Pray

For people struggling to escape being pulled down by muddy experiences.

159
Multiple enemies

Question time

Have you ever received punishment or derision for standing up for an innocent person?

Read Psalm 69:4-8

Comment

Imagine your boss calls a meeting of his employees. You turn up, hoping there might be news of a pay rise or pats on the back for good work. Instead, your boss tells you that he will be put on trial for a crime that he didn't commit, and that you, his employees, will receive the backlash and be persecuted yourselves, hounded by media, gossiped about by passers-by, derided and punished for being associated with your innocent boss.

David faced that kind of persecution. But listen to this: 'If people persecuted me, they will persecute you too . . . This, however, was bound to happen so that what is written in their Law may come true: "They hated me for no reason at all."' (John 15:20, 25).

That was Jesus speaking to his disciples, shortly before his arrest, trial and death. Anyone who is serious about loving God and obeying him, can expect persecution, bullying, ostracism, hatred – for doing nothing other than being a member of God's kingdom. David, Jesus, the disciples, and his followers through all ages, know that such trials are par for the course. David says those who hate him are more numerous than the hairs on his head. Jesus said that God knows us so thoroughly that he knows the number of hairs on our head.

Be encouraged

When we are God's, no enemy can overcome him – or us.

Pray

For persecuted Christians.

160
Insults

Question time

What would you regard as the worst insult somebody could give you?

Read Psalm 69:9-15

Comment

Take a look at the second phrase of verse 9. David is speaking directly to God when he says, 'the insults which are hurled at you fall on me'. The emphasis is on the *you*. This is a kind of comfort to those of us who are insulted because of our love for God. It is *he* who is the target of their attack. We are his representatives. They can't attack God himself so they attack us. We may feel outrage that anyone should dare to attack and insult our God but God is big enough to take it, and he's overcome the world anyway. The question is, are *we* big enough to take the insults on God's behalf? If in doubt, take it to the Lord in prayer, as David does in verses 13-15.

Jesus, in his meeting with the disciples before his death, talked at length with them, teaching, reassuring, encouraging and emboldening them to stick with him whatever happened. In John 16:33 Jesus says, 'The world will make you suffer. But be brave! I have defeated the world.'

Be encouraged

In John 17 Jesus then prays at length for his disciples who, fearful of what is to come and fearful of being left without him, are in need of strength, courage and determination to carry on. Jesus prays for us!

Pray

Thank you, Jesus, for your love for us, that makes you pray for us. May that sustain us as we face insults on your behalf.

161

Revenge

Question time

> Do you ever feel so angry that all you want is revenge on someone who has hurt you or slandered you?

Read Psalm 69:16-28

Comment

When angry, instead of immediately lashing out with a slap on the face or worse, it is better to count to ten or a hundred, or a thousand if necessary, and then make a more measured decision on how to respond.

David appears to be so incensed that he wants immediate revenge, though he doesn't intend to take revenge himself but urges God to do so. Is this the angry verbal lashing out that comes without careful thought? Or just an honest-to-God outpouring of feeling? Either way, it's better that David tells God all about it rather than going to bash his multiple enemies.

Challenge

Are you shocked by David's vehemence in verses 27 and 28? Do you ever ask God to keep someone out of his kingdom, to deny salvation to a person who has wronged you? Fortunately, God is open to hear our cries, but also all-wise and all-knowing and all-loving and anybody's eternal destiny is in his hands and not ours. Just as well . . .

Pray

For those who anger you.

Answers

Question time

> Do you regard letting go of anger to be defeatist or wise? Or what?

Read Psalm 69:29-36

Comment

It's a relief to move from David's anger – justifiable though it may have been – to his less frenzied words of verse 29. He confesses to God just how desperate he feels and asks God to lift him up and save him. There's no better way to deal with desperation than by giving it to God. Once we've done that, we're in a position to praise God. Our praise of God isn't dependent on how *we* feel but on *who God is*.

And so David praises, proclaims and pleases God with an attitude that focuses on God rather than on himself or his enemies. The whole tenor of the psalm changes as David moves from the minor key and discords of verses 22-28 to the major key and beautiful harmonies of verses 30-36. Look at the words used: glad, worship, encouraged, listens, praise, save, live, possess, inherit . . . All positives.

Be encouraged
However bleak our situation may be, God is still God and worthy of praise.

Pray
How can you use words and/or music to praise God right now?

163
Dismay

Question time

> How, practically, do you help change feelings of dismay to something more positive?

Read Psalm 70:1-5

Comment

During a general or local election, politicians beaver away at trying to get support for their cause. They canvas people on the doorstep, in the street, from their 'battle bus' and through leaflets, media and broadcast messages. The people vote and some of the candidates for election will be disappointed. And dismayed. It's happened throughout the history of the democratic process.

Here, David is in a mood of lament. He has put up with assassination attempts on his life and jeers of derision. He knows that God will save him and those who have been against him – and against God – will be dismayed by their defeat. Contrast that with the positivity of verse 4. Those who come to God are glad and joyful and thankful for their salvation. And will proclaim, 'How great is God!'

Challenge

Are you a jeerer or a cheerer? David experienced jeers but didn't retaliate in a similar way. The 'j' was replaced by 'ch' as he praised God. He knew that, however weak and helpless he felt, God was still his Saviour.

Pray

Use the word 'may' to preface phrases of a prayer, as David does.

164
A good example

Question time
🍃 What value do you put on your life, however young or old you are at present?

Read Psalm 71:1-11

Comment

My nephew wasn't impressed by long-life milk when he came to stay with me. 'It tastes different from fresh,' he said. 'True, but it lasts longer.' Unopened, it keeps in the cupboard for months so I know I'll never be caught out by not having milk in the house when unexpected visitors turn up for a cup of tea, a bowl of cornflakes, or a custard fix.

A homeless mum had been 'housed' in a cheap hotel where there was neither a cooker nor a fridge. The local food bank provided her with long-life milk so she could make breakfast for her children.

The old man in this psalm looks back over his long life and sees God's presence in it through the whole range of life's experiences. What a great example he sets! Despite the troubles and suffering he has had, he trusts God for strength for the day. God doesn't want us to worry about what might happen tomorrow. Long-life milk that stays in the carton isn't actually any use, other than as insurance. We need to open the package, pour it out, enjoy it and feel the good that it does us. As he reflects on long life, the elderly man appreciates God's long hold on him and the goodness he has shown him.

Be encouraged

That God's presence is with us at whatever age we are.

Pray

Praise God for the example of elderly Christians.

165
Tell it how it is

Question time

How do you feel about the prospect of your own old age?

Read Psalm 71:12-16

Comment

My 95-year-old dad was in hospital for several weeks before he died. His ageing body had been struggling to keep going. His mobility had decreased, his organs were gradually giving up, and he needed a lot of help. At the end of life 'attacks' may manifest themselves in an inability to eat or to manage bodily functions. The 'hurt' may be physical pain. The 'aid' may come in the form of a young doctor with a stethoscope slung round his neck or a nurse wearing an apron.

Despite the discomfort and pain, the psalmist still finds comfort in God; his life experience shows him how God has been there throughout. He is able to praise God and share his goodness with others.

My dad was unable to read in his last days on earth, but he indicated that he would like psalms to be read to him and for prayers to be said with him. These were witnessed by other patients and hospital staff. As in verse 16 can we, whatever our age and stage, join with the psalmist in witnessing to God's presence? – 'I will proclaim your goodness, yours alone.'

Challenge
Do you proclaim God's goodness?

Pray
For those who care for elderly people in care homes.

166
Lifelong learning

Question time

🍃 **What knowledge and life experiences do you like to share with young people?**

Read Psalm 71:17-24

Comment

Long-life milk, lifelong learning. In his first letter (2:2, 3), Peter, one of Jesus' disciples, wrote, 'Be like newborn babies, always thirsty for the pure spiritual milk, so that by drinking it you may grow up and be saved. As the scripture says, "You have found out for yourselves how kind the Lord is."' The scripture Peter quotes is from Psalm 34:8.

This remarkable old man in Psalm 71 continues to proclaim God's power and might. He wants to share it with younger people too, perhaps in fulfilment of the old laws which encouraged the people of Israel to pass on the faithfulness of God and his practical rules for living, down the generations.

The psalmist is a realist. He doesn't pretend that his life with God has been perfectly wonderful. He has a bit of a go at God in the first phrase of verse 20, then follows it with a 'but' and an expression of confidence in the God who has been with him throughout life.

Challenge and Encouragement

A lifelong desire for the milk of God's word is crucial for our spiritual development. The Israelites grew up with the oral tradition of passing on words. We have the benefit of the written word, the Bible, and all these wonderful psalms to draw upon for encouragement, challenge and to help us grow in faith.

Pray

Praise God for your life and vow to keep drinking from his goodness.

167
The kingdom

Question time

🍃 What promises or vows have you made during your life?

Read Psalm 72:1-11

Comment

'I declare before you all that my whole life, whether it be long or short, shall be devoted to your service . . . God help me to make good my vow, and God bless all of you who are willing to share in it.' That was Princess Elizabeth speaking on the radio on her twenty-first birthday. She was already preparing her heart, mind and soul for her future role as monarch. It was a three-stranded comment. She spoke about herself as a servant, she spoke about God as her strength and stay, and she spoke of the people for whom she would have responsibility during her reign. It is unlikely that anyone would dispute Queen Elizabeth II's dedication over decades in fulfilling that commitment.

Psalm 72 is attributed to Solomon, David's son, as he took up the reins of reigning (as it were). He was anointed by Zadok the priest in the presence of Nathan the prophet in a loud and joyous ceremony (1 Kings 1:40). Handel's coronation anthem, *Zadok the priest*, was sung at Queen Elizabeth II's coronation in Westminster Abbey, and uses these very words from the Bible.

It's good to have Solomon's prayer here. We see his intentions, under God's guidance.

Challenge

Whatever our role in life, do we dedicate ourselves to God and seek his guidance?

Pray

For those taking on new and important public roles.

168
King for ever

Question time
How confident are you in God's sovereignty?

Read Psalm 72:12-20

Comment

David's final words to Solomon were, 'Be confident and determined, and do what the Lord your God orders you to do' (1 Kings 2:2, 3). Verse 20 of the psalm suggests that perhaps it was David rather than Solomon who wrote it. Maybe it was David's prayer for his son and Solomon shaped it into the psalm. What matters are the words which point to dependence on God and a willingness to live God's way under his guidance. But there's more! The words point to a future king – Jesus – who was to come, whose reign would usher in peace and where the king was constant, faithful and unchanging. He would be a universal king whose kingdom would last forever and whose glory would fill the whole world.

How does this psalm impact your faith in God's sovereignty? At the turn of the most recent millennium, the Queen said, 'To many of us, our beliefs are of fundamental importance. For me the teachings of Christ and my own personal accountability before God provide a framework in which I try to lead my life.' On Christmas Day 2014 she said, 'For me, the life of Jesus Christ, the prince of peace, whose birth we celebrate today, is an inspiration and an anchor in my life.' Pray for the Queen as she seeks to live out her testimony.

Challenge

Can you echo those words of the Queen?

Pray

That Jesus may inspire and anchor you.

169
God won't know

Question time

🍃 Have you ever covered up a wrongdoing, thinking that nobody will know?

Read Psalm 73:1-12

Comment

Psalm 50 was attributed to Asaph. And now we come to a section of a number of psalms grouped together that come from the pen of Asaph who was a musician.

Every now and again you hear of a famous person who declares that they have lost their faith. A sportsman or singer who once witnessed boldly for God now has doubts and voices them. In verse 2 Asaph says how he'd lost confidence and his faith was almost gone. Why? Because he saw that the wicked were doing OK and the God-followers weren't. Do you sympathise with him? Do you feel hard done by as a believer? Don't be afraid to say so to God!

There is a sober warning at the end of verse 10: 'Even God's people turn to them (the wicked) and eagerly believe whatever they say.' How easily are you swayed by what other people say? Does it make you question your faith?

Challenge

God knows. God knows everything about everyone. He is all-seeing, all-loving, all-caring. He sees our good points, and he sees when we veer off his path. Which verse best describes you: 1, 2, 3 or 10?

Pray

That you'll lead a life of integrity.

170
Too difficult

Question time

- Where do you go to think things through?
- Do you have a special chair, or room, or somewhere outside in the garden or countryside?
- Maybe you like to find a church with an unlocked door to go and sit in quietly?

Read Psalm 73:13-17

Comment

The psalmist is struggling to avoid saying, 'It's not fair!' He's tried to follow God's ways, to keep himself pure and on God's track, but things still go wrong (verses 13, 14). He's tempted to talk and act as the godless people of verses 4-12, yet he knows that if he behaved like that, he wouldn't be acting as a believer should. Do you have that dilemma?

Poor Asaph. He tried to think the problem through but without success. It's too hard. Does he give up thinking or give up God? No. He went into the Temple. What reminders would he have found there of the faithfulness of God? What reminds you of God's faithfulness in your 'special' place? Who or what helps as you ponder the mysteries of life? We have to accept that there are no easy answers to some of the questions we have. That's where faith comes in. We have to trust and obey *in* the trying circumstances.

Challenge
It's easy-ish to trust God when all is going well. The tests of faith come in the trials.

Pray
That you'll not let anything or anyone prevent you from continuing to be a pilgrim.

171
Bitter thoughts

Question time

Who has been the best instructor or teacher in your life?

Read Psalm 73:18-24

Comment

Megan was nervous. She stood stock still, front legs apart, back legs rigid, and refused to move forward. She was afraid of a mechanical hoist. The hoist was to help disabled children and adults to mount their ponies safely and easily. It made little noise and the mechanism moved slowly but Megan the pony was uneasy. Megan's handler stood by her nose, holding her tightly, and talked in a quiet, reassuring voice. After a minute or two, Megan took a faltering step, then another towards the unfamiliar apparatus.

Have a look at verses 21-24. On the one hand is bitterness, hurt, stupidity, lack of understanding.

On the other, the closeness of God, his holding hand, his guidance. And look at the privilege at the end of verse 24!

Are you bitter, feeling hurt or stupid? God loves each of us for who we are, not for what we do, nor for the qualifications we may have or the status that may be afforded us by other human beings. The life and love he gives us are unique. You are special to him! As one commentator puts it, 'Our self-worth is not based on our ability to perform; it is based on our identity as God's children.'

Be encouraged

Bask in that knowledge, thank God for it, and be comforted that, whether we face success or failure, joy or disappointment, fun or fear, health or illness, his love is close and constant.

Pray

I'm encouraged, Father God, that I am valued by you for who I am – your child. Thank you.

Weakness and strength

Question time

Who was the closest person in your life to have died? Think of that person now.

Read Psalm 73:25-28

Comment

A friend's daughter had been ill for months, and was dying. She was in her forties with a husband and two small children. In her last couple of weeks she was barely conscious, couldn't speak or eat or do anything for herself at all. Verses 25 and 26 could be applied to her. And also to her family who would grieve her departure from earth to heaven.

When we experience the loss of a loved one, or when we have something else that troubles us and weighs us down so that we can barely think for ourselves, these words are a comfort. When all else fails, God is. He is the great Yahweh, the 'I AM'.

Jesus, in John's Gospel, describes himself variously as, 'I AM the bread of life; the light of the world; the gate; the good shepherd; the resurrection and the life; the way, the truth and the life; the vine.'

Nothing can negate the grief we have when a loved one dies, or the fear that we experience on the loss of a job, or of not having enough money to put food on the table.

Be encouraged

When human life throws its worst at us, we might echo the psalmist: 'What else have I in heaven but you? . . . God is my strength; he is all I ever need.'

Pray

For those who are grieving the loss of a loved one today.

Hands behind back

Question time

🍃 Think of a time in your life when God appeared to have his hands behind his back.

🍃 What was your reaction?

Read Psalm 74:1-11

Comment

For those of us who live in democratic places where there is freedom of worship and little overt opposition to Christianity, reports of persecution of Christian people and their places of worship in other parts of the world comes as a shocking reminder of the cost of following Christ.

The psalmist goes into graphic detail of the disregard some people have for God and of their destructive thoughts and actions, including the burning down of places of worship. It is still happening today. There have been recent examples in Egypt and Sri Lanka. No wonder the psalmist questions why God appears to keep his hands behind his back and fails to intervene on behalf of the believers.

Do you cry out for the beleaguered brothers and sisters who have to keep their faith secret and who live in fear of attack? Or are you indifferent as it doesn't happen on your patch? Are you keeping your hands behind your back?

Challenge

Maybe you're reading this in a secret place, afraid that you might be found out for daring to be a follower of Jesus. The Devil is like a roaring lion, seeking to destroy. And God appears to be blasé . . .

Pray

For strength and courage for those who are under attack.

174
Mighty creation

Question time

How do you react when you can't work out how to do something?

Read Psalm 74:12-17

Comment

I like doing jigsaw puzzles. It helps if you have a picture of what the whole thing should look like when complete. But if you don't, you can scrutinise one jigsaw piece and it's hard to see how and where it fits into the bigger picture.

With that lovely little 'But' at the beginning of verse 12, we see the psalmist pondering the bigger picture of life. The destruction and mayhem of the earlier verses have to be balanced with the universal picture; one little piece of jigsaw in the muddle of all the pieces in the box, but one little piece of which, when the jigsaw is completed, you'll be able to say, 'So that's how it fitted in.'

When we're bogged down with the puzzles of life, it's good to get out into the created world and see the sea, or walk by a river, or consider the seasons. As I write, it is snowing. Each little snowflake lands on a shrub outside my window and others join it to make a heap – lots of pieces for the picture. A naturalist once said, 'We can look at the big picture – great landscapes, a mountain range, but sometimes we can learn by looking closely at the tiniest detail.'

Be encouraged

God is king. We can remember that by looking at a snowflake or a mountain, an acorn or an oak tree. It's a matter of perspective.

Pray

Thank God for naturalists who help us to see and understand some of the detailed wonders of the universe.

175

Rouse yourself!

Question time

- How do you speak to God?
- What manner do you adopt?
- Chatty, reverent... or what?

Read Psalm 74:18–23

Comment

This section starts with another 'But'. The previous section was the filling in the sandwich. Now the psalmist has another go at God. See what he says to God: 'Remember... Don't abandon... Don't forget... Remember... Don't let the oppressed be put to shame... Let those poor and needy people praise you... Rouse yourself, God... Defend your cause... Remember... Don't forget...' There's a lot of telling God what to do here!

Is it cheeky to speak to God like this? Or irreverent? Or disrespectful? If you think God is impassive, deaf and blind, you may feel at exploding point and speak like this in frustration or sorrow or fear. It's all right to do that.

Our emotions can be like a wave on the sea, sometimes up, sometimes down, and sometimes angry with white horses spewing foam. It is into this situation that the God who seems to be asleep, can be roused. Like Jesus in the boat on the lake when the storm blew.

Be encouraged

God is ever-present; it's just sometimes we don't see his activity and think he's gone absent without leave. Perhaps then it's the time to be still and allow him back into our churned-up state.

Pray

Close your eyes and think how he's shown his presence in your life in the past, and ask him to come into your present situation now.

176
Fairness

Question time

🍃 **Have you made a promise to someone and then failed to keep it?**

Read Psalm 75:1-10

Comment

Does it irritate you, as it does me, when someone in a TV drama says to a companion, 'Don't worry. It'll be fine; I promise.' No human being can guarantee that everything will be fine and so the promise is invalid and deserves a raised eyebrow or an angry retort.

God's promises are different. He alone has the authority to make promises such as we read in verse 2. In our 'now' world, we don't like to wait for God to act. We want answers now and we want action now and we want everything to be OK now.

Peter quotes Psalm 90 in his second letter (3:8): 'There is no difference in the Lord's sight between one day and a thousand years; to him the two are the same.' Jesus made it clear, when talking about the second coming, that it is God who sets the time for judgement. Peter goes on in verse 9, 'The Lord is not slow to do what he has promised, as some think. Instead, he is patient with you, because he does not want anyone to be destroyed, but wants all to turn away from their sins.'

So verse 2 is reassuring for those of us who are impatient. Not only will God judge, but he will judge with fairness.

Challenge

Meanwhile, we have a gospel to proclaim! Good news for everyone.

Pray

That God's good news will reach everyone on earth.

177
Silence

Question time

🍃 Do you like or dislike silence?

Read Psalm 76:1-12

Comment

I sometimes ponder what it would have been like to live in the world before the Industrial Revolution. It would have been a quieter place. It must have been a shock to workers in factories to go from their quiet dwellings into a building with noisy machinery. Miners, working in the pits, had the constant sound of tools banging on rock, and with the arrival of motor vehicles, it wasn't long before our roads throbbed with the sound of car and lorry engines.

People make noise. But in verse 8 we read that when God judged, 'the world was afraid and kept silent.' Can you imagine that?

When Jesus returns to the world, what will happen? Will he appear on TV, on Smartphones, or on whatever technological device is trending at the time? Will there be so much noise that nobody hears his arrival? How many of us will be shocked into silence – either because we fear his judgement or because we're completely overawed by the sight of him coming in glory?

Edmund H Sears wrote the Christmas carol, 'It came upon the midnight clear', where his take on the first Christmas was that, 'The world in solemn stillness lay, to hear the angels sing.' In the second verse he talks about the 'weary world' and 'its Babel sounds'.

Challenge

Are you ever quiet enough to hear God's voice?

Pray

That we may all hear God's voice above the clamour of modern life.

178
Sighing

Question time
What makes you sigh?

Read Psalm 77:1-10

Comment

'A sigh is just a sigh,' according to the song 'As time goes by', by Herman Hupfeld, from the 1942 film Casablanca. But is it? Psychologists ask the question, 'Why do we sigh?' It might be a sigh of pleasure on eating a freshly picked strawberry, or exasperation at not understanding some computer instruction, or sadness because your dog has died, or frustration that the trousers that once fitted you are now too tight round the waist.

A sigh, however, while being an emotional response, is also a useful reflex to help lung function. So in verse 3 the psalmist sighs as an emotional response to the lack of comfort he's getting from God, but in doing so, he's probably also helping his breathing. Different sorts of breathing are used for crying and for meditating. Short and sharp on the one hand and long and calm on the other.

The breathing and emotions of Asaph are not calming him, alas. He cries, he sighs, he's discouraged, he's wakeful when he wants to sleep, he thinks, he meditates, he questions, and he appears to doubt God (verse 10). What anguish is expressed here! No wonder he sighs.

Challenge

Can you identify with Asaph? Are there times when you feel as desperate as he did? Hold on . . . as God holds on to you.

Pray

For God's still small voice of calm.

179
I will

Question time

Where there's a will there's a way. Is that true?

Read Psalm 77:11, 12

Comment

In these short poems it's tricky to work out what time-span is involved in the troubles expressed. Depression can last for days, weeks, months, years. A feeling of abandonment can make us feel isolated from God and from friends. But there is resolve here on the part of Asaph.

'I will.' Asaph gives himself a talking to as he talks to God. Do you talk to yourself? In your sighs, do you say, 'I will persevere,' or 'I will conquer this wretched computer,' or 'I will think of good things'? What are Asaph's 'I will' sayings? 'I will remember . . .'; 'I will recall . . .'; 'I will think about . . .'; 'I will meditate . . .'.

Challenge

What does Asaph recall? God's great deeds, the wonders God did in the past, all that God has done, all God's mighty acts. Could you do the same?

Pray

Praise God for the wonders he has done in your life.

180

Past presence

Question time

What do you understand by holiness?

Read Psalm 77:13-20

Comment

God is holy. Everything he does is holy. God is set apart from human beings. He is unlike us because we are fallible, fallen beings. But God, in his holiness, engages with human beings, even to the extent of coming among us as Emmanuel: God is with us, one of the names given to Jesus. The psalmist acknowledges God's holiness and then recalls the history of the chosen people of God. God is past, present and future.

Peter wrote, 'Be obedient to God, and do not allow your lives to be shaped by those desires you had when you were still ignorant. Instead, be holy in all that you do, just as God who called you is holy' (1 Peter 1:14, 15). Later he writes, 'You are the chosen race, the King's priests, the holy nation, God's own people, chosen to proclaim the wonderful acts of God, who called you out of darkness into his own marvellous light' (1 Peter 2:9).

Whatever our situation and whatever our emotions, if we belong to God – and his invitation to be part of his family extends to all people of every generation and every nation – then we are called to be holy and to live holy lives.

Be encouraged

Think of God's presence in the past, thank him for his holy presence in your life today, and pray for his Spirit to continue to work on your holiness in the future.

Pray

God of the past, present and future, help me to live a life that is worthy of you.

181

The generation game

Question time

Which member of your family would you most like to have on your team in the local pub quiz? Why?

Read Psalm 78:1-4

Comment

In TV quiz programmes where two contestants play as a team against other duos, a pair which is made up of different generations will often do better than a pair of the same generation. For example, the question, 'Which prime minister said, "I'm an optimist, but I'm an optimist who takes his raincoat."?' might be answered correctly (Harold Wilson) by a man in his sixties, while his daughter in her thirties would be more likely to know that Rihanna had a hit in 2007 with the song, 'Umbrella'.

It's heartening to see generations working to absorb information, to ask questions and to discover answers. Asaph sees the value of generational communication. 'Things we have heard and known, things that our ancestors told us' (verse 3). And he's keen that stories and facts should be passed on to the next generation.

So what is it that needs to be passed on, not just in Asaph's time, but also in our time? Not the random quote from a politician or the title of a pop song. No. Let's 'tell the next generation about the Lord's power and his great deeds and the wonderful things he has done' (verse 4). In order to do that, we need to have heard and know these things ourselves.

Challenge

Does my knowledge of the Bible match my knowledge of other subjects?

Pray

For intergenerational cooperation.

182

Commandments

Question time

🍃 **What are the values (or not) of laws of the land?**

Read Psalm 78:5-8

Comment

Why do we have laws? When traffic lights fail to work, motorists don't know when to stop and when to go. Occasionally the junction works better when the lights fail, but that's not usually the case! We need rules of the road for the transport system to function efficiently and with as little damage, disruption or disaster as possible.

Similarly we need rules for living individually and as community. Before God gave Moses the Ten Commandments, the people had been wandering grumpily through the desert, even to the extent that they moaned they'd be better back in Egypt in slavery. As the community got larger, the need for an orderly way of living increased. The commandments were very practical and Jesus summarised them centuries later: 'Love God'; 'love your neighbour'; and later to his disciples, 'Love one another'.

The people of Israel were to respond to God's gift of instructions by teaching them to their children, resulting in generations of people putting their trust in God. Good intentions. Do you have such good intentions? Do you trust God?

Challenge

Do you want your children, godchildren, grandchildren, to trust him too? What are you doing about it?

Pray

For law-makers and law-upholders.

183
Miracles

Question time

> Do you believe that miracles happen today?

Read Psalm 78:9-16

Comment

How frustrating it is to read the history of the people of Israel! How wayward they were! One day they'd declare their allegiance to God, the next they'd be rebelling. One moment they'd be trusting God, the next they'd be disobeying him.

Let's not point the finger. How blameless are you? Is your trust in God constant? Is your obedience constant? The people here were sometimes deliberately rebellious, other times they were just forgetful. Even when they recalled or saw the miraculous works of God, they didn't stay on course.

Think about what God has done in your life. What miracles has he done for you? How have you seen his hand at work as you look back through your life?

Challenge

The greatest miracle that is worth pondering is the very fact that God loved you so much that he came to save you. Just as he saved the people of Israel from the oppression of Egypt, so he makes it possible for the whole of the human race to be saved – if they trust him.

Pray

Thank God for what he has done for you and ask him to keep you faithful.

Demands

Question time

What demands did you make of your parents?

Read Psalm 78:17-20

Comment

'I want a new bike'; 'I want a piece of cake'; 'I want my own bedroom' are some of the demands a child might make. And we say to them, 'That's no way to ask.' And they'll say, 'Pleeeeeeeeeease', and then as the adult you may give them what they ask for, or you may say, 'No, not this time, even though you've said please!'

Is the child being audacious or just trying his luck? What about the people of Israel in these verses? Demanding, in their case, was a result of sin and rebellion. They failed to trust God to supply their needs. Perhaps they didn't trust that he knew their wants, perhaps they just wanted to test him (verse 18). Either way, it wasn't a gracious or appropriate thing to do! They begrudgingly acknowledged that

God had provided water for them, but questioned whether he could also provide food.

Grumpiness can infiltrate our families, our home groups, our churches. And it's then that we start to make demands of other people: our parents, our leader, our vicar – and God himself.

Challenge

In Philippians 2:14 Paul wrote, 'Do everything without complaining or arguing.' In 4:19 he says, 'My God will supply all your needs.' Needs are different from wants!

Pray

That God will help you to distinguish between wants and needs – and to act accordingly.

185
Angel food

Question time

- **What is the most nutritious meal you've prepared or eaten?**
- **What made it so good?**

Read Psalm 78:21-31

Comment

I remember, as a child, having angel cake for Sunday afternoon tea. It was a striped treat of yellow, white and pink sponge. Some foods were still rationed after World War 2 when I was a small child and so when such luxuries as angel cake were available, it really was like manna from heaven.

Now, if you'd been God, would you have given in to the people's demands for food? He did. But he was angry about their demands as it showed their lack of faith in him. Yet he provided for them with 'the food of angels'. He spoke to the sky and commanded its doors to open. Picture that in your mind. How might you paint a landscape that depicted this drama in all its glory? God gave them all they wanted. Manna: the food of angels, and then a huge flock of birds.

Why would God do that? Do you give in to a petulant child and give him what he's demanded? And then, when the child is still not satisfied, give him more? Maybe, in your exasperation, you do. And then you watch as the child gorges on yet more ice cream or sticky bun or beef curry or whatever.

Challenge

Twice we're told, 'God gave . . .'. That is his nature. To give. And to keep on giving. What is our response to God's generosity?

Pray

For an attitude of gratitude.

In spite of...

Question time

Did you ever rebel against your parents?

Read Psalm 78:32-37

Comment

A friend's son left home when a teenager and went to live in a squat. For some years he led a hedonistic lifestyle, doing what he wanted without any guidance or constraints. He'd left the security and love of his family and gone his own way.

The lad's family was heartbroken. In spite of his parents' love and care over the years of his childhood, he'd broken loose and left their love behind him, preferring to do his own thing even if it meant a life of crime and poverty.

Despite God's giving love, the people of Israel kept sinning and failed to trust him. When disaster befell some of them, there would be a temporary repentance and some earnest prayer, but it wasn't sincere, didn't last and there was a lack of loyalty to the one who had provided for them over generations.

The boy's parents never gave up on him and one day he returned to the family fold, did some studying, got a job and worked his way up the ladder to become a respected and useful member of society.

Be encouraged

God never gives up on his people. He longs for them to return to him and gives them every opportunity to do so. Thank God for his faithful love for you.

Pray

For rebellious teenagers and their parents.

187
Mere mortals

Question time

🍃 How would you describe yourself in your attitude to others?

🍃 Compassionate, impatient, intolerant, gentle, dismissive, forgiving, judgemental?

Read Psalm 78:38-51

Comment

If I want to learn the words of a song, I may do so by using YouTube. One of its joys is that after you've heard the song once, you can click and play it again, and again, and again. There's a song sung by a group of tenors that I play often; so far it's had nearly a million views (and they're not all mine!). You can also share the link with your friends and get them enthused about it too.

Asaph, in this long psalm, is keen for 'only mortal beings' to hear God's message. He records the history of the people and God's part in it. Look at verses 40-43. 'How often they rebelled . . .'; 'How many times they made him sad . . .'; 'Again and again they put God to the test and brought pain . . .'; 'They forgot his great power . . .'.

If Asaph lived today I wonder whether he might put his message on YouTube so that the people could play it over and over again. He'd want to get it into their heads so they wouldn't forget it. He'd want them to share the message with their family and friends. But would the people beam up YouTube? Would they bother to listen?

Challenge

You are a mere mortal but one who is loved by God. How might you remember God's words in times of rebelliousness?

Pray

For Christian songwriters and thank God for the help they give in getting us to think of God.

188
Sat Nav

Question time

What do you use to guide you when you're travelling?

Read Psalm 78:52-55

Comment

When I was a teenager we sang a song by Sidney E Cox (1887-1975) called, 'My Lord knows the way through the wilderness; all I have to do is follow'. I sang it with great enthusiasm, not really knowing what wilderness I might have to be guided through during my life. Today car drivers use Satellite Navigation to guide them. Some of us still use maps! What did God use to guide his people through the wilderness? And why did he bother?

It seems extraordinary to us humans that God should go to such lengths to save his people. Such rebellion! (verses 40-42). Yet God did not abandon his people. He led them safely into the promised land, divided up the land and provided homes.

Jesus described himself as The Good Shepherd who leads his flock. He guides his followers through life on earth and then provides them with a heavenly home.

Challenge

What are your desert or wilderness experiences? Do you ask God to act as your Sat Nav to guide you through life? Do you call on Jesus the Good Shepherd for your needs? Do you believe the Holy Spirit helps you?

Pray

For God's guidance each day.

189
Anger

Question time

🍃 What makes you angry?

Read Psalm 78:56-64

Comment

How could people who've been rescued be so fickle in their acknowledgement of God's provision? Let's not judge. How often do *we* test God's patience? Think about what might make God angry with you? How do you disobey God? How are you disloyal to him? Are you reliable as one of his followers? Are you consistent in your witness? Do you worship idols? In other words, do some things in your life take the first place that should be God's?

Anger is mentioned three times in these few verses. Do you find it distasteful that the God of love can be angry? There can be anger without sin. In the case of God, who cannot sin, his anger is righteous anger. Paul warns us, 'If you become angry, do not let your anger lead you into sin, and do not stay angry all day' (Ephesians 4:26). James says, 'Everyone must be quick to listen, but slow to speak and slow to become angry. Human anger does not achieve God's righteous purpose' (James 1:19, 20).

Challenge

God's anger is because he doesn't want his attributes of righteousness, justice and holiness to be compromised. God's overwhelming desire is for a restoration of the relationship between himself and human beings that sin messed up.

Pray

Help me, God, to control my anger and to be quick to patch up a relationship that may have been damaged by my anger.

190
God's choice

Question time

🍃 If you were choosing a national sports team, how would you go about it?

Read Psalm 78:65-72

Comment

Sometimes, for sports teams, there's a chief selector, sometimes a manager. Sometimes a squad is selected, from which a team will be chosen. In some sports talent-spotting scouts are sent out to regions to find fresh talent. It can be a daunting task to choose the right people.

In the slightly comical verse 65, we have a picture of God waking from sleep and the image of him as a strong man, intoxicated by wine, as he puts his plan into place. He chose a small tribe, Judah, and David, the youngest son to be king. It was an unlikely choice and eyebrows were probably raised, as they would be if the choice of cricket or rugby captain hadn't matched your choice.

David was to be king and would draw on his shepherding experience to care for his people.

Challenge

When you see an unlikely candidate leading a worship service or taking some other responsibility in the church, do you raise an eyebrow and think, 'I wouldn't have chosen her', or do you offer encouragement to that person?

Pray

For young leaders.

191
Burning fire

Question time

🍃 What do you like about a wood burner, coal fire, or bonfire?

Read Psalm 79:1-7

Comment

Childhood memories of November 5th include having a bonfire in the back garden. Newspaper was stuffed in with the wood and fabric and anything else that might burn well, a match was struck and the fire began to burn, slowly at first then with immense energy. Crackles, spits and sparks would fly and the heat became intense.

That kind of energy may be seen when someone is angry. In this psalm, it is God who is angry (verse 5). He's had to deal with the waywardness of his people, but the psalmist pleads with God to have mercy on his people, and to turn his anger onto the people who continually reject him in their thoughts, words and actions, on those who even desecrate his Temple.

Are you indignant at the way in which God is rejected by so many people, are you angry at those who target Christian individuals and communities? The psalmist, as has been the case so often in the psalms, doesn't seek vengeance himself, but turns to God in prayer.

Challenge
We're called to be light, not fire, to shine rather than burn.

Pray
That your face, smile, and words may bring light to others.

192

Payback time

Question time

Is there a place in modern life for national days of prayer?

Read Psalm 79:8-13

Comment

This psalm is headed, 'A Prayer for the Nation's Deliverance'. On 26 May 1940, at the request of King George VI, a National Day of Prayer was observed in Great Britain. The British Army was in trouble in France under Nazi fire and needed to escape. Storms had been forecast in the Channel but it was calm and lots of boats, large and small, crossed the Channel and rescued over 330,000 soldiers.

Would anyone today have the courage to request a day of prayer during a period of national crisis?

Asaph's prayer for the nation's deliverance acknowledges the failures of former generations, but then focuses on the present. 'Have mercy on us now.' Why? 'For the sake of your own honour.'

Those of us who base our lives on God long for all people to give honour to him. We know we fail to do this ourselves and we have to confess our failure to honour God. Honesty is a good policy with God. 'We have lost all hope,' says Asaph. 'Rescue us and forgive our sins.' He longs for God to 'pay the other nations back seven times for all the insults they have hurled at you'. 'At you' – God. Not at us.

Be encouraged
We pray. God acts.

Pray
Pray for your own country's deliverance from either its rejection of God, its apathy for God or for its ignoring of God.

193
A plate of sorrow

Question time

🍃 Is there anything you don't eat?

Read Psalm 80:1-6

Comment

'Is there anything you don't eat?' I'd been invited to a meal at someone's home and she was kind enough to pose the question. My reply would have sounded somewhat pathetic, even weird: 'Green peppers, onion, honey, wheat . . .' It would be my worst nightmare to have that combination on a plate. And would cause me the same sort of fear and sorrow I faced at school when told I must eat every scrap of gristly meat and over-boiled cabbage.

Asaph, in this Prayer for the Nation's Restoration, speaks of God giving the people 'sorrow to eat', and 'a large cup of tears to drink'.

Have you eaten a plate of sorrow recently? Maybe someone close to you has died, perhaps you've had the loss of a job, or a broken relationship, or maybe you're lamenting because of something you've done that you know will have displeased God. What is the solution to such a distasteful meal?

Be encouraged
Look at verse 1. Who is your leader?

Pray
Ask God to listen to you, to hear your cries as you acknowledge him as the great Shepherd, your leader, and the awe-inspiring Almighty God who, yet, cares for you.

194

Deep roots

Question time

🍃 Next time you're outside take a look at exposed tree roots or try digging out the root of a dandelion. What is noticeable about such roots?

Read Psalm 80:7-13

Comment

Grapes. Ah, that sounds more palatable. Way back, God sent twelve men to do a recce on the promised land. Ten of them came back with negative reports, two – Joshua and Caleb – were much more positive. One of the items they brought back was a bunch of grapes that was so heavy it had to be carried on a pole by two men. When the Israelites eventually entered the land they found it to be a pleasing contrast to the desert. Here was a land full of agricultural potential.

Asaph likens the Israelites themselves to a grapevine with deep roots, but – to switch metaphors – things went pear-shaped and the nation was discombobulated.

Paul urged the Christians of Colossae to keep their roots deep in Christ and to build their lives on him and become stronger in their faith 'as you were taught'. The people of Israel in Asaph's time had certainly been taught God's ways, but it seems that their roots were not always as strong as they might have been.

Challenge

Let's make sure we put down deep roots that won't be wobbled. We need to be strong plants for Christ, bearing fruit for him.

Pray

For those who help us to put down deep roots in Christ – church leaders, Bible study companions.

195

Grapevine

Question time

🍃 **What do you do to keep your body strong?**

Read Psalm 80:14-19

Comment

When I first attended a gym class I was introduced to the Grapevine. I had no idea what it was until the teacher demonstrated it. It's a lateral step movement that is often included in a warm-up before a more vigorous workout. Although it is easy to do, it works the quads, hamstrings, calves, and core muscles of the body and, basically, helps to strengthen the body.

This section of the psalm continues the imagery of the grapevine for the body of people. God had planted the grapevine, he'd made it grow strong. Now Asaph asks for its preservation and protection (verse 17). In return he says, 'We will never turn away from you again.' We all have good intentions to be faithful to God but, like the people of Israel, we have to keep returning to the Lord.

Jesus described himself as the true vine and his followers as the branches. It's when we keep fixed to him that we will grow, be strengthened and thrive in our faith.

Challenge

'Remain united to me,' Jesus says, 'and I will remain united to you. A branch cannot bear fruit by itself; it can do so only if it remains in the vine. In the same way you cannot bear fruit unless you remain in me' (John 15:4).

Pray

For a fit body and a fit soul.

Moon time

Question time
What's your favourite kind of party?

Read Psalm 81:1-5

Comment
Party time! The people of God knew how to celebrate. A number of festivals were held each year, including the New Moon Festival which marked the beginning of a new month and was a time when an offering was brought to God. It was a time of noisy music, singing and shouting, not in praise of the people themselves, nor of the moon, but of God.

We may love to look at the moon in its different phases but, while it can give us joy in its brightness, it is not something to be worshipped. Worship belongs to God alone. The moon depends for light on the sun; it has no light of its own.

As God sheds his light on us, we can reflect his glory. One way we can do this is as we worship and celebrate his goodness. Does your church celebrate God in a way that will point other people to him?

Challenge
Does your God-attitude to life show him to others and shed his light on them?

Pray
For genuine joy in worship that will make others want to join the 'party'.

197
Load of bricks

Question time
How many bricks do you think you could carry in a rucksack?

Read Psalm 81:6-10

Comment
Tests to join the army may include doing 50 sit-ups in two minutes, 44 press-ups in two minutes and a 1.5 mile run in a specified time depending on which unit you have applied for. If you pass these, and other tests, you may be accepted for training and that's when the hard work really begins. Television programmes show trainees struggling to carry weighted backpacks. It's become trendy for civilians wanting to increase their fitness to undertake similar tasks. They might load their backpacks with sandbags or . . . bricks. The burden is colossal, the task unimaginably hard and demanding physically and mentally.

Look at verse 6. When the Israelites were in Egypt they'd been burdened by bricks and treated harshly by slave drivers as they undertook massive building projects for their masters. God relieved them of the burden and saved them from their oppressors. The psalm reminds us of God's work to relieve and save his people.

Challenge

What bricks are you carrying in your proverbial backpack? What burdens has God offered to lift from your back? What is your response to his care? Do you respect him and give him your obedience? Do you worship him wholeheartedly?

Pray

Thank God for the skill of bricklayers and pray for house builders.

198
Wish list

Question time

- Do you have a wish list?
- For your birthday?
- For things you want to do before you die?
- For your ideal partner in life?

Read Psalm 81:11-16

Comment

The people of Israel had a wish: to do whatever they wanted. What are the dangers of doing that? How can you avoid selfishness or covetousness or a hedonistic lifestyle?

God has a different wish. The people don't listen to him, and don't obey him. They are stubborn and think they know best! God's wish is in verse 13. What does he wish for? That the people would listen to him and then that they would obey him.

Challenge

Think about the things you wish for. How many of them are really valid? How do you balance the fact that Jesus said he came that we might have fullness of life, with our own agendas of desire which may not always be in harmony with his ways?

Pray

Heavenly Father, giver of all good gifts, make me thankful for and content with what I have.

199

Rights

Question time

🍃 What are your rights?

Read Psalm 82:1-8

Comment

'I know my rights', said the 8-year-old to her teacher. The child had broken a school rule repeatedly but the teacher had limited options for disciplining the child who . . . knew her rights.

The United States Declaration of Independence of 1776 states, 'We hold these truths to be self-evident, that all men are created equal, that they are endowed by their Creator with certain unalienable rights, that among these are Life, Liberty, and the Pursuit of Happiness.' What's unalienable can't be taken away or denied.

It's not just children and Americans who talk about their 'rights'. We all have a tendency to do so. But the Bible makes clear that we have to look out for the rights of certain groups of people in society who are often the voiceless: the poor and the orphans, the needy and the helpless (verse 3). How can we, in practical ways, defend the rights of these groups of people?

Challenge
What are you doing in your own neighbourhood to defend the rights of the people that God speaks of?

Pray
For those who have no rights.

200

Revolt

Question time

> When is there a place for questioning authority?

Read Psalm 83:1-4

Comment

Wat Tyler led the Peasants' Revolt in England in 1381, Guy Fawkes plotted to blow up the House of Lords and kill King James I in 1605, and boys at Rugby School rebelled against their headmaster in 1797 when a Justice of the Peace had to read the Riot Act. In the twentieth and twenty-first centuries there have been other plots and revolts and rebellions, not just in the UK, but around the world.

In this psalm we see the people rising up against authority – not the authority of national leaders but of God. Asaph, in talking to God, describes the people as 'your enemies' (verse 2). Asaph couldn't bear to see God's laws being flouted and God's people put under duress and God's own authority challenged.

Challenge

Do you campaign for causes that you feel passionate about? How much are you prepared to stand up for God's good causes in the face of opposition? Do you bring matters of concern to God in prayer and ask him to give you his wisdom to know what to think, what to say and how to act? Perhaps you're a rebel yourself. Are you rebelling against God or someone or something else?

Pray

For those who are prepared to stand up for God in the face of opposition.

201
Shame

Question time

- 'You should be ashamed of yourself!' Did anyone ever say that to you when you were a child?
- Had you done something you shouldn't have done?
- Did you know what you'd done wrong?
- And were you contrite when told off?

Read Psalm 83:5-18

Comment

It seems from this list of peoples from different areas that they had no shame at all for their misdemeanours. Look at verse 12: 'We will take for our own the land that belongs to God.' They knew it was God they were defying but carried on anyway.

Do you deliberately flout God's laws? Do you fail to love him with your whole being? Do you fail to love other people? Love should be at the forefront of our thinking, our speaking and our doing if we acknowledge God as our Lord. It's disrespectful and shows a distinct lack of love for God when we disobey him – and it impacts on the lives of those around us: in our families, our workplaces, our churches.

Asaph pleads with God in verse 16 to shame the rebellious people, to make them acknowledge God and to know that the Lord is to be respected, loved, trusted and obeyed.

Challenge
Is there anything you need to confess to God now?

Pray
Ask God to restore you into a right and active relationship with him.

202
Keep close

Question time
What are the attractions of home-making?

Read Psalm 84:1-7

Comment

A pair of robins has taken up residence in a bird box on the garden fence. Every morning they flit in and out, building a home. They don't venture far, but come out to sit at the top of the apple tree to sing their joyful song before swooping onto the vegetable patch for a worm or two. This pattern is repeated over and over.

The psalm of the sons of Korah expresses a longing to be close to the Lord, a desire to be in his house, to sing praise to him. Look at the words that describe this desire: love, want, long, sing, near, happy, live, strength, eager ... All positive words.

Do you enjoy making the journey to church? Perhaps you walk, or cycle, or go in the car, or use public transport. Do you go with anticipation?

Or do your feet drag? Do you worship God without distraction? Do the surroundings help or hinder your worship? Are you able to sing praise to God whatever your own personal circumstances?

Challenge
How much do you long to be in the presence of God?

Pray
For eagerness to worship God and to be close to him.

203

A thousand days

Question time

What's the longest time you've spent in any one place?

Read Psalm 84:8-12

Comment

2.73973 years is the same as 1,000 days. So that's roughly just over two and a half years. Have you ever spent that long in one place – apart, perhaps, from your own home? I've spent several years in one place in north-west Wales, but not on consecutive days. It's been a holiday destination for decades so, added up, I've spent many years there! Now if I'm honest, would I rather spend a thousand days there or one day in church?

We know that our human hours and days and years are not the same as God's. But the psalmist makes the point well. His priority above all else is to be in God's presence. I could argue – and probably would – that I can be in God's presence more effectively in north-west Wales than I can in a city or even in my own home. I see God as creator in the magnificence of sea and mountains. I can worship him more easily there than in many places. And it's certainly difficult or challenging to worship God where he is not acknowledged.

Challenge

Wherever we are, let's echo the psalm's sentiment.

Pray

Why not turn verses 11 and 12 into a prayer of praise now, and then ask God to help you to long for him as the sons of Korah did.

204

Fury and forgiveness

Question time

🍃 What infuriates you?

🍃 What might infuriate God?

Read Psalm 85:1-7

Comment

It's fascinating to see the sequence of psalms and the swaying between praise and lament, thanksgiving and vindication, trust and wisdom, and so on.

From the joy and desire of Psalm 84, we move swiftly to a song of lament. The first three verses focus on God, the next four verses on us. The sons of Korah emphasise God's goodness: 'You have been merciful...'; 'You have made Israel prosperous...'; 'You have forgiven...'; 'You stopped being angry...'.

God doesn't waver like we do. He is constant in his love and constant in his faithfulness to his people. But we are not like that. And so in verses 4-7 we read, 'Bring us back . . .'; 'Stop being displeased . . .'; 'Will you be angry for ever?'; 'Make us strong . . .'; 'Show us your constant love . . .'.

Is waywardness an inevitability of being human? Romans 3:23 indicates that that is the case: 'All have sinned . . .', as we've seen before in pondering the psalms. So what can we do about it? First of all, nothing! It is God alone who can forgive sins. Our role is to come to him and admit our shortcomings. And for Christian believers, it is the Holy Spirit who can transform us, slowly but steadily, into the likeness of Christ. It's a lifelong process.

Challenge

Have you asked God to forgive you?

Pray

For a willingness to let the Spirit of God take charge of your life.

205

Two-way loyalty

Question time

🍃 With whom do you have a meeting of mind and heart?

Read Psalm 85:8-13

Comment

A child puts his hand into his dad's hand and looks up at him. 'I love you, Dad,' he says. Dad looks down at his son. 'I love you too,' he smiles. They walk on, hand in hand, to the park or the shops, or to a football match.

Here is a lovely picture of the relationship we can have with God and that he can have with us. Verse 8 tells us it involves listening, a promise of peace, and a warning to keep on the right path. God is always ready to save – and he demonstrated that in the most dramatic way by sending his son to be the Saviour of the world. How we long for a world where there is love and faithfulness, righteousness and peace!

Like a child we can reach up and hold onto God's righteous hand as he looks down with tender love to us. This two-way loyalty is worth striving for. Look at verse 11. I would rather have my hand in God's than in anyone else's! But remember that all love comes from God and when we love we are showing God-love to someone else. So to hold hands with someone close to you is a small example of God's love in action.

Be encouraged

To show someone your love and loyalty and thereby demonstrate God's love.

Pray

Praise God for the way he reaches out to us.

206

Down and up

Question time

🍃 **What is your experience of hospital?**

Read Psalm 86:1-7

Comment

If you need to be in hospital, the chances are that you feel helpless and weak. David didn't have the advantage we have of a National Health Service where, despite its inadequacies, there is still the opportunity to receive good treatment and to be cared for in a compassionate way when we're in need.

My local hospital is perched on a hill and surrounded by agricultural fields where the appearance of the fields reflects the time of year. Hospital workers walk the byway to reach the hospital, dog walkers and joggers enjoy strolling or running in the countryside nearby. If they look up they'll see the hospital chimney. You can tell which way the wind is blowing by looking at the plume rising from the chimney. Sometimes, but not often it rises straight up.

David is feeling down, much like many hospital patients. He turns to God in his need and knows that his prayers rise up to God – like the smoke from a chimney.

Be encouraged

Whatever your feelings today, be assured that your prayers rise to the God of compassion who hears and listens to us in our need.

Pray

For medical practitioners.

207

Unique

Question time

🍃 **Do you sometimes feel you're just a number?** You have a National Insurance number, an NHS number, a hospital number. They can make you feel that you are not of significance, that your number is more important than your name, that you're just one of many.

Read Psalm 86:8-10

Comment

In these verses we see the uniqueness of God. There is no other god like him. No other being does what he does. In Isaiah 44:6b-8 we read, '"I am the first, the last, the only God; there is no other god but me. Could anyone else have done what I did? Who could have predicted all that would happen from the very beginning to the end of time? Do not be afraid, my people! You know that from ancient times until now I have predicted all that would happen, and you are my witnesses. Is there any other god? Is there some powerful god I never heard of?"'

Challenge

Consider the uniqueness of God in the light of these verses, and praise him for it. And then remember that you are made in the image of God and that you, too, are unique as one of God's precious creative beings.

Pray

For each person in your family or for your close friends and thank God for the uniqueness of each one.

208

Devotion

Question time

How would you define devotion?

Read Psalm 86:11-13

Comment

Devotion: Love, loyalty, enthusiasm, steadfastness, allegiance, dedication . . . And in addition, or complementary to those, we might add – as far as our relationship with God is concerned – a commitment to godliness and holiness and becoming more Christ-like. No wonder we need to be taught how to serve God with complete devotion! It's a tall order.

Think of another human being to whom you feel devotion. Your spouse, your son or daughter, your godchild, your parents, your sister or brother. How does that devotion show itself? Is it more than merely an attitude of mind? Does it show itself in the way you speak and the way you behave towards that person?

Challenge

How do you serve God with complete devotion? Would you do anything for him because you love him so much? Do you like to spend time with him? Do you want to serve him as Christ served people – spending time, offering compassion and kindness? Have you worked out what your gifting is so that you can use those gifts in God's service?

Pray

As David did, that God will teach you how to serve him with complete devotion.

209
Just like mother

Question time

- What did you learn from your mother? How to make jam tarts ... how to tie your shoelaces ... how to sew on a button ... ?

- And what example did she give you to follow? How to look after a family ... how to pray ... how to be a good friend and neighbour?

Read Psalm 86:14-17

Comment

David talks to God about his mother, someone of whom we know very little. She isn't named in the Bible, unlike Timothy's mother and grandmother whom Paul mentions in his letter to Timothy: 'I remember the sincere faith you have, the kind of faith that your grandmother Lois and your mother Eunice also had. I am sure that you have it also' (2 Timothy 1:5).

You may or may not know much about your mother. You can be sure she is known to God by name. And you, as the son or daughter of your mother, are also known by name and loved by God. Your mother may have been a devotee of God, as was the case with David and with Timothy; if so, be thankful. Whatever our relationship was with our mother, we can still ask for God's mercy, strength and saving power in our lives, and dedicate ourselves to serve him.

Be encouraged
By God's patience, kindness and faithfulness.

Pray
For mothers.

210

Citizenship

Question time

🍃 Have you ever applied for citizenship in a country?

Read Psalm 87:1-7

Comment

Applying for citizenship can be a complicated procedure and you may be required to answer test questions about the life and constitution of that country. Anyone wishing to leave the UK for a holiday overseas needs a British passport with details of their status, their photo and signature to prove that they're a bona fide Briton.

How do you apply for citizenship in God's kingdom? It seems from this psalm that people from all nations belong in God's special place! In the New Testament this is confirmed when Jesus told Nicodemus in John 3:16 that 'God loved the world so much that he sent his only Son.' Jesus told his Jewish disciples, 'Go . . . to all peoples everywhere and make them my disciples' (Matthew 28:19).

Jesus said, 'I will never turn away anyone who comes to me' (John 6:37). We are put right with God through faith in Jesus Christ, acknowledging that he came into the world to save the world from sin, believing that he is the Saviour and committing to him as Lord of our lives.

Be encouraged

We live in God's kingdom through his grace, something that Paul confirmed, 'We, however, are citizens of heaven, and we eagerly wait for our Saviour, the Lord Jesus Christ, to come from heaven' (Philippians 3:20). Are you a citizen of heaven? If so rejoice! If not, how about it . . .?

Pray

For those applying for citizenship in your country.

211

Feeling like death

Question time

You may feel like death physically, mentally, or spiritually or in a way that affects your whole being: holistically. Can you think of occasions when you've felt like death?

Read Psalm 88:1-12

Comment

I was in a supermarket many years ago, filling my trolley with the family's needs for the week. I picked up, by the lid, a plastic bottle of bubble bath. The lid came off, the bubble bath bottle bounced to the floor and spewed its bright red contents up into my eyes. I was blinded. Somebody called an ambulance and I was whisked off to A & E, leaving the contents of my trolley and a red mess on the floor of the supermarket. Apart from the pain and loss of sight, I was concerned that I wouldn't be home in time to collect my young daughter from school.

Depression can make you feel like death. So can cancer. And the loss of a job. Or the pain of knowing you've committed a misdemeanour that has repercussions on other people. In this psalm notice the words: cry, troubles, abandoned, forgotten, depths, darkest, deepest, heavy, crushed, repulsive, suffering.

Questions to God follow in verses 10-12.

Be encouraged

Never be afraid to cry out to God when you feel like death, and don't be afraid to ask the questions.

Pray

For anyone you know who, today, is feeling like death.

212

Darkness

Question time

- Have you ever been afraid of the dark?
- In what circumstances?

Read Psalm 88:13-18

Comment

'Darkness is my only companion' (verse 18). In that ambulance, unable to open my eyes that smarted with pain, darkness seemed to be my only companion. It was frightening and lonely. The paramedic was with me in the back of the ambulance but I couldn't see him.

Job, in his dark days, found his friends weren't much help: 'I have heard words like that before,' Job says to them, 'the comfort you give is only torment' (Job 16:1, 2). He agonises, 'God has handed me over to evil people. I was living in peace, but God took me by the throat and battered me and crushed me. God uses me for target practice and shoots arrows at me from every side – arrows that pierce and wound me; and even then he shows no pity . . .' (Job 16:11-13). After 37 despairing chapters God answers Job's cries. God describes graphically his work in creation, his power in sustaining the universe, and his long-term care for people.

We may not always hear the answers to our cries. We may not always see light when we're in darkness, but the message of the Bible is that, however awful the darkness, there is light.

Be encouraged

One day the Light of the world will return and a new heaven and earth will be formed, where there will be no more darkness – ever.

Pray

That the light of Christ may penetrate the deepest darkness.

213

Heaven sings

Question time

🍃 **What is your favourite hymn or Christian song?**

Read Psalm 89:1-7

Comment

Psalm 89 introduces us to another songwriter, Ethan the Ezrahite. He's mentioned in 1 Kings 4:29-31 in connection with King Solomon: 'God gave Solomon unusual wisdom and insight, and knowledge too great to be measured. Solomon was wiser than the wise men of the East or the wise men of Egypt. He was the wisest of all men: wiser than Ethan the Ezrahite . . .'.

Ethan uses his God-given talent to offer a hymn of praise and thankfulness: 'I will sing . . .'; 'I will proclaim . . .'. But who is the focus of his singing and proclaiming? God! Have you ever tried to write a song of praise to God? This is one of the longer psalms and includes a mixture of subject matter.

Could you take a phrase from one of the first two verses and write a praise song to God?

Challenge

Think of your favourite Christian song or hymn. Why do you like it? What or who is its focus? How do the words – and the tune perhaps – help you in your worship of God?

Pray

Praise God for the gift of music and the talent of musicians.

214

Your world

Question time

🌿 When you look objectively at the world we inhabit, do you see it in negative or positive terms?

Read Psalm 89:8-14

Comment

Anna Bartlett Warner (c.1827-1915) was born near New York city in the 1820s. The actual year of her birth is unclear. She wrote a number of well-known children's songs including, 'Jesus loves me, this I know' and 'Jesus bids us shine'. And this one: 'The world looks very beautiful and full of joy to me; the sun shines out in glory bright on everything I see. I know I shall be happy, while in the world I stay, for I will follow Jesus all the way.' Sentimental? Naively optimistic?

The psalmist describes God's world as powerful and angry but also that it sings for joy. God's kingdom is based on righteousness and justice and

is shown through his love and faithfulness. In this one section of the psalm we have an outburst of praise for God's power in the created world. And it can look very beautiful.

Subsequent verses of Anna Warner's song move to the reality of pilgrimage. 'They tell me I shall sorrow meet before my journey's done. The world is full of sorrow and suffering, they say.' She concludes that despite her tears en route, it is with joy that she will follow Jesus.

Challenge

Our experience may echo that of the psalmist and of the nineteenth-century songwriter. Can we rejoice even through our tears, because we know that God is in charge?

Pray

Lord, whatever the state of the world, may I remember that it is your world and so rejoice in its beauty while praying for its pain.

Kindness

Question time

🍃 **What was your last act of kindness?**

Read Psalm 89:15-18

Comment

Mother was suffering with a migraine. Her 12-year-old daughter came home from school, offered to go and meet her younger sister from primary school, then came home, cooked the family's evening meal, and made sandwiches for the following day's lunch boxes. She didn't think twice about her action; she just did it.

When we think about God and his kindness, do we see it in human terms? What does it mean to 'live in the light of his kindness'?

A kind person is someone who puts the needs of others before her own needs or wishes. Whether it's acting in loco parentis as the 12-year-old did, or being a good Samaritan to a person who has fallen in the street, or giving a cup of coffee to a rough sleeper, or writing a letter to a far-flung relative, these acts of kindness bring light to the recipient.

Challenge

Think of examples of human kindness that have been shown to you. Now think of the ways in which God shows his kindness to you.

Pray

Thank God for the kindness he has shown you through the actions of others.

216

Promises, promises

Question time

> How much do you trust the promises someone makes to you?

Read Psalm 89:19-29

Comment

I had to peer closely at a £5 note to see whether it still says what I remembered from the distant past . . . And it does: 'I promise to pay the bearer on demand the sum of Five Pounds.' This phrase dates from a time when banknotes represented deposits of gold. If you were rich enough you could exchange a banknote for that value in gold – five gold coins: sovereigns. Sadly, you can no longer do that, but the wording remains on the banknotes.

Promises, promises. What about the promises you make? Are they reliable? How much trust do you put in the person making a promise to you?

What about God's promises? There are plenty in this section of the psalm. Glance through the verses and see how many times the word 'will' occurs. These promises were made to King David but they also point forwards from his reign to the reign of an even greater King: God's own Son, Jesus Christ, the King of kings.

British banknotes have a picture of Her Majesty the Queen on them, reminding banknote holders of her position in British life. In early adulthood she made promises to serve God and serve her people.

Be encouraged

God promises a new kingdom and a new King. His promises are true, dependable and lasting.

Pray

Praise God that his promises are always kept.

217

Non-stop love

Question time

Why do people think they can get away with flouting laws?

Read Psalm 89:30-34

Comment

More promises here, but they are warnings. Rules for living are, on the most part, put in place for the good of society and for the good of individuals. This isn't always true of human laws, but it's true of God's laws. Time and again he warns people of the folly of disobedience, but time and again they ignore the warnings and have to take the consequences.

There are warning signs everywhere. Traffic signs are the most obvious, but there are warnings on electricity pylons, warning cones about wet floors, warnings about sharks, avalanches, the dangers of straying onto railway lines . . . But people still get electrocuted, slip on wet floors, bathe in shark-infested waters, climb mountains in adverse weather conditions and get hit by trains. Why do we do it? Because we think we'll get away with it? Or because we're just daft?

The astonishing facet of Almighty God's character is that he never stops loving – despite human folly and disobedience.

Challenge

Does this give us licence to do as we please, or does it make us have more respect – and thus obedience – to such a God?

Pray

Praise God that, despite our flouting of his ways, he still loves us.

218

More promises

Question time

How can variations between light and dark and different weather conditions focus your mind on God?

Read Psalm 89:35-37

Comment

As I write, there is thick fog outside. It is cold, clammy and all-enveloping. But the weather forecasters have promised that the sun will burn off the fog by mid-morning and already the sky shows hints of a yellow tinge through the thinning fog. On foggy or cloudy days we can think that the sun has vanished. But it hasn't.

God promises David that he'll watch over David's kingdom 'as long as the sun shines'. It was from David's line that Jesus came and his reign has no end. It will last, yes, 'as long as the sun shines'. And then we have a lovely image of the moon as 'that faithful witness in the sky'. Last night, before the fog, there was a clear sky with a half moon shining brightly. It had been visible since late afternoon as the evening sun dipped below the earth's horizon but still shone on the moon.

Be encouraged

Whatever the fog or cloud of our everyday situations, let's remember this imagery and relax in the promises of God, that his kingdom, his rule, his supremacy, his faithfulness, last for all time.

Pray

Praise God for the lights of sun, moon and of the great light: Jesus.

219

Rejection

Question time

- Behemoth (Canada), Apollo's Chariot (USA), Colossus (England), Dragon Khan (Spain), Hair Raiser (Hong Kong) . . . These are all famous roller coasters. Have you ridden any of them?
- Would you want to?

Read Psalm 89:38-45

Comment

This psalm is an example of a roller coaster with elated highs and desperate lows. And in these verses, we're in a deep dip. This is a lament when everything seems appallingly bad. If a ride on a famous roller coaster makes you feel sick, and your companions and random passers-by laugh at your discomfort, it pales in comparison with what the king in this psalm is going through. Everything has gone wrong, such that it seems God has made him 'old before his time'.

When you sink to a low in life, how do you deal with it? Do you hope that you'll slowly be hauled up to the heights again? And then find you plummet headlong down again and that the pattern is repeated? Will the builders of the ride or the people who take your money gloat with delight at your discomfort?

Challenge

When you sink, metaphorically, to rock bottom, is it because of something you've done, or are there external influences that bring you low? Don't despair . . .

Pray

Remember that, as the psalms demonstrate, there is room for lament in our prayers. If you need to, pray a prayer of lament now.

220

Deliverance

Question time

🍃 **Think of a situation that you've desperately wanted to get out of!**

Read Psalm 89:46-52

Comment

I couldn't wait to get off. Well, I had to wait, actually. There was no way I could escape before the end of the ride on the Big Dipper at Battersea Fun Fair way back in the mid-twentieth century. It was the first time I'd ever been on a roller coaster. I thought it would be the last. Years later I ventured on one with my children just to show I wasn't scared. Never again!

The psalmist is desperate to get out of the situation he's in. He knows he can't do it by himself so he turns the whole thing over to God. He asks a series of questions, including, 'Where are the promises . . .?' This is not the sort of fear and self-pity that I felt on the Big Dipper. The psalmist certainly wants a change from his current situation, but there's more to it than that. He is indignant at the way he is being treated because it is God himself who is being insulted, as it was God who had chosen the king: 'Your enemies insult your chosen king, O Lord.'

Be encouraged

It's been a long, up and down psalm. But look at the last seven words! And a double 'Amen' to emphasise that God is to be praised. Whatever the situation. Can you do the same?

Pray

Use the words of verse 52.

221
One-day weeds in God's home

Question time

- What is your favourite flower?
- What makes it so attractive to you?

Read Psalm 90:1-6

Comment

Psalm 90 is the start of the fourth section of psalms and the next dozen or so psalms are mostly of an upbeat nature and include what are probably some of many people's favourite psalms.

Beauty is in the eye of the beholder, according to the proverb. What is one man's weed is another's flower. Take the humble daisy, for example. Its little flowers grow in lawns and on commons, adding delight to the nature lover and wrath to the lawn purist who wants his grass to be devoid of anything other than perfect grass.

Verse 5 describes humans as weeds. I'd like to think of myself as a daisy rather than as Japanese knotweed or deadly nightshade. We have been put in the world which verse 1 describes as God's home. Yes, it's his world, his home – and we're a part of it, each of us for just a short time. His longevity is immeasurable; our life, in comparison, is brief.

Challenge

Let's make sure that, while we have life, we bloom where we're planted, not to draw attention to ourselves but to God in whose home we live.

Pray

Praise God for the variety of flowers we see in the countryside and in our gardens.

222
Short life

Question time

What do you most value about your life?

Read Psalm 90:7-12

Comment

I'm 70 years old. I've reached my three score years and ten. And I'm grateful to God for letting me live to reach that milestone. Anything beyond that I will regard as a bonus, as verse 10 suggests. I've had friends who have not reached 30, some who have not reached 40 or 50 or 60. Others are considerably older than I am. Whatever our age we are aware that life is finite and we need to live it with due respect for God and in obedience to him.

It's for that reason that the psalmist prays in verse 12 that God will teach us to value each day that we're given on Planet Earth and for us to live each day wisely. What practical steps can you take to achieve that? How and from whom would you expect to receive wisdom?

Life sometimes fades away like a whisper (verse 9); sometimes it is cut short suddenly. The only certainty about life is death.

Challenge

If you're a believer you will know that there is life beyond the grave, but that is no excuse for not living life wisely and thankfully now while you have it.

Pray

You alone, Lord, know how many days you've allotted to me for life on the planet. May I live each day in gratitude to you, and for you.

223
Future generations

Question time

🍃 What is your greatest desire for future generations of your family or of your godchildren's families or neighbours' children or whoever is precious to you?

🍃 Perhaps you'd like the world to be a kinder place, or for there to be political harmony or peace or fairer shares for all?

Read Psalm 90:13-17

Comment

The psalmist has a different desire. He longs for his descendants to see God's 'glorious might'. How could this come about? Perhaps there's a clue in verse 14. If and when we are filled with God's 'constant love' that will rub off onto our children and their children. Do those closest to us witness us singing because of God's love and of a deep-seated gladness or joy that overrides the challenges and disappointments of life in a fallen world?

When we focus on God or fix our eyes on Jesus, we will see the world and its inhabitants in a different way: as people whom God loves, of a God who is the sustainer of the world and of a God who cares, not just for us, but for future generations.

Challenge

Let's pass on the knowledge and love of God to our children and pray that they will pass it on too.

Pray

For young people, that they may be shown your love and come to acknowledge you.

224

Whoever

Question time

Do you have a right to a long and threat-free life?

Read Psalm 91:1-6

Comment

In recent months an alarming number of friends have had life-threatening illnesses to contend with; some friends have died. And some have been young. So how can these verses speak about God keeping us safe from deadly diseases (verse 3)?

There's safety . . . and there's safety. None of us is immune from the ills of this world. Some have a rougher time than others. Can God keep us safe?

Timothy Dudley-Smith wrote a hymn based on this psalm: 'Safe in the shadow of the Lord'. In the shadow of the Lord. And this is where safety comes from – whatever our bodily situation. Whoever goes to the Lord is protected by him, not *from* the ills of this world, but *through* the ills of this world. It's a matter of trust. Whoever goes to the Lord.

Challenge

Have you gone to the Lord for safety? Can you trust him for protection even if you go through very dark times, and even when you face death itself?

Pray

Lord, may I go to you for safety and protection. May I trust you and be freed of fear.

Angelic protection

Question time
What do angels mean to you?

Read Psalm 91:7-13

Comment

I've mentioned the stripy angel cake before. A slightly different angel cake is angel food cake which is made of whisked-up egg whites and is entirely white. We associate angels with brightness and light, a contrast to the Devil and his associated darkness, and illustrated by devil's food cake, which is a very dark cake.

'God will put his angels in charge of you to protect you wherever you go' (verse 11).

I love the Bible verses that refer to angels – and there are many of them. A favourite is when the angel announces to Bethlehem's shepherds that Jesus has been born. The shepherds are told where to find the newborn Saviour of the world. And off they go to find him. Jesus, at the start of his adult ministry, was ministered to by angels following the Devil's tempting of him. And again, in the garden of Gethsemane, an angel appeared and strengthened Jesus. Light in darkness.

Be encouraged

Light for the journey leads to lightness of spirit.

Pray

Thank you for your promises. I know I need never walk alone.

226
Long life

Question time

How concerned are you to know what the future holds in store for you?

Read Psalm 91:14-16

Comment

When I was an adolescent, a 'tweeny' as they call it these days, the girls in my class at school were hooked on horoscopes. Magazines had a horoscopes page which we scrutinised to see whether we would meet a handsome boy, come into an inheritance or achieve the job of our dreams. Why this obsession with the future?

None of us knows what will happen to us in the next minute, let alone the next week or month or year! Would you really want to know what will happen to you? Only if it's something nice, I guess.

In this psalm God makes promises. 'I will save . . .'; 'I will protect . . .'; 'I will answer . . .'; 'I will be with them . . .'; 'I will rescue them and honour them . . .';

'I will reward them . . .'; 'I will save them . . .'. And one of those promises is for long life. So does that mean that if we go to the Lord, he'll give us extra years on earth? Not necessarily. But then this earthly life, while worthwhile and to be lived to the full, is not the end. Our true 'long life' is kept for us in heaven. So whether you live to be 20 or 90, the long life promised can be ours when we go to the Lord and give him our allegiance.

Be encouraged
By the 'I will' sayings.

Pray
Praise God for his promises.

227
Deep thoughts

Question time

Can you guess how deep the deepest part of the sea is?

Read Psalm 92:1-8

Comment

The deepest part of any ocean on the planet is about 36,000 feet down. It's called the Challenger Deep and is at the southern end of the Mariana Trench in the Pacific Ocean. The deepest part is 7,000 feet deeper than Mount Everest is tall. It is completely dark and as difficult to penetrate as Everest is to climb.

Unfathomable comes to mind. A fathom is approximately six feet and is a measure used to calculate the depth of water. We use the word unfathomable to mean something that we can't comprehend. So when the psalmist writes, 'How deep are your thoughts!', the depth of the sea is a useful analogy. Just as I would struggle to climb Everest or plummet the depths of the ocean, so it's impossible for us to know the depth of God's thoughts. And yet . . .

We give thanks for, and praise God for, the facets of his being that we *can* understand, albeit in small measure: his love, his faithfulness, his mighty deeds. Are we fools or stupid because we don't comprehend everything about God? Elsewhere, the Bible says that fools are people who say God doesn't exist.

Be encouraged

While those who believe in God can't know everything, we can still rejoice about the things we do know of him.

Pray

Praise God for the vast dimensions of his thoughts.

228
Flourishing

Question time

Which species of plants and trees flourish best in your area?

Read Psalm 92:9-15

Comment

Take a look back at Psalm 1, verse 3. In Psalm 92 we have a similar sentiment expressed. The psalmist refers to righteous people – those who trust and obey God – who will grow like the cedars of Lebanon. King Solomon used timber from numerous cedar trees when building the palace and Temple in Jerusalem. More cedars were used in the rebuilding of the Temple after the exile.

What is special about the cedars of Lebanon in Old Testament times? The wood is aromatic and disliked by insects so it stays bug-free. It is also resistant to fungus diseases and strong enough to be used in the construction of ships. Reread verse 12 and apply these qualities to people who follow

God who are protected from the ravages of enemies, can resist the Devil and receive their strength from God himself. Cedars grow to immense heights and their fruit – the cones – are produced in their mature years, often not before they are forty years old.

Challenge

How well are you flourishing as a person of God? What encouragement and challenges are there in these verses?

Pray

That you may flourish as a believer.

229
Immovable

Question time
What is your favourite period of history?

Read Psalm 93:1-5

Comment
Assyrian, Greek, Roman, Aztec... Think of some of the great empires of the past. They seemed immovable in their heyday but kingdoms rise and fall. If your schooldays history reached as far as Victorian times (and many of us didn't get much beyond Henry VIII) you might have learned about the British Empire. In fact, the British began to establish overseas colonies in the sixteenth century, and in the eighteenth century its expansion was rampant. In school atlases the British Empire was coloured pink and there was a lot of it! Like empires before, it rose and fell. Regimes that seem to flourish today will also, at some point, decline, and others rise to take their temporary place.

In comparison, God's kingdom, God's world, is immovable. He set the universe in place, he keeps it going, he reigns supreme. It may not always seem so. You may question why the world is in such a sorry state of disarray. This psalm shows us the bigger picture and the last verse of the psalm sums up the longevity of the kingdom. More than longevity, it is eternal. It lasts for ever and ever. God is king! Long live the king. And his people will live with him in the eternal kingdom where all will be perfect.

Be encouraged
That God's kingdom is one of peace and righteousness.

Pray
The Lord's Prayer.

230

Eyes and ears

Question time

How many different parts of the eye can you name?

Read Psalm 94:1-11

Comment

Sclera, iris, cornea, pupil, lens, conjunctiva, retina, optic nerve, cones, rods . . . The eye is a complex organ that gives us sight. More of the brain is involved in helping us see than in any of the other senses. So when the psalmist says in verse 9, 'God made our eyes – can't he see?', there is a touch of irony, even if in those far-off days, the writer didn't have the scientific knowledge that we have today. He recognised God's creative work in the anatomy of the human body.

Yes, God made us in all our complexity. So of course the inventor and creator of the ear and eye hears us and sees us. It's completely logical but we don't always want to admit that he hears all we say and sees all we do.

Spend a bit of time learning about the eye or the ear and thank God for his creative power. Ask him to help you to use both pairs of organs wisely.

You may, however, have lost, or never had, the ability to see or hear.

Challenge

Are you still able to praise God, as Fanny J Crosby did? Though blind, she was a prolific hymn writer.

Pray

For opticians and eye surgeons.

Corruption and constancy

Question time

What are the contrasting features of members of your family?

Read Psalm 94:12-23

Comment

'Compare and contrast . . .' was an instruction in English literature exam papers. We might have to compare and contrast two characters in a novel. For example, Elizabeth and Jane in *Pride and Prejudice* by Jane Austen, or Helen and Jane in *Jane Eyre*. You have to analyse the differences or similarities between the two characters. You might be asked by a friend to compare and contrast two possible holiday destinations or the merits or otherwise of two food items or garden plants.

Here, the psalmist contrasts corruption and constancy. His world is full of injustice, wickedness

and corruption. Life in God's surroundings is about his protection, his presence, his love, his comfort, his defence of righteousness. It is in that context that the psalmist can say in verse 19, 'Whenever I am anxious and worried, you comfort me and make me glad.' If only it were that easy! How often, if you're anxious or worried, do you churn over negative thoughts and grapple with trying to pull yourself up. God's way is to rest in him, to trust him and to be assured of his presence despite the things that frighten or depress us.

Be encouraged

Learn to be mindful of God in the everyday and when we have those anxious moments, to pause and pray rather than pause and panic.

Pray

Lord, help me to focus my mind on you in times of anxiety.

232
Bow down

Question time
🍃 **How good is your posture?**

Read Psalm 95:1-11

Comment

'Think about your posture', the health and fitness instructor tells us. 'Head up, shoulders back and down, stomach in, breathe . . .' Many of us sit hunched over our laptops, shoulders rounded and head down, not ideal for more than short bursts, but often we're like it for hours on end – only getting up to fetch a cup of coffee.

What about posture for worship? Verse 6 tells us to 'bow down' to worship God, to 'kneel' before him. My mother recalled how her mother had taught her to kneel by the side of her bed to say her prayers at night. Perhaps you kneel to say yours.

Bowing and kneeling have been associated with worship and reverence for centuries. The Hebrew word for worship means 'bow down'. Abraham had visitors one day; he recognised them as being from God and he bowed to welcome them. When it comes to our worship of God, bowing and kneeling may be helpful, but they're not the only postures we might adopt for worship. Sitting, standing, walking, lying down, raising our hands or faces to heaven, could all be valid postures as we acknowledge God as the supreme being.

Challenge

The outward posture and expression of our reverence for God must come from an appropriate inner attitude. Who and why we worship are as important as how we worship.

Pray

If you can, get down on your knees now to pray.

233

Good news

Question time

- How do you like to receive good news?
- Personal messenger, text, WhatsApp, letter...?

Read Psalm 96:1-6

Comment

There's a song, based on Isaiah chapter 6, which uses the words, 'I see the Lord and his train fills the Temple.' I have to admit that the words make me laugh, as I have this image in my head of a steam locomotive with some beautiful Pullman carriages roaring into the Temple.

In modern versions of the Bible it talks about God's *robe* or the train of his robe filling the Temple. It's a wonderful image of the complete awe-inspiring majesty of God. In verse 6 of this psalm we read that, 'Glory and majesty surround him; power and beauty fill his Temple.' And it is from this awesome God that we have good news.

The psalmist urges the whole world to sing to the Lord. We sing in honour of our God. We praise him. And because he is wonderful we proclaim him to others. Why? Because he is a God who brings us good news. He is good news – personified in Jesus Christ the Saviour.

Challenge

If we fret about lack of numbers in churches and ponder how we can get people to church, maybe we could read this psalm and think not how to get bums on seats, but what, or who, it is we want to communicate and why.

Pray

Reread verses 1-3 and pray for wisdom in sharing the good news – preferably in words that people understand and without steam trains.

234
All creation

Question time

What elements of the created world fill you with most joy?

Read Psalm 96:7-13

Comment

A few days ago a storm blew across the Atlantic and hit British soil. I staggered along the road trying to keep upright and listened to the wind blowing through a line of beech trees; the sound was alarming, the volume deafening and the noise carried a long way. The sea was whipped up into an angry white-tipped frenzy and people were knocked sideways as they walked along pavements.

The noise in this psalm is not an alarming noise from creation. It is the noise of gladness and joy, and it is the noise of *all* creation. When the wind of God blows and he comes to rule the earth, the trees will shout for joy! In the fields, everything will be glad: harvest mice, field fares, snails, waving barley, sheep . . .

We have glimpses of the future rule of the King of kings. We live in the in-between times after Jesus' first arrival and before his second arrival.

Be encouraged
Look for signs of Jesus' kingship now in the created world.

Pray
Thank God for his plan to rescue the world and to be its fair judge.

235
Gladness

Question time

- What makes you glad?
- A sunny day, a task completed, a new baby in the family, a good meal?

Read Psalm 97:1-12

Comment

Have a look at the number of times 'glad' or 'gladness' are mentioned in these verses. What makes the psalmist glad? The fact that, 'The Lord is king!' All the nations see his glory. One glad day that will indeed be the case. Revelation 21 verse 5 states that, 'The one who sits on the throne said, 'I will make all things new!' In chapter 22, right at the end of God's word, we learn that life – the water of life – sparkles as it flows from the throne of God and of the Lamb (that is Jesus, the Lamb of God who takes away the sin of the world). What a picture! What a wonderful sight.

We can rejoice now with gladness because God's promises are true. We've already had the incarnation – the coming of God as man into the world – and the subsequent sacrifice of Jesus for the sins of the world, and his resurrection – the promise of new life. And one day we will see the consummation of God's work.

Be encouraged

There's no reason not to be glad *now* for what God has done, what he is doing and what he will do.

Pray

Praise God for the things that make you glad.

236

A new song

Question time

🌿 Do you have a favourite worship song or hymn?

Read Psalm 98:1-9

Comment

This is a wonderfully upbeat section of the psalms. Full of praise and thanksgiving, full of promise of great things, full of exuberant joy. How can you express your thankfulness to God? Are you a writer? A painter? A composer of music? Use your God-given creative juices to think how you, like the psalmist, can pour out your joy and gladness.

If you can't write or paint, try singing. There are plenty of songs you can use that have been penned by other people. Find some on YouTube or in a hymn book, or use one of the psalms to read aloud. Listen to a choir or orchestra making music for God, learn from children how to praise; they're often less inhibited than adults!

You don't have to feel in tiptop condition to praise God. He is worthy of praise irrespective of how we feel.

Challenge

You might like to choose a word from this psalm and ponder that word. It might be, 'new' or 'wonderful', 'power' or 'strength', 'promise' or 'loyalty', 'love' or 'joy'. Give it a go!

Pray

Use the psalm as your prayer.

237

Supreme

Question time

> What comes to mind when you think of the word 'supreme'?

Read Psalm 99:1-5

Comment

A boneless and skinless piece of chicken is called the 'supreme'. Not sure why, other than, perhaps, it is tender, succulent and tasty. Chicken supreme can also mean a piece of chicken breast cooked in a rich cream sauce. It is special. The dictionary defines supreme as 'highest ranking' or 'very great' or the 'greatest'.

The psalm is headed, 'The Supreme King'. Nobody matches God's greatness. Nobody matches him in power and authority. Nobody matches him in holiness or in justice, righteousness or fairness. Which is a great comfort in a world where there seems so much misused power, where there is a lack of holiness, where there is much injustice and unfairness.

Challenge

Think of geographical areas where there is injustice, of areas where there is unfairness. Is there something you could do to bring about change, however small?

Pray

Specifically for those places and for people you may know of or know personally who struggle in the face of adversity. And thank God for his supremacy.

238
Cloud-speak

Question time

🍃 Do you notice the clouds?

🍃 Have you ever seen shapes of animals or maps when you look at the clouds?

Read Psalm 99:6-9

Comment

I love the variety of clouds that tell us the kind of weather to expect: cirrus, cumulus, stratus . . . or in more colloquial language: mares' tails, herringbone pattern, cotton-wool or cauliflower clouds.

God spoke to the people of Israel through the clouds and through fire. He speaks through different elements in his created world, showing his supremacy over everything. The godly leaders recognised God's 'words' demonstrated in so many different ways.

Today we have the Bible, God's word, and the Word himself, Jesus Christ. Jesus communicates to us and his Spirit interprets and teaches us God's ways.

Challenge

Think of the ways in which you listen to God. Is there one particular way which you find most helpful? Through creation, through the Bible, through sermons? Take time to listen, as Samuel did.

Pray

Instead of talking to God, be still in his presence and just listen.

239

Enter

Question time

> Can you say, honestly, that you worship God with joy? If so, why? If not, why not?

Read Psalm 100:1-5

Comment

Here is a wonderfully exuberant song of praise that urges people to enter the Temple gates with thanksgiving. Frederic E Weatherly (1848-1929) wrote the lyrics for 'The Holy City', a sacred song with music composed by Michael Maybrick, also known as Stephen Adams (1841-1913) and his hymn reminds me of Psalm 100. The lyricist writes of standing beside the Temple in old Jerusalem and hearing children singing like angels in praise of God. The second verse speaks of the hush from praise at the lonely place of the cross. And the third verse talks about the Holy City at the end of time – yet to come – when, 'The light of God was on its streets, The gates were open wide, And all who would might enter, And no one was denied.'

I sang the song at my Uncle Philip's house when I was a teenager, at a family gathering round the piano. And the thought of people streaming through the gates of the new Jerusalem was uplifting and something I looked forward to so much – and still do. What a wonderful day it will be when, with the light of God shining, we will sing, 'Hosanna in the highest, Hosanna for evermore!'

Meanwhile, still on earth, we can enter into God's presence to worship him with songs of joy and praise.

Challenge
Read this psalm just before you go to a worship service.

Pray
For joy in worship services in your community.

240

Loyalty

Question time

- To whom do you feel most loyalty?
- How do you show it?

Read Psalm 101:1-8

Comment

I happen to be writing this on Ash Wednesday, the day when people vow to give up something for Lent or do something positive for Lent. It's a bit like New Year resolutions; easy to say you'll do or won't do something, harder to keep that promise.

In this psalm King David makes all sorts of promises to God, even with the bold statement of verse 2 that his conduct will be faultless. How many of David's promises might you be able to make to God – and would you be able to keep them? Let's take a look at just a few of them:

'I will . . . live a pure life . . . never tolerate evil . . . not be dishonest . . . have no dealings with evil . . . not tolerate anyone who is proud and arrogant . . . approve of those who are faithful to God . . .'.

Challenge

Do we dare make any such promise to God? You may have sung the hymn, 'O Jesus I have promised to serve thee to the end', but how well do we keep that promise? When we make a promise to God, it's a very solemn thing.

Pray

Maybe you could say a prayer along these lines: 'I will do my best to live your way, Lord. I know I can't do it in my own strength. May your Spirit teach and challenge, comfort and encourage me as I commit my life to you.'

241

A lonely bird

Question time

- Which birds do you see on their own?
- Which are in groups?

Read Psalm 102:1-8

Comment

Very often a lone blackbird will sit on the apex of the roof of the house opposite and sing its evening hymn of praise, but the picture of a bird in this psalm (verse 7) is of a lonely and sad figure. The psalmist is weary and troubled and pours out his song to God; it's not a song of praise but a song of sorrow.

The imagery in verses 3-5 paints a bleak picture of someone who is in physical distress and, in verses 6-7, lonely, abandoned and lacking spiritual nourishment. It's a pitiful description. Is it one you can empathise with? Have you experienced such rock-bottom feelings of despair and sorrow? Is it any wonder that the psalmist cries out to God, begs God to listen to his prayer and to hear his cries for help?

I met such a lady in a care home. She was frightened, didn't really know where she was, and cried out over and over again, 'Help me! Someone, please help me!' Sometimes she had to wait before anyone came. When a carer did come, the lady would be pacified, and calm would be restored – until the next time. The psalmist urges God to 'answer me quickly'. How we long for that reassuring touch.

Be encouraged

To show empathy to someone who feels alone.

Pray

For someone you know who is lonely.

242

Ashes and tears

Question time

What might make you feel you're only fit to be thrown out as rubbish?

Read Psalm 102:9-17

Comment

I have a mental picture of my father kneeling by the fireplace and sweeping up the cold ashes from a once brightly burning fire. I think he threw them out into the dustbin. If the ashes are mixed with water – left out in the rain – the whole thing turns to a sticky grey sludge that is useless. There are, however, some plants that benefit from dry ashes.

The psalmist feels wretched and describes food and drink as ashes and tears. Not a good mix. Fit only to be thrown away. The troubled young man of the psalm is at rock bottom or, as he puts it, like dry grass and evening shadows.

Thankfully, he starts the next sentence with one of the wonderful link words, 'But' (verse 12) and we

know that God hears us when we feel like rubbish and that he hears our cries and listens to our prayers. There is always hope for those who trust God and who communicate with him, whether in songs of praise or songs of lament.

Be encouraged

Look at verse 16. It's not *if* God rebuilds, but *when* he rebuilds. He can rebuild broken lives.

Pray

For yourself or for someone you know who feels they're rubbish.

243
Write it down

Question time

- When was the last time you wrote a handwritten letter or card to someone?
- What was its purpose?

Read Psalm 102:18-28

Comment

I'm writing about my family history. There are many skeletons in cupboards, some of which I knew nothing about until I started researching. It's important that my writing is honest. There's no point in glossing over failures and scandals; they're as important as the achievements and joys.

The Bible is a book of books and they're all there to communicate God's engagement with people. It was important to pass on God's story and his message to future generations. I'm profoundly thankful that the Bible doesn't omit the unsavoury bits. We get it all and, in this psalm alone, we have emotions of anger, anguish, pity, forsakenness, but also protection, security, worship and hope.

The emotions and experiences of life that we read about in the Bible resonate with our emotions and experiences today. How remarkable the Bible is! And how constant God is!

Challenge

It is good to write down what God does for us and to share it with our family and friends. My Bible is stuffed with wise and helpful snippets from my adult children and grandchildren, based on their emotions and experiences of God in their lives. Write it down; pass it on!

Pray

That you'll make time to write down messages that will help younger members of your family know God better.

244

Healing

Question time

🍃 Why doesn't God heal everyone?

Read Psalm 103:1-5

Comment

'Why doesn't God heal everyone?' is an often-asked question. Although we know we'll all die at some point, we somehow expect to live a long and healthy life and feel cheated if we don't. It can be even worse if someone close to us succumbs to illness and death before we think they should.

So why does the psalmist here say that God, 'heals all my diseases'? (verse 3) Perhaps the clue is in verse 1 where we read, 'All my being . . .'. We tend to think in terms of physical or mental healing where we might be better to think of ourselves as holistic beings.

In the Gospels we read about Jesus healing individuals from physical disability or mental suffering, but they would all eventually die. Maybe it was more important to see what Jesus released them to be and do, rather than to just see his release of their immediate affliction.

I don't in any way wish to negate or minimise the effect that bereavement has on grieving parents or siblings or friends of a loved one. Remember that Jesus wept at the death of his friend Lazarus. But, seen holistically, we can rejoice that God forgives our sins and, in that respect, heals us.

Be encouraged

God also keeps us from the grave in that we will live forever in his presence, once the shell of our earthly bodies has been shed.

Pray

Praise God for your life and pray that you will live each day as a gift from him.

245

A father's love

Question time

- What sort of relationship did you have with your father?
- If you're a dad yourself, what sort of relationship do you have with your children?

Read Psalm 103:6-14

Comment

Anna Maria told Henry about the love of God when he was a tiny child, reading him Bible stories and praying with him. His father abandoned the family and his mother died. Aged 9, young Henry was without either parent. His early Bible knowledge stood him in good stead.

Have a look at verses 11-13. You can imagine what the words of this psalm might have meant to young Henry, speaking as it does of the love of God. The words so inspired Henry that, later in his chequered and challenging life, he penned the words of, 'Praise my soul, the king of heaven', based on this psalm.

This is the same Henry – Henry Francis Lyte – who wrote, 'Abide with me'. Some of the most memorable poetry comes from people whose sensitivity and creativity is shaped and utilised by sad or troubled circumstances. It makes it all the more special and amazing that they are able, as the psalmist does, to praise God.

Be encouraged

Perhaps you feel abandoned by loved ones, or are weak from illness, or have had an unexpected tragedy strike your life. You can experience the fatherly goodness of God, as Henry did.

Pray

For fathers, that they may take their example of fatherhood from our heavenly Father.

246
Seed sown

Question time

- Do you have 'green fingers'?
- How do you look after seeds and plants?

Read Psalm 103:15-22

Comment

'Bloom where you're planted.' 'Harvest to those in need.' I have those words written on bookmarks in my Bible. In verse 15 we read of human life flourishing like a wild flower. The seeds of a wild flower spread even though the parent plant may die. Only God knows what seeds have been sown by one of his faithful followers. Hundreds of people turned up for the funeral of a friend of mine. She was young but her life had touched the lives of many other people. She bloomed where she'd been planted. What influence for good and for God might you have on your child or a friend or someone you get chatting to on a train?

Followers of God are encouraged, even commanded, to spread the good news of Jesus, to sow seeds of his love while they have the chance of life to do so. We may never see the harvest ourselves, but we might in heaven when someone turns up and says, 'You helped me to a better understanding of God's love.' Read verse 17 again. Even when our earthly life is snuffed out, God's love lasts and his goodness is passed on to future generations.

Challenge
Reread the whole of this wonderful psalm and marvel at God's love for you.

Pray
That you will flourish where you've been planted – for good and for God.

247

Living creation

Question time
What do you use water for in your daily life?

Read Psalm 104:1-18

Comment

I'd love to be able to write poetry as beautiful as this psalm! What a joyous celebration of God's creation! Every day we have reminders of God at work. Yesterday we had glorious sunshine where I live, not a cloud in the sky. The birds sang and all seemed well and bright. I walked with a light step and a joyful heart. Today there's a gale blowing with gusts that take your breath away and your feet from under you if you dare to step outside. Moreover, it's pouring with torrents of rain that bash relentlessly on the window, distracting me from the task in hand.

Whatever the weather, and there's plenty in this psalm about water, it reminds us of a power that is beyond human control. Pictures of the blue planet from space show us that it is dominated by water, but that water gives life. And so we also read in this psalm about animals whose thirst is quenched, grass that grows for cattle, and crops for us: a lovely mixture in verse 15 of wine, olive oil and bread to make us happy, cheerful and strong.

Challenge

Whatever is going on outside your window today, take a look. What are you contributing to the well-being of the nature, creatures and people you see?

Pray

Thank God for his creation.

248
Order

Question time

🌿 Do you live in an orderly way or in a muddle?

🌿 What are the advantages or disadvantages of each way?

Read Psalm 104:19-23

Comment

There is meaning, order and purpose in God's created world, and we see something of it expressed in these few verses. We're all familiar with the phases of the moon and how the moon marks the months and influences the tides. We know that the sun rises in the morning and sets in the evening, and that is true whatever our location on Planet Earth. For a harmonious, balanced and regulated life, we follow the orderliness of Earth. We get up in the morning, do our work, and go to bed in the evening. Or most of us do. We're grateful for those who work shifts and have to juggle with sleeping during the day, which isn't the natural way of doing things.

A lack of order results in disquiet and can lead to chaos, whether in damaged relationships, a hoarder's untidy home or a leaderless office. In private and public life we know the unease that comes with disorder.

The picture in these verses reminds me of chapter 11 of Isaiah's prophecy where we read of the Peaceful Kingdom. Harmony, peace and order.

Challenge

Let's work together, in the often chaotic scenarios of our human lives, to bring order to the fore, for the benefit of all.

Pray

Let's thank God for the meaning, order and purpose he gave in his creation of the universe and thank him too that parts of his created order still prevail by his sustenance.

249
New life

Question time

What's the funniest or most peculiar creature you have ever seen?

Read Psalm 104:24-30

Comment

God has a great sense of humour. Who else could have thought up the giraffe's long neck, a dolphin's playfulness, a waddling penguin, a bright pink flamingo. As God's creatures made in his image, humans have a sense of humour thanks to him. So we can enjoy the things he enjoys. In this psalm it seems that he made some parts of his creation just for the fun of it! Leviathan, in some translations, is described as 'that sea monster you made to amuse you'.

God didn't just create. He sustains. So he gives breath to living creatures, he provides them with food, they live their life – with its mixture of hopes and fears, joys and distress, laughter and tears – and then die. The circle of life: 'for dust you are and to dust you will return' (Genesis 3:19, NIV).

There is a hint here, though, of something more. At the end of verse 30 we read that God gives 'new life to the earth'. This is emphasised in the Gospels with the arrival of Jesus the Saviour – the Resurrection and the Life – and in Revelation when we're told there will be a new creation.

Be encouraged

To enjoy the diversity of God's creation while we have breath.

Pray

For endangered species and our responsibility as stewards. Pray for conservationists.

250
Volcanic power

Question time

- Have you seen, in reality, or on television, pictures of an erupting volcano?
- What emotions did the sight conjure up?

Read Psalm 104:31-35

Comment

A volcanic eruption is one of the most dramatic sights on earth. When the earth was being formed it was volcanic activity that created a major part of earth's surface, forming mountains and, as the rocks are broken down, providing fertile soil through their nutrients, for life to grow and thrive. Volcanic activity can be both constructive and destructive. In 2014 a new island appeared, following the eruption of a submarine volcano. The island, in the Pacific, has the splendid name of Hunga Tonga-Hunga Ha'apai. But when Krakatoa erupted in 1883, it's estimated that more than 36,000 people died.

Any volcanic eruptions, sudden and dramatic as they are, remind us of the awesome power of God but also warn us of our need to acknowledge his authority. The earth is the Lord's, not ours. We are to be its stewards on God's behalf.

Challenge

We know, through illness and crime and unexpected 'natural' disasters that we live in a less than perfect world. But, along with the psalmist, we can praise God for his power, his presence and his love for the world which is so immense that he offers life to us that goes beyond the human experiences of our short earthly lives.

Pray

Thank God for today and commit your life, however long or short it may be, to him.

251

Remember

Question time

- How good is your memory?
- Were you good at exams?
- Can you recall facts and figures with ease?

Read Psalm 105:1-11

Comment

When my eldest daughter left university she vowed never to take another exam. It was so stressful. I made a similar vow when I left school. I'd found taking exams a dreadful ordeal, mostly because I couldn't remember facts and figures that needed to be reproduced on paper at a desk in the assembly hall. The result was poor exam results and a feeling of failure. All because I couldn't remember.

The Bible often urges its readers to see the bigger picture of God's plan for life by remembering the past: its people and events; God's promises and laws; our place in that picture. Here the psalmist recalls –

and encourages his readers to recall – history. Or, as we could put it His-story. This is God's story of his 'agreement' with Abraham, his 'promise' to Isaac, and his 'covenant' with Jacob.

Challenge

What is your story in His-story? What do you remember of your ancestors, if anything? Who helped to shape your world-view? What influences can you look back on – bedtime prayers, Sunday School stickers in an attendance book, singing Christian songs in a youth group, listening to the Bible being taught in church, the friendship of a praying relative?

Pray

Thank God for his story in your past, ask that you may live in the present for him, and anticipate the total fulfilment of his promises for the future.

252

I am only one, but I am one

Question time

- Have you ever felt you're in a minority?
- Even a minority of one?
- What were the circumstances?

Read Psalm 105:12-15

Comment

God's people were few in number. At one stage in their history they were described as the remnant. I have various bits of material and wool stuffed into my sewing basket. They are remnants – random bits that might come in handy one day. Kept for a purpose. You may feel that yours is a lone Christian voice in the work place, that you're the only churchgoer in your street, that you're ridiculed or ignored or persecuted because of your faith. God won't abandon you! His presence is with you, whatever your circumstances. So persevere in your walk with him.

John Wesley wrote: 'Do all the good you can, By all the means you can, In all the ways you can, In all the places you can, At all the times you can, To all the people you can, As long as ever you can.'

A similar sentiment is expressed in this anonymous piece: 'I am only one, but I am one. I cannot do everything, but I can do something. What I can do, I ought to do, and what I ought to do, by the grace of God I will do.'

Challenge

Write out one of these two quotes and keep them by you.

Pray

For strength to persevere even if you're the only believer on your front line.

253
Proved right

Question time

If proved right about something, what is your reaction?

Read Psalm 105:16-22

Comment

The story of Joseph, in Genesis, is given to us in great detail. He was a spoilt child, thought he was better than his brothers – and told them so. They were incensed and sold him to traders and he was taken to Egypt. He was falsely accused of violating Pharaoh's wife and thrown into prison. And forgotten. Eventually a fellow-prisoner, on release, put in a good word for Joseph. He was released, found favour with Pharaoh, and became Prime Minister. His family, stuck in Canaan where there was famine, travelled to Egypt for food. Joseph provided for them and the family were reconciled. Throughout the story, the words 'God was with Joseph' are there for us to read.

All's well that ended well for Joseph but he had many sticky moments in his life and was dependent on God's goodness and presence through all the changing scenes he faced.

Can you look back and see God at work in your life? Maybe you were a spoilt child, maybe there was sibling rivalry to work through. Perhaps you were accused of something you didn't do and were punished for it. Did you feel hard done by, or did you ask God to help you through?

Challenge

What is the status of your walk with God today?

Pray

For God's presence with you each day, whatever your circumstances.

254

Horrible history

Question time

- Which historical or fictional figures are your heroes?
- And your anti-heroes?

Read Psalm 105:23-36

Comment

World history has heroes, people who have stood up and been prepared to take on unenviable roles of leadership. Alexander the Great, Mahatma Gandhi, Martin Luther King, Nelson Mandela, Winston Churchill . . .

Joseph's father, Jacob, took his family to settle in Egypt. All was OK to start with but as the clan grew they were resented by the Egyptians. Moses and Aaron were chosen by God to be leaders of the growing Israelite clan as they prepared to leave Egypt and move towards the promised land.

As with other more recent leaders, Moses and Aaron had a hard time. The intransigence of Pharaoh brought great hardship on the Israelites and great distress on the Egyptians. Moses and Aaron needed cool heads, compassionate feelings, wise words and dependence on God for deliverance.

Challenge

To grapple with the difficult passages of scripture and to try and see the bigger picture of God's love and plans for the world.

Pray

Whatever you may think of your country's leaders, it's good to pray for them. Pray that they may put God first and rely on him for guidance and wisdom in the difficult decisions they have to make.

255
A new land

Question time

What has been easy or hard about moving house?

Read Psalm 105:37-45

Comment

Moving house is one of the most stressful things we do in life. Moving thousands of people all at once was a logistical challenge, but it was God who led the people out of Egypt. Yes, Moses was their human leader but he was working under God's guidance. God guided them and provided for their needs. Despite this, the people grumbled a great deal and even went so far as to say they'd be better off back in Egypt! How fickle human beings can be! The move would take more than forty years and many who left Egypt would never see the promised land and settle into a new home themselves. And that included Moses.

There were bright moments on the journey. Moses and Aaron had a sister, Miriam, who was a musician. She led the women in song and dance. What a joyous spectacle! The people were thrilled to be on their way to God's promised future.

Challenge

We may get frustrated or despondent when our move doesn't seem to be progressing as fast or as smoothly as we might like. God never promised a life of ease. It's how we deal with the challenges, how we manage the mishaps, how we breathe deeply in moments of panic, that will shape our peace of mind.

Pray

That God's presence will bring peace even in the most trying circumstances.

256

Poor memory

Question time

How would you like to be remembered after you're gone?

Read Psalm 106:1-8

Comment

There's a lot in the Bible about remembering – and forgetting. We're quite happy to ask God to remember us in what we're doing and how we're feeling, and to remember our loved ones. But how often do we remember God and what he has done and how he feels towards us and our loved ones? All communication is two-way.

The first three verses of this psalm are full of praise for God. The psalmist then asks God to remember him though, all credit to him, he asks in the context of appreciating – and saying – that all good things come from God and that we are his creatures. The emphasis is on God.

Then comes a confession in verses 6 and 7 of past misdemeanours by ancestors as far back as when the Israelites were still in Egypt. And the sad acknowledgement that human nature doesn't change. Sin and wickedness and evil still prevail. A poor memory of who God is and what he has done results in rebellion. And yet, in verse 8, we have a God who saves – despite our wrongdoing.

Be encouraged

Jesus the Saviour's work was the result of God's love for people and we do well to remember that.

Pray

That you will not forget God's memory of you.

257

I want

Question time

🍃 Why would a parent give a child something they want, irrespective of whether it is good for them?

🍃 Perhaps so they might learn from their clamouring and from their foolish demands?

Read Psalm 106:9-15

Comment

The people believed God's promises and sang praises to him (verse 12) but then forgot what he'd done for them. They decided to go their own way, failed to ask for advice, and then got into a pickle. The parent in this case was God and the Israelites his wayward children.

An exaggerated modern example of this might be a parent in a supermarket with a toddler saying, 'I want . . .' – crisps, sweets, chocolate, biscuits, a new toy. The toddler throws a wobbly and the parent allows the child to have what it wants. And then has to deal with the aftermath: being sick, rotten teeth, obesity, or whatever.

A teenager, instead of remembering his parent's kindness and patience, might exert some new-found independence and get mixed up in foolish behaviour. What does the parent do? Let them find out the hard way? Pick up the pieces when the prodigal returns home?

Be encouraged

To keep close to our parent God and seek his advice for your life on a daily basis.

Pray

Help me, Lord, to be wise in my use of the freedom you give.

258
Swap

Question time

 Do you have a box of treasures?

Read Psalm 106:16-23

Comment

When I was about 8 years old I had a box with random bits in it: a drying-out acorn, some no-longer-shiny conkers, an old bracelet, a picture card from inside a box of tea . . . In the school playground we girls would get out our respective boxes and swap treasures with each other. The exchanges were generally fair and there was nothing of particular monetary value. It was all just a bit of fun.

We read here of the Israelites' shenanigans. Not only did they forget God, they spurned his chosen leader, Moses, and his chosen priest, Aaron. Jealousy can have drastic consequences. Verse 20 shows the folly of their choices when they swapped the glory of God for the image of a metal bull. This was no playground game, however. Daft? Irresponsible?

Ungrateful? Verse 21 says that, yet again, the Israelites had forgotten the God who had saved them.

Rather than judging the Israelites, we should look at their story and learn from it.

Challenge

How much do we focus on material things rather than on God? How can we avoid worshipping things rather than God? Where does God come in the pecking order of home, family, work, pleasure, food, holidays?

Pray

Father God, none of us deserves your love, yet you give it constantly. Thank you that you are a God of love and mercy. Help me to live in the light of that love.

259
Grumbling

Question time

What do you grumble about?

Read Psalm 106:24-27

Comment

'They rejected . . .'; 'They did not believe . . .'; 'They grumbled . . .'; 'They would not listen . . .'.

Are you a grumbler? We all grumble from time to time. Some grumble more than others! Grumbling is contagious and in a group situation everyone can end up murmuring. It doesn't make anyone happy but we still do it!

In the New Testament Jesus fed thousands of people and afterwards said, 'I am the bread of life.' In a long discourse Jesus explained how he'd come down from heaven, was doing the will of his Father, and that it was God's plan and desire that nobody should be exempt from his love. Anyone who believed in Jesus would have eternal life. Wow! What fantastic news! But what did the religious leaders do in response? They grumbled. (See John 6:35-51.) They grumbled because Jesus said he'd come from heaven, they grumbled because they couldn't see he was anything special – after all, they knew he was the son of a carpenter, Joseph of Nazareth. Jesus responded to their grumbles with a further explanation and referred them to their ancestors for whom God had provided food in their journey from Egypt to the Promised Land. And what had those ancestors done? Grumbled. History repeats itself!

Be encouraged

The good news is that people can have new life when they start believing in Jesus. Eternal life starts as soon as you put your trust in God through Jesus. And everlasting life beyond death is guaranteed. Why grumble?

Pray

That you won't contribute to a snowball effect of grumbling.

260

Think before you speak

Question time

🍃 Can you think of a time when you wished you hadn't spoken hastily?

Read Psalm 106:28-33

Comment

If you had been promised a new land to live in and then spent forty years getting there, how would you feel and how would you react? Patience tested, physical energy challenged, mental positivity at breaking point . . .? Moses had a hard time as God's leader of the people. Did he get weary of the role, weary of his tiresome flock? Is it any surprise that he was bitter?

In the New Testament followers of Jesus were warned that going his way was no stroll in the park. They would face opposition and persecution and the pathway was likened to a narrow road. It was a road, however, that would lead to life. Many chose it but then found it too hard to keep going and gave up. Others persevered because, as Simon Peter, put it to Jesus, 'To whom would we go? You have the words that give eternal life' (John 6:68).

Challenge

How is your walk with God? Are you happy in your travels? Or do you sometimes find it so tough that you mouth off at someone? Sometimes it's our fellow-travellers who test us to the limit. And it's then that we may speak without stopping to think.

Pray

Ask God for his grace and patience, and for love for him and for all those who are travelling his pilgrim route.

261

Adoption and abandonment

Question time

🍃 What ethos have you adopted in living your life?

Read Psalm 106:34-42

Comment

Adoption has two meanings. It can be the action of legally taking another person's child and bringing it up as one's own, or it can be the action of choosing to take up, follow, or use something.

These verses don't make pretty reading. God's people had turned their backs on him and decided to do whatever they wanted, live with whomever they chose, and murder children as sacrifices to false gods. They were unfaithful to God. God was so disgusted with their behaviour that he abandoned them. What a bleak picture.

If you read news reports, you may be horrified by some of the practices that occur today – the exploitation of children, the murder of young people by others of their own age, adult behaviour that sickens us. Do you live in a culture where ungodly ways have been adopted? How does God look on what we do? Does he abandon us as a lost cause?

Challenge

You may live somewhere where God is honoured by many or you may live somewhere where God is largely ignored. How do you react and interact with them?

Pray

For your neighbours and friends, your local and national leaders, and pray that God may be recognised and honoured.

262

Distress

Question time

- Have you ever given up on someone as a lost cause?
- If you're a teacher, is there a child in your class who is so disruptive that there seems no way of getting through to him?
- Are you a parent with a rebellious teenager?
- Have you given up on her?

Read Psalm 106:43-48

Comment

God, as we've already discovered, never gives up. Despite repeated bouts of bad behaviour by the Israelites we read that 'many times' he rescued them. And then they chose to rebel again. Each rebellious episode drew them deeper into sin. Boggy ground on Dartmoor is a hazard. Step on a bog and you start to sink. You take another step and sink further. And need to be pulled out. Which is what, metaphorically,

God did for his people. He heard their cries, he saw their distress. If it's your child that is sinking into the bog, your instinct is not to think: well, he's getting what he deserved, but to go to the rescue because you love your child.

Be encouraged

God's children are precious to him and he holds out his hand to rescue them and save them. And they praise him for his goodness.

Pray

This is the end of Book Four of the Psalms and it ends with praise. Can you join in the 'Amen!' of verse 48?

263
Wandering

Question time

- Are you wandering through a 'trackless desert' in your life at the moment?

- Have you given up hope?

Read Psalm 107:1-9

Comment

Book Five begins with praise! How often do you say the words of this first verse? God is good. He is eternal. So we give thanks. Often. God's goodness is constant and continues irrespective of our human circumstances, which may not be good all the time.

God doesn't give up! Ever. And it is his constancy that can keep us when we're being tossed about on a seemingly relentless turbulent ocean of fear, discouragement, uncertainty or disappointment.

With God we don't have to run a marathon all in one go. The pilgrim way is certainly more of a marathon than a sprint but all we need to do is take one step at a time. Call out to God as his people did here in this psalm and what does God do? He leads them by a straight road. The weary wanderer becomes the strong stepper. And it is God's strength and presence and guidance that take us safely along his road – one step at a time.

Be encouraged
We can repeat verse 1 and say that the Lord is good.

Pray
Spend some time thinking about and praising God for the things in your life that show he is good.

264
Gloom

Question time

🍃 Have you ever experienced spiritual imprisonment because of your rejection of God – even if only temporarily?

Read Psalm 107:10-16

Comment

Bodmin Jail in Cornwall is chilling (in both senses). It was built by prisoners in the 1700s and in use until the 1920s. Today it is a museum and you can visit the cell blocks and imagine what life was like for the occupants: dark and cold, with plenty of fear and misery thrown in.

The psalmist describes the imprisonment that resulted from rebellion against God and a rejection of his instructions. Today there are people in jail for crimes they've committed, but any of us might experience spiritual imprisonment because of our rejection of God.

By way of contrast, in Acts we read of Paul and Silas in jail in Philippi. They'd done nothing wrong but were severely beaten then thrown into jail. The jailer was ordered to, 'lock them up tight' (Acts 16:23). They were thrown into an impregnable inner cell and chained. Dark and cold. Battered. Bruised. Bleeding.

The psalmist recalls how the people called to the Lord and he saved them from their imprisonment. 'They must thank the Lord for his constant love, for the wonderful things he did for them' (verse 15). Paul and Silas dealt with their imprisonment by praying and singing hymns. They too were released.

Challenge

How would you react if imprisoned?

Pray

For prisoners of conscience and those illegally or unjustly imprisoned.

Reprieve

Question time

* If somebody has wronged you, how do you react?

Read Psalm 107:17-22

Comment

Offenders sometimes receive a suspended sentence. It serves as a warning. You've been reprieved, so long as you don't re-offend.

God reprieved his people on numerous occasions, an indication of his merciful nature and love. Would we be so patient? How do you treat someone who has been foolish and got into trouble? Do you seek revenge? Do you want justice to be meted out? Do you let them off?

Many years ago our house was burgled by three men who were on their way home from their father's funeral. At the wake they'd imbibed more alcohol than was perhaps wise, and decided to target a random house. I was out at the time and returned home to find the front door open and an absence of electronic equipment. My 5-year-old daughter was upset because a plant that had been on the hall window ledge had been knocked onto the floor. My concern was for the safety of my children. The hero of the day was a neighbour who had chased the men up the road on foot, shouting at the top of her voice. She was outraged by what had happened and determined that they should be apprehended. Which they were. There was no reprieve for them.

Different reactions to misdemeanours.

Be encouraged

God doesn't tolerate sin but he never stops loving the sinner and when there is repentance he saves.

Pray

Praise God for his saving grace.

266

Raging storm

Question time

What images of a rough sea can you recall, from personal experience or from paintings or films?

Read Psalm 107:23-32

Comment

Images of the sea are portrayed in paintings, poems and music. *Sea Fever* by former Poet Laureate, John Masefield (1878-1967), captures the draw of the sea when he writes, 'I must go down to the seas again ...'

The seas, however, can be hazardous as we know from fact and fiction. *Christmas Morning*, an oil painting by John Brett (1831-1902), depicts a shipwreck. The sailors have abandoned ship and taken to the lifeboat and are tossed in a menacing sea. But in the background the dark clouds are breaking to reveal a brighter dawn. In the psalm the sailors were terrified and their skills to no avail. The men called to the Lord and he saved them.

It was Presbyterian minister, William J H Boetcker (1873-1962) who said, 'A man without religion or spiritual vision is like a captain who finds himself in the midst of an uncharted sea, without compass, rudder and steering wheel. He never knows where he is, which way he is going and where he is going to land.'

Be encouraged

God is the lifeboat coxswain, the one who saves, when help is called for. He calms the storm and the waves and brings the sailors to a safe harbour. His saving power is still there for us in our storms.

Pray

For those in peril on the sea.

267

Be wise

Question time

🍃 **Where or from whom do you seek wisdom?**

Read Psalm 107:33-43

Comment

At the end of this very long psalm we have a picture of peace and prosperity, of rescue and righteousness. The psalm is titled, 'In praise of God's goodness'. There's been a lot about the ineptitude and enterprise of human beings and of oppression and optimism. The good news is repeated frequently: God is good, God is constant, God is merciful, God is love, God is wanting to provide a good and full life for human beings in relationship with him.

Look at verse 43. Are you wise? Do you think? In Proverbs 7:3, 4 we read, 'Keep my teaching with you all the time; write it on your heart. Treat wisdom as your sister, and insight as your closest friend.' In today's lingo, it's a no-brainer, but it's not easy!

Challenge

Spend a bit of time rereading the whole psalm. Notice how many times the reader is told to, 'thank the Lord for his constant love'.

Pray

Thank God for his constant love and ask him to give you wisdom and faith to follow him day by day.

Greatness of the sky

Question time

Think of a sunset you've witnessed. What is it about sunsets that we appreciate so much?

Read Psalm 108:1-6

Comment

When my father was ill in hospital I visited him most days. My route took me, on foot, uphill and across fields. It was autumn and the weather was fine, such that every evening the sun went down in a blaze of red, orange and yellow glory. This seemed apt, for my father had been a research scientist specialising in colour. He would have loved the sight of the vast and colourful sky! One night, after some weeks in hospital, he died. Words of the hymn 'For all the saints' came to my mind: 'The golden evening brightens in the west; soon, soon to faithful warriors cometh rest; sweet is the calm of paradise the blest. Alleluia! Alleluia!' (William Walsham How, 1823-1897).

I can echo the words of verse 5. I saw God's glory in the skies over England's fields and hills that autumn. I don't have a harp or lyre (verse 2) but I played that hymn a lot on the piano to remind me of God's faithfulness to his living people and also to those who have lived for him during their earthly life and are now safe in the glory of heaven.

Be encouraged

'But lo! there breaks a yet more glorious day; the saints triumphant rise in bright array; the King of glory passes on his way. Alleluia! Alleluia!'

Pray

For those nearing the end of their earthly life, that they may see God's glory.

269

Worthless help

Question time

> What practical help have you received from other people?

Read Psalm 108:7-13

Comment

The local hospital has just raised £1,500,000 for a new MRI scanner. The money has come from people in the neighbourhood who have received help from the hospital and who want to offer help themselves in the form of monetary provision for the scanner. It will enhance the lives of countless people.

Verse 12 says that 'human help is worthless'. And that is sometimes the case. Not every patient gets better, nobody is immune from troubles in their lives. Famine, poverty, disease, war, anxiety, fear . . . Sometimes human help is limited in its scope. We still have to do what we can, responding to appeals from charities, in an effort to make the world – or at least the lives of one or two people – better.

The emphasis in the psalms is on God. He is appealed to, he is praised, he is grumbled at, he is pleaded with. Look back at verse 1. Where does help come from? Ultimately it comes from God. In our prayers, as well as praise and thanksgiving and confession, we ask for his help, his presence, his comfort, his equipping of his people to be his representatives of compassion, kindness and love.

Challenge

What fundraising activity might you be involved in with your local hospital?

Pray

For hospital technicians and other support staff.

270

Opposition

Question time

🍃 Have you ever felt under attack from people you have prayed for and whom you love?

Read Psalm 109:1-5

Comment

Rugby internationals are major events. The Wales team, for example, show solidarity when they sing their National Anthem and then when they're on the field of play. Though individuals, they run as one, working together, rooting for each other and playing to win. Yet they all come from different rugby clubs where, when not on international duty, they are set against each other in matches. So a player for Scarlets may be up against a player from Cardiff Blues in a club match when they'll attack each other and oppose each other.

Here we see the psalmist David complaining to God about the opposition he is up against: 'They oppose me, even though I love them and have prayed for them. They pay me back evil for good and hatred for love.' It was bewildering for David and very painful.

The fickleness of human nature is such that we hurt each other – sometimes unintentionally, often deliberately. Our behaviour can be as rough as a rugby ruck or maul or scrum and we may come out of it with metaphorically bloodied noses and broken bones.

Be encouraged

To turn to God, following David's example, when you face opposition.

Pray

For those who oppose you.

Ouch!

Question time

🍃 Have you ever been so badly hurt by someone that it physically hurts?

Read Psalm 109:6-15

Comment

Oh dear! This is the cry of a desperate man who is at the end of his patience and the end of his tolerance. He's had enough! Nine times he comes up with a 'May he . . .' or a 'May his . . .' and wishes the worst on those who mistreat him.

I like David! I like his feistiness, his honesty, his belligerence, because they ring true. Can you honestly say that you've never felt extreme annoyance, dislike, even hatred, towards another person? If that is the case, then you're an unusual saint! Maybe you're more mild in your words – spoken or in your head: 'He drives me up the wall . . .'; 'I could murder her . . .'; 'I don't mind if I never see or hear from him again . . .' and you don't mean to carry out a killing or total ostracism. But the thoughts are there. And David puts his thoughts on paper or parchment or whatever – for all the world to read for generations to come!

David's words are truly shocking. But let's not judge him. Rather, be thankful that the Bible doesn't fudge issues, that God's people try their best to be godly but don't always manage it. We see that God still loves. And if he still loves, who are we to abhor loving his creatures, however tiresome they are?

Be encouraged

To vent your anger towards God rather than towards your enemies, and let God deal with the situation.

Pray

For God to calm you down when you're angry.

272

Scorned

Question time

🍃 Think of a time when you have been a bully.

🍃 You reckon you haven't? Think again . . .

Read Psalm 109:16-25

Comment

Freddie was bullied at school. Whenever possible he avoided those who taunted him but sometimes they caught him on his way home and made his life a misery. One day he plucked up courage to tell his parents, who told the head teacher. Freddie had a generous heart and he didn't want to make trouble for those who'd caused him trouble. He concentrated on making life better for others who were scared or lonely or upset. School staff dealt with the bullies.

'I am poor and needy; I am hurt to the depths of my heart . . . When people see me, they laugh at me; they shake their heads in scorn' (verses 22, 25).

Be encouraged

God is stronger than the Devil, good will prevail over bad, one day there will be an end to injustice, fear and pain. David acknowledges God's part in meting out justice.

Pray

For those who are bullied – and for the bullies too, that love will replace hate, and that compassion will take the place of cruelty.

273
Loud

Question time

🍃 Think of someone you don't like. Is there a chance you could love them?

Read Psalm 109:26-31

Comment

David has moderated his tone slightly. He still wants justice, but he's calm enough to ask for God's help, to acknowledge God's love and saving power. He wants his persecutors to know that it is God who saves.

Jesus said, 'But I tell you who hear me: Love your enemies, do good to those who hate you, bless those who curse you, and pray for those who mistreat you' (Luke 6:27, 28). It's a big ask! If you feel hard done by through the actions or words of a fellow human being, it's not always easy to let it go. But if we allow our anger to fester, it just makes us feel worse. A vicar once commented – and it was a relief to hear him say – 'As Christians we don't have to *like* everyone, but we are called to *love* everyone.'

Challenge

Jesus said, 'I tell you who hear me . . .'. Are we hearing and listening to the voice of Jesus in our indignation? Talk to him, tell him how you feel, as David told God his thoughts and feelings. Then take a deep breath and remember that God loves that person who you struggle to like. Be loud – not in your protestations, but in your thanks and praise to God, because, 'the judge of all the earth has to act justly' (Genesis 18:25). In the end it's God's call, not ours.

Pray

Relax and breathe deeply. Then tell God you're submitting to him and allowing him to do his job.

274
Drink for strength

Question time

🍃 What do you know about your local water supplier?

🍃 If the company has a magazine do you read it? Find out today who supplies your water and learn what they do.

Read Psalm 110:1-7

Comment

More than half the human body is water. It's important to replenish the water if we want to maintain good health. It's recommended that we drink about 2 litres of water a day which is equivalent to about 8 glasses. If we feel thirsty it's usually an indication that we're already dehydrated.

Jesus said, 'Those who drink the water that I will give them will never be thirsty again. The water that I will give them will become in them a spring which will provide them with life-giving water and give them eternal life' (John 4:14).

In this Messianic psalm, we see pictures of David the king, but also a prophetic vision of the king who would be the Saviour and Priest, Jesus Christ himself. The book of Hebrews uses quotes from this psalm to explain Jesus' role as priest.

The king is strengthened from drinking water from the stream. Jesus, in John 7:37, 38, says 'Whoever is thirsty should come to me, and whoever believes in me should drink. As the scripture says, "Streams of life-giving water will pour from his side."' These words can also be translated, 'Streams of life-giving water will pour out from within anyone who believes in me.'

Be encouraged

Water is essential – physical and spiritual. The tap may be the source of the first, Jesus is the source of the second. Tap into it.

Pray

Praise God for the water you have on tap and pray for those for whom water is a rare luxury.

275
Wonderful actions

Question time

What's the kindest or best thing that someone has ever done for you?

Read Psalm 111:1-6

Comment

The kindest thing someone has ever done for me is probably the occasions when my dad took me to Wimbledon to watch tennis. Or the surprise fiftieth birthday party my daughters gave me. Or the positive comments a teacher made about my story-writing. Or the gift of a series of classic novels when I left a job . . .

None of those compare with the kind and wonderful things that the Lord God does. I wonder what the psalmist had in mind in verse 2? What was so wonderful about God's doings that made the psalmist so delighted and yet wanting to understand more? Maybe it was the immensity of the universe, looking at the stars and seeing different worlds, or the faithfulness of God in guiding the psalmist through the turmoil of everyday life, or the provision of his presence at all times.

The psalmist publicly thanks God for his goodness, 'in the assembly of his people'(verse 1).

Be encouraged

Thankfulness is catching. If one person expresses thanks to God, it prompts other people to think about God's wonderful works. Such a snowball effect could revolutionise our worship gatherings. And impact our neighbours and friends who don't yet know God.

Pray

Let's be ready to proclaim God for who he is and for what he does.

276
Dependable

Question time

- How well do you trust your local political representative?
- Or your nation's government?
- Do they offer 'sound judgement'?
- Are they 'truthful'?
- Are they dependable?

Read Psalm 111:7-10

Comment

There's much scepticism about leadership, local, national and global. Where do we turn for dependable government?

Let's list God's credentials as shown in these few verses: he is wonderful in his actions, kind, merciful. He provides, remembers, is faithful, just, dependable, timeless, truthful and righteous. He sets people free and makes promises and covenants that last forever. He is holy and mighty.

Is it any wonder, then, that the psalmist urges us to 'honour the Lord' as the way to become wise? Politicians may do their best but it's sometimes a self-interested best.

Be encouraged

God's best is not subjective but objective. All that he does he does for people. Why? And this is how he, perhaps, differs from politicians: he does it out of love.

Pray

As you thank God for all that he is, pray for your political and church leaders, that they may honour God and seek his wisdom.

277

A good person

Question time

- How would you define a 'good' person?
- Do you think of yourself as a good person?

Read Psalm 112:1-10

Comment

If asked, many people claim to be good people – though what they say about themselves sometimes seems self-indulgent! The most moving quotes I've read about being good describe people other than the person speaking. Some cite their dad or their mum as being a good person, some mention a famous figure from the past who has been seen to be doing good.

In this psalm it is not so much what a person does as what his characteristics are. Look at verses 4 and 5. The good person is merciful, kind, just and generous – all human traits to which any of us might aspire. But there's more to the good person than just demonstrating those assets of character in action.

Faith is involved. The good person 'honours the Lord' (verse 1), his faith is strong and 'he trusts in the Lord' (verse 7).

James, in his letter, writes about the connection between faith and actions: 'My friends, what good is it for one of you to say that you have faith if your actions do not prove it?' (James 2:14).

Challenge

Faith or action? It isn't an either/or for those who acknowledge God as their Lord. The two go together. And it all starts with God.

Pray

Start your prayers today with praise, as in verse 1.

278

East to west

Question time

How can we praise the Lord in whichever part of the globe we happen to be?

Read Psalm 113:1-9

Comment

I've been watching some spin-off programmes from Blue Planet II, the iconic series produced by the BBC's Natural History Unit in Bristol. The current programmes go out live from three different locations: the west coast of Mexico on the Pacific Ocean, Heron Island on the Queensland coast of Australia, and the Bahamas in the Caribbean. Live links take us from one location and one presenter to another location and a different presenter. Each is connected to the others and supported by camera crews on land, sea and in the air. It's a remarkable feat of technology.

In the psalm we are told how praise of the Lord is connected from east to west. The programmes I watch have shown huge whales and tiny baby turtles, sun-bathed clear waters and dark deep ocean depths. The variety of wildlife is mind-blowing. We're told elsewhere in the psalms that *all* creation praises the Lord and seeing these programmes you can believe that. The psalm, however, speaks particularly of human beings praising the Lord's name all around the globe. Wherever we are on God's earth, he is there too – in the clear waters of the oceans, in the mud of flooded landscapes, in the beauty of the skies, in the poverty of famine-stricken places.

Challenge

We praise the Lord in words and action. How much do you show his love and care for his creation – whether as stewards of the physical world or carers of people?

Pray

That good stewardship of God's world may happen globally, from east to west and from north to south.

279
Trembling

Question time
What makes you tremble?

Read Psalm 114:1-8

Comment

The exodus from Egypt is one of the most dramatic migration stories we have. In this psalm, sung at the Passover festival, there is vivid imagery to convey something of the awesome nature of God's intervention in the recalcitrance of the king of Egypt to let God's people go.

The supposedly solid steady run-of-the-mill landscape is depicted as moving and trembling: mountains skipping like the goats that run on them, the hills jumping like the lambs that frolic there, and the sea taking on the form of a person who looks and runs away! Poetic imagery to make the reader or singer realise the enormity of God's action.

For many life is chaotic and stressful and when a major happening occurs, we may wonder whether

God is present, whether he is acting out of anger or whether he doesn't care about our situation. The psalm makes clear that we need to be aware that we live in God's world and that he does have the control to do whatever he chooses. Most of the time he allows human beings to get on with their lives – with or without his guiding hand.

Challenge

When life is tough we call to him in fear or distress but let's not forget him when life is easy. We need God and need to have reverence for him in all circumstances.

Pray

For those undertaking migratory journeys.

280

No sense

Question time

- Sight, hearing, touch, taste, smell . . .
- Do you have all your senses?
- Which do you most value?

Read Psalm 115:1-8

Comment

A friend was in a car accident many years ago. He spent more than two months in intensive care and was in hospital for nearly six months altogether while doctors tried to piece his body back together. He lost the sight in one eye. Another friend, in her old age, has lost her hearing, and her senses of taste and smell. She would love to be able to smell a hyacinth or a rose, she would like to be able to distinguish the difference in taste between lemonade and coffee. Her loss of hearing distances her from other people.

The psalmist describes gods that are limited in their scope. They are inanimate objects without senses. God, in comparison, sees, hears and touches the lives of the people he loves and cares for. He is faithful and to him alone glory must be given.

Are you tempted to worship something other than God? Your car, perhaps, or your technological gizmos? Your football team, your possessions, food or drink? Maybe you're a shopaholic or a hedonist? Anything that gets in the way of God and giving him first place, could become an idol. Ultimately none of those things will offer what God offers. They're all transitory and have no sense.

Challenge

Chillingly, we may become as senseless as the idols we put in place of God.

Pray

Lord Jesus, help me to have the sense to love God and love others as you said when you summarised the Law.

281
Triple trust

Question time

🍃 How is trust in a human different from trust in God?

Read Psalm 115:9-18

Comment

I trust my window cleaner to wash my windows effectively. I trust my plumber to unblock my sink. I trust my bank to look after my money. All of these do a good job most of the time but they're not infallible. So my trust is somewhat guarded; it's not total trust.

The psalm changes tack in these verses – from the inanimate nature of idols to the animated Lord of the universe! The psalmist urges people to trust the Lord. What does that mean, exactly?

First, you have to believe and put your life in his hands. Second, you have to believe what he says – that he has your best interests at heart. Third, if you have faith in him, you will follow his guidance today and commit to him for the future.

That's a rough and quick guide to faith. For someone to have faith in God the benefits are huge. Here we have the same trust statements, repeated three times for different groups of people. In each case they are called to trust the Lord because he helps, protects, remembers, and blesses.

Challenge

Do you trust him because of what he does for you or because of who he is?

Pray

Lord God, I trust you. Please increase that trust day by day.

World of the living

Question time

What do you understand by the biblical phrase, 'the world of the living'?

Read Psalm 116:1–11

Comment

I was dressed in white from neck to ankle. No, it wasn't my wedding day and I wasn't dressing up as an angel for a Nativity play. The robe I wore was hardly trendy 1960s fashion; it was extremely unprepossessing, and made – I imagine – from an old sheet. On this particular Sunday, clad in the ghastly garment, I trod carefully down steep steps into a rectangular pool of hip-deep water, the voluminous sheet threatening to rise up and reveal my knees, or worse. A pair of strong arms clasped me and plunged me backwards into the water, dunking me completely then pulling me upright again.

I opened my eyes, spluttering – and grinned. I had been baptised and there, before the church family, I declared my faith in Jesus Christ. The symbolism of being 'buried' – dying to sin – and 'rising' with my sin washed away was a memorable occasion. To mark it, I was given a card with my name and the date and this verse: 'I will walk before the Lord in the land of the living' (Psalm 116:9, KJV).

This psalm could be my testimony. With a few detours on the way, I have tried since 11 April 1965 to walk in the presence of the Lord where he's put me. I trip up often but I know I'm on his road and that he walks with me.

Challenge
What would be your testimony to share with others?

Pray
That you will know how to give an answer to anyone who asks you about your faith.

283

What can I give him?

Question time

Which hymn would you like to have sung at your funeral? Why?

Read Psalm 116:12-19

Comment

A friend said that, at her funeral, she would like the Christmas carol, 'In the bleak midwinter' to be sung. She died in April but the carol was sung, respecting her wishes. She particularly liked the last verse: 'What can I give him, poor as I am; if I were a shepherd, I would bring a lamb; if I were a wise man, I would do my part; yet what I can, I give him, give my heart.' Christina Rossetti (1830-1894) penned the words and they have been sung at carol services ever since.

The question is posed in the psalm: What can I offer the Lord? In Old Testament times sacrifices were made to God for different reasons and occasions. What was important was the attitude behind the offering. In the prophecies of the Old Testament we read that God disliked sacrifices that were made without thought and given just because that's what they did. True worship involved the heart of the person or people giving the offering.

Challenge

'What can I give him?' What can you offer the Lord? He gives each of us gifts to be used in his service. It may involve the giving of money or you may have the gift of writing, music, art, praying, listening, gardening or carpentry. Whatever your gift is, use it to worship God and offer it to him as a gift for him to enjoy and for others to benefit from too.

Pray

Praise God for the gifts he has given you and ask how he wants you to use them for him.

284

Triple praise

Question time

Do you like statistics? If so, you'll be keen to know that this psalm is the shortest out of the one hundred and fifty. It also happens to be the 595th chapter in the Bible, out of a total of 1189 chapters. So this short psalm is at the very centre of the Bible.

Read Psalm 117:1, 2

Comment

What could be more appropriate to have at the centre than the praise of God! Is the praise of God at the centre of your life? When you wake in the morning is your first thought to praise God? And at the end of the day?

We've already had plenty of clues in previous psalms of why we should praise the Lord. Let's use this psalm as a reminder. All nations must praise God. Every part of the globe. All peoples must praise him. So think about the country in which you live.

Is it one nation? It may be, but how many 'peoples' are within it? Many, if not most countries today, have a mixture of peoples of all creeds and nationalities. Some were born and bred in that country, others are temporary visitors, some are refugees, some are permanent migrants. All are created by God and all are encouraged to praise the Lord.

Be encouraged

God's love is strong; his faithfulness is eternal. No wonder the psalmist says, a third time, 'Praise the Lord!'

Pray

Think of three things that you can praise the Lord for now, then do it.

285
Eternal dependability

Question time

- Have you ever had to go on one of those team-building exercises that many companies think will help their staff to bond?

- What was involved?

Read Psalm 118:1-9

Comment

In a team-building exercise you may have been asked to pair up with someone else. You stand in front of your partner with your back to him and let yourself fall back into his arms. At the critical moment his mobile phone rings and he fishes in his pocket, pulls it out and puts the phone to his ear, just as you crash onto the floor in front of him.

The psalmist says it's better to trust in the Lord than to depend on human beings, and in the team-building exercise that went wrong, you can see why!

Maybe you've been let down, metaphorically, by someone you trusted. It may be in a personal relationship; your partner has left you for someone else, or the company you work for is doing dodgy dealings, or the friend who said she'd pick up your child from school forgot to do so.

Challenge

How trustworthy are you? We're not always very reliable or trustworthy or careful in our dealings with family, friends, neighbours or workmates. When others fail us and when we fail other people, let's acknowledge our fallibility but thank God for his dependability.

Pray

Praise God for his eternal dependability.

286

On the victory side

Question time

How does it feel when you're part of a winning team?

Read Psalm 118:10-20

Comment

Some of the psalmists went through tiring and tiresome times and expressed their frustration and fear in these poems and songs. I've found writing poetry a helpful way of unravelling my own emotions in times of crisis or bewilderment. Talking to God in that way helps.

This particular prayer of thanks for victory is shot through with the phrase, 'the power of the Lord'. In the early verses of the psalm we learned that it was the Lord who helped, the Lord who was with the psalmist, the Lord who could be trusted. And in this section it's the power of the Lord. The psalmist takes no personal credit for success; rather, it the Lord's power, his help, he who saves.

As a result of God's presence and power, the psalmist wants to let others know what God has done, who he is, what he is like. Paul, writing to the Christians in Corinth, and who went through times, like the psalmist, when he was opposed and hounded by those who took against him, writes, 'Thanks be to God who gives us the victory through our Lord Jesus Christ!' (1 Corinthians 15:57).

Be encouraged

It's the antidote to triumphalism to acknowledge that it is only in God's strength that we are able to win. He has the power to change situations and to change lives.

Pray

Praise God for his victorious reign and his power in your life.

287

Stones and branches

Question time

- Do you know how the Old Testament fits with the New Testament?
- Why is it important to know the Bible's whole story?

Read Psalm 118:21-29

Comment

I had an email one day from somebody I'd never met who lived over the other side of the world. He'd read a meditation I'd written for a magazine that is published in more than 30 languages and distributed worldwide. I was humbled to think that my little thought for that particular day had impacted somebody's life enough for him to write and let me know.

I wonder sometimes what the psalmists would think if they knew how their poems and songs were still being read and loved centuries after they were written. It's exciting enough to think that this psalm was not only familiar to the gospel writers and to many Jews in first-century Palestine, but also to Jesus himself. He quotes verse 22 and we can read it in the context of his storytelling and teaching in Matthew 21. What's more, he was the fulfilment of these verses! Look at verse 27 and we picture the entry of Jesus into Jerusalem when people tore branches off the trees to wave as flags and lay as carpet for him to ride through the city – on what we know now as Palm Sunday.

Be encouraged

This is one of the so-called Messianic psalms that looks ahead to prophecy about the coming of Jesus the Messiah, Saviour and King.

Pray

Let us, like the psalmist, give thanks to the Lord because he is good.

288

Pleasure in obedience

Question time

🍃 **Do you delight in obedience or are you a rebel who likes to go your own way?**

Read Psalm 119:1-16

Comment

From Psalm 117, the shortest, and the exciting Messianic 118, we now come to the longest psalm in the Bible which focuses throughout on the Law of the Lord or the word of God. Each of its 176 verses refers, in some way, to God's word or law, using different imagery and insights into what it means to trust and obey the Lord.

As it's getting on for 300 days since we read Psalm 1, you might want to just take a quick look back at the first two verses of that psalm and see how it resonates with these verses of Psalm 119. To be honest, it all sounds a bit too good to be true.

Is your life faultless? Do you never do wrong? Most of us are only too aware of our shortcomings!

The emphasis here is on God and his instructions for living. If we follow them we will be blessed. In verse 5 the psalmist hopes that he'll be faithful and, in verse 6, that he'll pay attention to what God has to say. It's a learning process (verse 7).

Be encouraged

When we take pleasure in God's word and obey it, we will indeed be blessed.

Pray

Praise God for his instructions, pray that you'll be obedient to them. Thank him for the blessings that brings.

Open eyes

Question time

Is it a waste of time making your appearance look good?

Read Psalm 119:17-24

Comment

She put on her make-up, dressed in her best, felt confident and went out looking good – and nobody took any notice. Was it a waste of time making an effort? Making an effort means you value yourself and want to make the most of the day. But do we make an effort with God? Have a look at verses 18 and 19. We only have a limited time to open our eyes to see God's wonderful truths.

John Keating, the radical English teacher (played by Robin Williams) in the 1989 film, *Dead Poets Society* told his students, 'Carpe, carpe diem, seize the day boys, make your lives extraordinary.' His unusual methods startled the boys: 'I stand upon my desk to remind myself that we must constantly look at things in a different way.'

God wants us to live life to the full. The psalmist recognises this but also recognises the brevity of life and the need to value each day and make the most of it, to see things in a new way: God's way.

Challenge

Delve into the Bible, God's communication tool par excellence – and discover its wonderful truths. This is more exciting than the boys' experiences in *Dead Poets Society*. How does the psalmist want to live the day? By hearing God, listening to him and seeing the treasure that is in God's word. That will set him up for the day more than any clothes parade, make-up or poetry.

Pray

For a greater love for, and understanding of, the Bible.

290

Wrong way

Question time

Do you sometimes feel defeated by your own failings?

Read Psalm 119:25-32

Comment

My husband tells the story of his first visit to China on a business trip. Not only did he not understand the language but he hadn't a clue about the signage in the streets. It was only too easy to go the wrong way. Fortunately for him, the organiser of his trip who spoke Chinese, wrote down the hotel's address and said, 'Just show this to the taxi driver and he'll take you the right way.'

The optimism of verses 1-9 seems to have plummeted into a sense of failure in today's verses. Do you sometimes feel defeated by your inability to go the right way and measure up to God's standards? You grovel around in the dust, dirty and thirsting for revival. There is always hope. The psalmist admits his failure, confesses his wrongdoing, and claims God's promise for revival. He asks God to teach him, to help him understand. In return the psalmist promises to meditate on God's teaching, reiterates his choice of being a follower of God, and lets God pick him up from the dust and move on.

Be encouraged

God's words are there in our own language for us to read, mark, learn and inwardly digest. They will lead us the right way – unless we ignore the instructions – in which case we'll end up in the wrong place and needing help to be set on the right path again.

Pray

Praise God for the Bible in your own language and pray for translators who work to provide Bibles for those who don't yet have it in their own language.

Explain

Question time

🍃 Do you listen to explanations or tune out?

Read Psalm 119:33-40

Comment

I'm happy to listen to explanations if I think the additional knowledge will enhance my life. At school I found Maths extraordinarily difficult to comprehend. I didn't understand the teacher's explanation and, frankly, found it all so irrelevant that I couldn't be bothered to listen properly to the explanation anyway.

On the other hand, when somebody explained the rules of rugby to me I listened carefully because I wanted to understand what was happening on the field of play so that my enjoyment of the game might be enhanced.

The psalmist asks God to explain his laws. He wanted to know because he knew it was the way to happiness and a fulfilled life to follow God's ways. What is your attitude to God's word? Do you want it explained to you? Do you really value God's words? Does your worldview depend on what God says to you about the world, himself and your relationship with him? If so, allow him to explain. Hear his word, listen to it and, if you're still lacking understanding, find someone to discuss it with, or read a commentary, or ask for advice from someone who's further along the pilgrim way.

Be encouraged

God offers new life in him. If we want to claim that life, we need to hear and obey what he says.

Pray

Lord, give me clarity when I explain the Bible to others, and help me to listen when others explain it to me.

292
Meditate

Question time

- What does it mean to meditate?
- Is it something you practise?

Read Psalm 119:41-48

Comment

There are a number of '-ate' verbs that have similar meanings: cogitate, contemplate, ruminate, deliberate, and meditate. Meditation, in twenty-first century culture, can sometimes mean to empty your mind of clutter and concentrate on breathing and relaxing. In biblical times, particularly as portrayed in the Old Testament, it had the idea of murmuring and sighing God's words, repeating what we know of God from his word and from his activity in the world and in our lives.

So when the psalmist says he'll meditate on God's instructions, he will deliberately focus his concentration on what God has to say and reflect on its meaning. If we cogitate, we think deeply about something; if we contemplate, we look thoughtfully at something for a long time. If I deliberate (using the word as a verb with the emphasis on the last syllable) I'll concentrate on what God is speaking to me.

When we meditate on God's instructions he will put his thoughts into our minds. We will see how much he loves us, we will know he saves us, we know we can trust him, our hope is in him, and we'll live in freedom.

Challenge
Give yourself time to meditate on God's word.

Pray
With your Bible open so you can let God put his thoughts into your mind and heart.

293

Compose songs

Question time

> What piece of music moves you physically and emotionally?

Read Psalm 119:49-56

Comment

It's decades since I did 'O' Level Music. We studied a movement from a Brahm's symphony, a movement from Elgar's *Cello Concerto* and *Dido's Lament* from Purcell's *Dido and Aeneas*. To be honest, at that time, I was much more interested in the Beatles and the Shadows, and found the classical repertoire somewhat tedious.

By the time my children did GCSE Music, the Beatles were on the syllabus, along with Queen. *Bohemian Rhapsody* was played frequently at home as preparations were made for the exams. In addition, the students had to compose a piece of music. It all seemed a lot more fun and more stimulating than when I was doing Music!

The psalmist composed songs. Maybe he was the ancient equivalent of the best of today's Christian songwriters whose lyrics are based on God's word.

Challenge

Have you ever had a go at composing a song in praise of God, or a song of lament, or a prayer? If you don't have a tune in your head, you could try using a hymn tune that you know and fit words to it. Or rewrite an old hymn in your own words. If that's not your thing, then just have a good sing in church or in the bath, choosing your favourite sacred song.

Pray

In song.

294
Conduct

Question time

🍃 **Does your home have a naughty step?**

Read Psalm 119:57-64

Comment

I've never quite got the idea of the naughty step. Children are sent there in the same way I was sent to my bedroom for my misdemeanours. I never minded because I could sit on the bed and read a book. In both cases the aim is that the child should think about their wrongdoing, have a chance to calm down (or, more likely, for the cross parent to calm down) and then return to the bosom of the family with an apology and a smile and all's well that end's well.

The psalmist says, 'I have considered my conduct' (verse 59). How often do you consider your conduct before God? In church on a Sunday in the confession? Or in the season of Lent? Perhaps it's best to consider our conduct at the end of each day, bringing to God anything that has not been honouring to him through the day. God is merciful: 'If we say that we have no sin, we deceive ourselves, and there is no truth in us. But if we confess our sins to God, he will keep his promise and do what is right: he will forgive us our sins and purify us from all wrongdoing' (1 John 1:8, 9).

Challenge
Let's keep short accounts with God.

Pray
If you wake in the night, praise God for his constant love, then go back to sleep in peace.

295

More than money

Question time

🍃 **What would you do with a monetary prize?**

Read Psalm 119:65-72

Comment

Quiz shows on television ask the competitors what they would do with the prize money if they won the quiz. Top of the list tend to be: have a holiday, buy a motorbike/guitar/house, go on a binge night out, or go travelling.

How much does money mean to you? There is much poverty in the world where people don't have enough money for basic living; there is much wealth in the world where some people have huge properties, or a yacht, or a vast wardrobe of designer clothes. The unfair distribution of wealth is of great concern.

The psalmist shows that money isn't the be all and end all of life. He would rather have wisdom and knowledge and delight in God's law than all the money in the world.

A well-educated and privileged young woman once said to me, 'I like nice things.' She said that to justify her extravagant use of money. Contrast that with the homeless person who sits on the pavement and asks whether I have any spare change.

Be encouraged

God's provision for us isn't about how much money we have or don't have. His gift to us is love and his word should mean more to us than any pile of coins.

Pray

For those who struggle for lack of money.

296

Understanding

Question time

Can you distinguish between the real and the unreal, the true from the false?

Read Psalm 119:73-80

Comment

Apparently, if you drop a diamond into a glass of water and it sinks, it's likely to be real; if it floats, it's fake. Personally, I'd rather consult an expert than do an experiment. A friend was a diamond expert. He had to take diamonds to dealers and to customers and he carried an attaché case to which he was attached, so nobody could snatch the jewels from his hand.

It's important for us to know whether what we hear about God is true or false. His words are like precious diamonds and the psalmist asks for understanding so he can discern God's commands and know truth from falsehood. Paul, writing to the young pastor Timothy, instructs him to correctly teach the message of God's truth (2 Timothy 2:15). In order to do that, close study is required.

Be encouraged
Keep attached to God and his word and ask him for understanding. We may find some bits hard to understand; that's OK.

Pray
For understanding as you read God's word.

297
Tired eyes

Question time

How do you relieve tired eyes?

Read Psalm 119:81-88

Comment

My eyes are tired now after sitting looking at a screen for several hours. What is the best way to relieve tired eyes? Blink a lot, look away from the screen to something else at frequent intervals, drink lots of water, lie down with a slice of cucumber on each closed eye? Maybe you just need a good sleep.

The psalmist has tired eyes from watching for God's promises. But it's more than that. He's worn out, feels useless, is being persecuted, and has had death threats. Maybe your eyes are tired from looking for answers from God. You're going through a hard time: unemployment, bereavement, hostility from a family member or friend, illness. Whatever it might be, you look and look – like squinting at the sun – and find no relief, no answers.

What do you do in such circumstances? Hang on. God hasn't lost his grip on you even if it feels as if he has. Yet again, the psalmist comes back to the thought of God's constant love, a love that doesn't let go. Think of a limpet clinging to a rock. When the waves come, the limpet and rock are tightly stuck together. Try and prise them apart and it's almost impossible.

Be encouraged

When your eyes are metaphorically 'tired', be reassured by the clinging closeness of God's hold on you.

Pray

For specialists in vision and for the eyes they treat.

298

Through all ages

Question time

- What is your greatest source of joy?
- Your partner?
- Your child?
- Your holidays?
- Your home?

Read Psalm 119:89-96

Comment

The psalmist's greatest sense of joy is in God's law. He's had a desperate time, to the extent that he says he would have died from his suffering had it not been for the joy of God's word. What sustains you through the darkest times? We may have sustenance from other people but there is a limit, even with the closest of buddies. God is one hundred per cent for us. And that is true for believers today as much as it was in the times of the psalmist. Think of what Paul wrote after all the trials of life he'd experienced:

If God is for us, who can be against us? Certainly not God, who did not even keep back his own Son, but offered him for us all! . . . I am certain that nothing can separate us from his love: neither death nor life, neither angels nor other heavenly rulers or powers, neither the present nor the future, neither the world above nor the world below – there is nothing in all creation that will ever be able to separate us from the love of God which is ours through Christ Jesus our Lord.

Romans 13:31, 32, 38, 39

Be encouraged
Through all ages, God is there, faithful and true. Let him be your joy today.

Pray
For joy in God.

299

Sweet as honey

Question time

What is your favourite sweet treat?

Read Psalm 119:97-104

Comment

I can't abide the taste of honey so verse 103 is a bit problematic. If the verse read, 'How sweet is the taste of your instructions – sweeter even than chocolate', it would resonate in a more positive way with me!

The point of the words is that God's instructions to us are not unpleasant, they're not bitter or sour or salty. Rather, they are sweet in the sense of being delightful, satisfying, attractive, pleasant and acceptable.

Now, take the honey or chocolate analogy and apply it to these verses and consider how delightful you find God's instructions to you. How much do you crave his words in the same way you might crave chocolate? Do you come to his word and look at it with delight, taste it, savour it, roll it round your tongue, and swallow it?

The psalmist is willing to be taught by God himself. Are you? Do you 'gain wisdom' from God's word?

Challenge

Have a spoonful of honey or a piece of chocolate and think about its appearance, its colour, its texture, taste and how it makes you feel, and then reread this passage and ponder whether savouring God's word has a similar effect.

Pray

That your sweet tooth may find fresh sweetness in the word of God.

300
Light the way

Question time

 Would your preference be to live in a well-lit city or a dark rural area?

Read Psalm 119:105-112

Comment

When our family moved from London to a more rural part of the UK, our daughters said they didn't want to live in a place that didn't have street lights. They were used to a lot of artificial light from being townies and were afraid of the prospect of being in the dark, unable to see their way.

Dog walkers, going out late in the evening, wear head torches that shine light across fields and over hills and along tree-lined lanes. The light guides them in safety and in the right direction.

So it is with God's word. Verse 105 is often quoted. Perhaps it's a verse that you've learnt off by heart. It's a good one to put in your memory bank. When we're fumbling around in the metaphorical dark paths of life, we need light. And there's no better light than the light of God, most notably made manifest in Jesus who described himself as the Light of the World. He can be our torchlight. If we wear him on our head he'll enlighten our minds. If we hold him in our hands we'll walk in harmony with him. If we have his light in our hearts he will illuminate our whole being.

Challenge
Learn verse 105 by heart and apply it to your life.

Pray
Praise God for those who teach you the Bible and help you to see the light of Christ.

301
Hold me

Question time

How do you show physical affection, when appropriate, to a friend, relative or neighbour?

Read Psalm 119:113-120

Comment

An elderly lady lived in a care home. She felt very much alone although she was surrounded by other people. Her friends had all pre-deceased her, her few relatives lived at a distance, and she was isolated. I visited her one day and she was looking at a little gift book – *Words of Encouragement* was its title. It was beautifully illustrated with photographs and just short pieces of text. They were verses from scripture that brought her comfort in her loneliness, fear and sadness.

'Hold me, and I will be safe', says verse 117. Physical contact is a comfort but when there's nobody to give it, you can feel bereft. What a wonderful thing it is to know that God holds us. Here, the psalmist

asks God to hold him. Elsewhere in the Bible we're told that God has a good strong hold on us – not in an aggressive stranglehold but in the same way that a mother holds her baby: tenderly, gently, with love and compassion and kindness.

> God has always been your defence; his eternal arms are your support.
> *Deuteronomy 33:27*

Be encouraged

'"Can a woman forget her own baby and not love the child she bore? Even if a mother should forget her child, I will never forget you. Jerusalem, I can never forget you! I have written your name on the palms of my hands."'
Isaiah 49:15, 16

Pray

For someone who has nobody to give them a hug.

302

Watching

Question time

🍃 Do you sometimes wonder whether God hears your prayers, whether he sees your distress, whether he actually cares?

Read Psalm 119:121-128

Comment

Sometimes it seems that God is distant, that no amount of praying makes any difference, and we slump into weariness from waiting and watching for God's help.

You're not alone. The psalmist waits for deliverance from his feelings of oppression and from the actual oppression he is being bombarded with by those who are against him.

This morning was foggy and cold. But through the fog, I could see the pale round of the sun. It looked more like the moon. But it was the sun and I could look at it safely through the hazy fog that covered it. The fog was real but so was the sun. And

now, an hour or two later, the sun has burnt off the fog and it's a lovely day.

Waiting for the fog in our lives to dissipate can take a long time. We sit in the chill and may not even see a glimpse of an obscured sun, but we know that it is still there. Gradually we see a little more and eventually brightness is revealed.

Be encouraged

If you're in the bewilderment of fog at the moment – for whatever reason – take comfort that the psalmist understands and that God understands.

Pray

Thank you, Lord, that you are the bright morning star, the sun of righteousness, and that our watching will eventually bring deliverance.

303
Tears of sorrow

Question time
What makes you sad about people's attitude to God? Why?

Read Psalm 119:129-136

Comment
At antenatal classes we were taught different ways of breathing which would help us during labour. When that hard work time arrived – for that is what labour is – the midwife would instruct, 'Pant!' at the appropriate time. And I'd open my mouth and take short, quick breaths. The exertion was immense. In a similar way, an athlete completing an Olympic gold medal sprint, bends over at the finishing tape and pants to regain breath after his effort. On a hot sunny day, a dog sits in the shade and pants.

The psalmist pants with open mouth in his desire to hear and respond to God's commands. Do you have that similar yearning? Do you make every effort to learn from God's word to you? But the psalmist takes it further. His concern isn't just for the benefits he knows he will receive from God, but his concern is also for those who don't know or heed God's law. His tears for them are pouring down like a river in full spate. How much do you have such feelings of emotion for your family members, friends, neighbours, work colleagues, who don't know God?

Challenge

We receive God's word for ourselves but, with that privilege, comes the responsibility to share it with those around us.

Pray

That your friends and neighbours may long for God.

304

Just instructions

Question time

- What do you think of yourself?
- When you look in the mirror do you like what you see?

Read Psalm 119:137-144

Comment

Outward appearance is not as relevant to God as it is to us or to those who look at us and make judgements. God is more interested in the real me, the inner me, and he knows that me better than I know myself.

The psalmist describes himself as angry, unimportant and despised, filled with trouble and anxiety. He's being real before God, knowing that God knows him anyway so there's no point in pretending that all is well when it isn't.

Despite his negative feelings, the psalmist balances those with what he knows and has experienced of God. He describes God as righteous,

fair, full of promises, truthful, and just. And so he is filled with joy – even in his anxiety. Happiness I think of as being superficial and transitory. We can have moments of supreme happiness but they don't last. Joy is more deep-seated; it's an inner contentment and peace that comes from knowing that God is in control whatever we may be feeling like or going through.

Challenge

Let's hang on to God's just instructions and his living presence.

Pray

Thank you, Lord God, that you are a God who is just and your instructions for living are wise. Help me to live well in your sight, in anticipation of the joy it brings.

305
Non-stop learning

Question time

🍃 What are you studying or learning about at the moment?

Read Psalm 119:145-152

Comment

The psalmist doesn't seem to get much sleep. Awake before dawn and awake at night. I love the time just before sunrise, particularly in winter when I get up and it's still dark. I go for a walk and see the sun rise as I offer my walking, waking prayers to God and commit the day to him. If I'm awake in the night, I'll sometimes have the words of a hymn or some Bible verses that come to mind and they soothe me and often send me back to sleep.

It's all about attitude. Of course we need our sleep and of course we have tasks to fulfil during the daytime hours. But we can still have God at the

centre of our being – a kind of God-awareness and God-awakeness.

I committed my life to Jesus when I was 8 years old. I was baptised when a teenager. One of my daughters recently had her fortieth birthday and said, 'Now I'm old!' 'What does that make me?' I muttered. 'Ancient!' And my own mother? Super-ancient. But when it comes to being disciples – learners – of Jesus, we're forever young: always learning, always at 'school'. Like the psalmist I agree with verse 152. Yes, I learnt God's instructions a long time ago, but I still go on learning. It's not an age thing.

Challenge

It's life-long learning to become more Christ-like. Are you happy to be a 'school child' in God's class for ever?

Pray

I'm so glad, Lord, that you continue to teach me your ways. May I be a good learner.

Perfect security

Question time

What makes you feel secure?

Read Psalm 119:153-168

Comment

My house has multiple keys and locks and apparently complies with police guidelines for security. I feel safe in the house, knowing that it is secure.

How secure do you feel in your relationship with God? Do you feel safe in his presence? Jesus told the story of the good shepherd who protects his sheep because he is the gate through whom his flock go in and out in safety. When on holiday in Wales I saw a tiny gate low in a stone wall on a hillside. It was a sheep gate. Too tiny for a human to pass through it, too daunting for predators to negotiate, just right for the sheep.

God knows that there will be times of danger and fear in our lives. He doesn't keep us exempt from those times. What he does is promise to be with us *in* the dangers and fears. He is the gate, there to protect and keep us safe.

Be encouraged

One way in which we can know that protection is by reading and studying and immersing ourselves in scripture. We are happy with God's promises, we learn by his instructions, we rest in the knowledge of his perfect security.

Pray

That you'll recognise that perfect security comes from loving and putting into practice God's instructions.

307

Lost sheep

Question time

🍃 Think of something you've lost. How did you deal with the situation?

Read Psalm 119:169-176

Comment

A neighbour's cat went missing. It was old and rarely strayed more than a few yards from its home. The neighbours were alerted, notices posted – along with a photo of the cat – and everyone hoped it would be found. Later, I heard that the cat had been found at a local petrol garage, a driver thought it was a stray and took it to his vet in a distant village. From there the cat was restored safely to its home.

This long psalm ends with the picture of a lost sheep. The bleating of a lamb that strays from its mother has a response in the deeper tones of her answering call. She keeps calling until the two are reunited. The psalmist is crying for help, pleading to be saved, ready to put himself into the safe, guiding hands of God.

Jesus tells the story of a shepherd who has 100 sheep, but one goes missing. The shepherd counts, and counts again to make sure. 99. He searches for the lost one, finds it, carries it home on his shoulders, then gives a party for his friends and neighbours who rejoice that the animal is safe and well.

The psalm is all about God and his word. Follow him, learn from him, keep close!

Be encouraged
Know that God is there to rescue you if you go astray.

Pray
For shepherds who seek to be good stewards of their portion of God's creation.

308

War and peace

Question time

How well do you understand the times and culture in which you live?

Read Psalm 120:1-7

Comment

A clash of interests may be the first trigger for conflict and lead to all-out war, affecting millions of people. But where does it start? With a point of view on any particular ideology or situation. That, however, is simplistic. The reality is more complex. This can be seen if we study war in history with its resultant violence and power-grabbing, or verbal conflicts, such as the years of Brexit with opposing sides reluctant to budge from their own viewpoint.

It happens in family life too, with a breakdown of communication or trust and differing views on anything from household budgeting to how to bring up your children. Most of us long, as the psalmist does, for peace. He can't understand why people hate peace. He is mystified and feels out of place: 'I have lived too long . . .'. He can't understand the present age he is in. He's weary of the effort in calling for peace when others clamour for war.

We're all prone to recalcitrance at some time. We want our own way, we want our opinion to be listened to and we want others to follow our lead. Beware! It could be the start of war.

Challenge

Let's follow Jesus' example and instruction to be lovers of peace and to work for peace, even when we're weary and disillusioned.

Pray

For peace-keeping forces around the world.

309

Wide-awake God

Question time

- Have you ever travelled the Camino de Santiago de Compostela?
- Or a similar long-distance path?

Read Psalm 121:1-8

Comment

The Camino route takes you across northern Spain from east to west. The walk can't be rushed but those who have taken it say what a wonderful experience it is of purpose, pilgrimage and companionship.

God's people of the Bible made an annual pilgrimage to Jerusalem and set their sights on the 'mountain' or the hills. They talked and walked and sang songs together as they travelled. What do you set your sights on? You may find it helpful to walk in mountainous areas, to be inspired by the hills, to focus on reaching the top, getting to your goal.

The mountains and hills themselves can't help us – other than to inspire us as part of God's created order, and they certainly do that. But it is as we gaze at them and walk in them that our thoughts turn to God and we recognise his help. A doctor will say to a person suffering from depression, 'Try and get out for a walk every day.' There's something about the outdoors that lifts the spirits.

Challenge

Give walking a go, whether it's a twenty minute walk or a lengthy pilgrimage. If you're unable to go for a walk, perhaps you can find a book of walks or look at some photographs of mountains and use your imagination to walk them.

Pray

For pilgrims that they will become closer to God as they journey.

310
Let's go!

Question time

Are you an initiator or a follower when it comes to going somewhere special?

Read Psalm 122:1-5

Comment

There's a mountain in Snowdonia that's a slog to ascend, although the views on the way up are stunning. You have to pause for breath frequently as you plod up the steep grass and rock, and the breaks give opportunities to enjoy the surrounding scenery – and for you to wish that you were as fleet-footed as the sheep who munch away and look at you nonchalantly, probably pondering why you're finding it hard work. When you reach the top of this particular mountain, it's a bit of a let-down. Instead of some rocky pinnacle, you find the summit is more like a football field, flat and boring – and it had looked so promising from down below.

In this psalm it wasn't a let-down when they reached their goal: 'I was glad . . .!'

The anticipation is palpable as you listen to the organ introduction of Hubert Parry's version of this psalm in his coronation anthem, *I was glad*. The introduction builds up to a rich climax as the choir comes in with those stirring words, 'I was glad.'

I like to imagine those pilgrims of old singing this anthem as they entered the Temple in Jerusalem. How excited they were to reach their destination! And they weren't disappointed. They were glad and thankful and full of praise.

Challenge
Do you feel 'glad' when you go to worship God?

Pray
For enthusiastic worshippers, that their joy may be catching.

311
Pray for peace

Question time

🌿 **Do you ever wonder how God must feel about Jerusalem?** It has an unhappy history with frequent periods of conflict and few times of peace.

Read Psalm 122:6-9

Comment

Jeremiah describes Jerusalem as, '"the Throne of the Lord" and all nations will gather there to worship me' (Jeremiah 3:17). God spoke through Zechariah and said, 'I will return to Jerusalem, my holy city, and live there. It will be known as the faithful city' (Zechariah 8:3). Jesus, however, wept over the city, 'Jerusalem! Jerusalem! You kill the prophets and stone the messengers God has sent you! How many times I wanted to put my arms around all your people, just as a hen gathers her chicks under her wings, but you would not let me! And so your Temple will be abandoned and empty' (Matthew 23:37, 38).

It was in Jerusalem on the day of Pentecost, one of the Festival days on which pilgrims gathered in the city from far and wide, that the Holy Spirit was given to the believers. It was from Jerusalem that they went out to fulfil Jesus' great commission to go and make disciples of all nations.

Be encouraged

One day Jerusalem will be reborn as the truly Holy City that will shine with the glory of God (Revelation 21:10).

Pray

As the psalmist did, for the peace of Jerusalem.

312
Look up

Question time

🍃 **What do you imagine heaven to be like?**

Read Psalm 123:1-4

Comment

Albert Midlane was born on the Isle of Wight in 1825. He wrote hundreds of hymns, one of which I recall singing as a child: 'There's a friend for little children, above the bright blue sky.' Subsequent verses told me that there's a 'rest' for little children, a 'home' and a 'crown' – all above the bright blue sky. This may sound like rather typical Victorian sentimentality but there is truth in the words of the hymn – apart, perhaps, from the blue sky bit.

We don't actually know where heaven is but in the days of Victorian – and subsequent – Sunday schools, there was a perception of God wearing a beard and a long white robe sitting on a cloud in the blue sky. The psalmist says he looks *up* to heaven.

My mother, in her nineties, was perturbed about heaven, saying she hoped people wouldn't have to wear long white nightshirts which she thought was inappropriate for a place of perfection. More helpfully, she recalled that when she was in her teens and war was looming, her Christian mentor told her – and others – to KLU. Keep looking up.

Be encouraged

However trying our circumstances, whatever our bewilderment about what heaven is like, we look up to him in trust in the same way that a child looks up – literally and metaphorically – to a loving parent.

Pray

That you'll keep looking up and trusting God for today and tomorrow.

What if...?

Question time

🍃 Ask yourself some 'What if...?' questions.

Read Psalm 124:1-8

Comment

Oh, our minds can be rattled by 'What ifs!' What if I'd been born in a war-torn country? What if we had no food to eat? What if I'd never made peace with my father? What if there was no sun? What if cricket had never been invented? What if I'd been attacked with a knife or a gun by a terrorist?

The psalmist uses the appalling picture of being swallowed alive. What if God hadn't helped his people? A tiger shark is capable of devouring a human, as is a polar bear. And we all know the story of Jonah. But the psalmist speaks of human killers. In the story of Jonah the fish spat Jonah out and Jonah lived to tell the tale and do what God had originally asked him to do. Sometimes people don't live after being attacked. We question why members of a

congregation are gunned down in a place of worship. We ponder why someone in a quiet suburban street is murdered. Questions to which there are no easy answers.

The psalmist felt they'd been caught in a trap and God came to their rescue. Maybe, with questions buzzing round our brain to which we don't have answers, we just have to commit each day to God and, at bedtime, thank him for its safe negotiation.

Challenge

God didn't promise an easy life. We have to trust that one day the 'What ifs' will be answered.

Pray

Lord, I have many 'What if' questions which I'd love answers to from you, but I guess that by the time I'm in heaven with you, those questions will no longer matter! Thank you for the prospect of that perfect place – the new creation.

314
Shaken, not moved

Question time
What shakes your faith in God?

Read Psalm 125:1-5

Comment

Selwyn Hughes was born in 1928 and died in 2006. He was a Christian writer whose belief in God rose above the grief he experienced during his lifetime. Like C S Lewis, Selwyn Hughes saw his life on earth as preparation for what was to come. The 'real story' as Lewis put it, was still ahead. Hughes' health was not good and he had had to cope with the death of both his sons. C S Lewis had described the death from cancer of his wife, Joy, as a time of spiritual fog. He looked to God and it was as if God had slammed the door in his face and bolted the door.

The psalmist says that those who trust in the Lord will 'never be moved'. We may in reality be shaken by events in our lives, but can remain intact if our lives are on God's foundation. Both Lewis and Hughes could witness to that. There is much that is inexplicable and horrible in life, but both saw a bright future. Indeed, Selwyn Hughes, with a mischievous sense of humour, showed curiosity about dying, death and heaven. He wasn't morbid about it but fascinated by it. Death, he acknowledged, wasn't far away for him. He looked forward to the reality of heaven with anticipation.

Challenge

Do you believe that God surrounds you? Do you believe that you're on the way to heaven? Can you honestly say that, even if you're shaken, you won't be moved?

Pray

For steadiness in your walk with God.

315
Laughter

Question time
🍃 What or who makes you laugh?

Read Psalm 126:1-6

Comment

I have three daughters and when the second one had her fortieth birthday, she wanted to celebrate it with members of the family. Three generations came together for what was a very happy occasion: a delicious meal, a country walk, a magnificent birthday cake with ice-cream, laughter and chatter and the joy of companionship and thankfulness to God.

Times of celebration are to be treasured and filed away in the memory bank. It happened that the day after that birthday bash was Mothering Sunday. All three daughters remembered their mum and I was profoundly thankful to God for each of them. The 40-year-old had reproduced, on a handcrafted card, a piece she'd written in Infants School about me, her mum. She'd kept the piece of memorabilia and I was able to read what she'd thought of me when she was 6! I was very touched.

Challenge

Weeping and joy. Either end of life's emotional wave. Think about a time when you have 'laughed' and when you 'sang for joy'. What was the occasion? What made you laugh? Did you acknowledge God's hand in your happiness? Did it occur after a time of testing or grief or sorrow? Seeds of sorrow may lead to a harvest of happiness.

Pray

Praise God for opportunities to party, and pray for times of sorrow, that in both circumstances you may remain on an even keel.

316
Building

Question time

 Who built your home?

Read Psalm 127:1, 2

Comment

In my childhood home there was a picture on the hall wall of an open window with a bowl of flowers on the outside ledge and a row of books on the inside ledge. Roses curled around the window frame which was painted blue. My imagination was fired into thinking about who lived in that house, who had placed the flowers in the bowl, what the titles of the books might be, and why the window was open on that particular day.

Decades later, the picture came into my possession and it now hangs in the hall of my home. It reminds me of the building blocks that formed my childhood home and on which I wanted to build my own family's home. Underneath the picture was a text from the book of Joshua, 'As for me and my house, we will serve the Lord.'

In the psalm it is the Lord who is the master builder. Is he the master builder of your home and of your life? We can strive to build a good home, have a nice garden or window box, open the windows to let in fresh air, fill the shelves with uplifting books, endeavour to keep a harmonious atmosphere, but if God hasn't been let in to join us and mastermind the making of a home, it's all rather futile.

Challenge

Will you allow God to be the master builder of your home?

Pray

That God may be at the centre of your life and of your home.

317

Children

Question time

> Are you from a large or small family?

Read Psalm 127:3-5

Comment

On our wedding day my husband and I received a telegram from a well-wisher who hoped we would be blessed with various things: good health, a happy home – and masses of children. I was somewhat alarmed by the thought of this friend's last blessing. Yes, we hoped to have children, but not too many! We were, indeed, blessed with three lovely daughters for whom we are forever thankful.

Do you have children of your own? What was your childhood family like? Were you adopted or fostered or did you grow up in a children's home? Your childhood may have been traumatic or tranquil, sad or satisfying, hopeless or hopeful. Children, the psalmist tells us, are a gift from the Lord: 'They are a real blessing.' In the past I've tended to read these verses from the point of view of a parent, but try reading them from the point of view of yourself as a child. Here is affirmation from God, the greatest 'parent' ever, that your arrival on Planet Earth was a blessing.

Challenge

Do you feel valued? Worthwhile? Remember what Jesus said. In the New Testament mothers wanted to bring their children and babies to Jesus for a blessing. His disciples gave the mothers a ticking-off. But Jesus called the children to him: 'Let the children come to me and do not stop them, because the Kingdom of God belongs to such as these' (Luke 18:15, 16).

Pray

For children who feel unloved.

318
Fruitfulness

Question time

🍃 Would you describe your family as successful?

🍃 What does that mean?

Read Psalm 128:1-6

Comment

Fruitfulness stems from living God's way and obeying his commands. If we have our roots in him, and grow in him, we will produce fruit in our lives for his glory.

The psalmist paints a picture of a rather magnificent family whose members all seem to be successful, resulting in blessing. We may look at other families and think they seem to have it all: a grand home, good health, well-paid jobs, apparently perfect children and a harmonious partnership between husband and wife. Outward appearances don't always tell the whole story.

Be encouraged by the fact that the partner in your life can be the same as that of the psalmist: God himself. It is he who provides for our needs (different from our wants and wishes) and blessings come from his hand. Are you partnering with God in being fruitful on your frontline, wherever that may be? It may start in the home but it could include your relationship with your neighbours, work colleagues, art class friends, or whoever. Are you able to be an encourager – someone who gives out kindness, who is patient, who bakes a cake for an ill friend, who takes the ironing off a frazzled young mum?

Challenge

Love is practical. Like learning to play a musical instrument, love doesn't always come naturally; we have to work at it! Sow the seeds and be fruitful.

Pray

For family life in your street.

319
Bless you!

Question time

- Do you sneeze quietly or loudly?
- Does this say anything about you?!

Read Psalm 129:1-8

Comment

Someone sneezed in my quiet yogalates class. 'Bless you!' said the instructor. Everyone giggled. The tranquility of relaxing had been broken by a sneeze. What do we actually mean when we say, 'Bless you!' What does God mean when he blesses us?

Blessings come in different forms and we need to be alert to recognise a blessing when it appears. The psalmist recalls past difficulties in his life. He prays against the enemies of his nation. Rather than blessing, he thinks his enemies don't deserve and shouldn't receive God's blessing.

Is anyone beyond the reach of God? Jesus told us to bless those who curse us. I like the psalmist's honesty. And if you're honest, aren't there times when you've ranted at God about people who've caused you harm or ignored you or insulted you? Do you wish to curse them rather than bless them?

Challenge

God is gracious and we have to learn to be gracious too. It's not easy. But with God's help we can leave the judging to him and, instead, look for ways of blessing those who irritate us.

Pray

Think of someone you would like God to bless now and bring their name to God.

320

Eager

Question time

- What do you wait eagerly for?
- A holiday?
- The arrival of spring after a long winter?
- The end of the working day?
- For the time when you can taste the bread rolls that are emitting a wonderful aroma from the oven?
- A pay rise?

Read Psalm 130:1-8

Comment

The psalmist waits eagerly for the Lord's help (verse 5). Why? He'd been in despair. It seems he was burdened by his wrongdoing: 'If you kept a record of our sins, who could escape being condemned?' (verse 3). In the New Testament Paul writes to the church in Rome, 'There is no condemnation now for those who live in union with Christ Jesus' (Romans 8:1). Earlier in the letter he'd reminded the recipients that it was 'because of our sins' that Jesus was 'given over to die, and he was raised to life in order to put us right with God' (Romans 4:25). As a result, people can have peace with God through Jesus.

The psalmist knew too of God's forgiving nature. God is always willing to save, always ready to welcome back the remorseful sinner. And so it is with eagerness that he waits for the Lord's help. He trusts God's word. He knows that God's love is constant. And, in a prophetic last sentence he says that God 'will save his people Israel from all their sins'.

Challenge

It's a matter of repentance, trust and obedience on our part to be put right with God.

Pray

Lord, give me an eagerness to receive your help and gratitude when you give it.

321

Given up

Question time

- Do you habitually give up something during Lent?
- If so, why? If not, why not?

Read Psalm 131:1

Comment

When I was at school friends told me what they were giving up for Lent. But they couldn't tell me what Lent was! So I gave up trying to understand Lent and gave up giving up anything.

The psalmist has given up his pride and turned his back on arrogance. Humility must surely be one of the hardest characteristics to aspire to. There's a tendency to think, 'I'm right', a tendency to puff ourselves up, to boost our ego. Perhaps rather than an indication of strength, it's a sign of insecurity. Can you think of a time when you've been proud or displayed arrogance? Think of someone you know who is truly humble. What is it about that person that is attractive? What draws you to him or her?

Do you need to give up pride? Do you need to do a U-turn on arrogance? How can you set about it? Do you have someone who will tell you to come down off your pedestal? How would you react to that? Rejecting pride and arrogance may require going to people and saying you're sorry for being too uppity. You may have to climb down from your high horse, as the saying goes, and eat humble pie, as another saying goes! And it isn't easy.

Challenge

Take your ultimate example from Jesus who humbled himself. He gave up the glory of heaven to come down to earth.

Pray

Show me, Lord, what unpleasant or unhelpful character trait I need to give up, and help me to do it.

322

Contentment

Question time

What makes you content?

Read Psalm 131:2, 3

Comment

The elderly lady's short-term memory was not good though she could still remember things from sixty, seventy, even eighty years ago. She was less able now to complete crossword puzzles, find her way around the town, or follow political arguments. She knew her limitations. And she was at peace. She had learned what was important in these days of restricted ability and mobility and she knew what she could let go of.

At the other end of the age spectrum a baby had been yelling loudly. Now he was exhausted and lay, subdued, in his mother's arms. She talked to him quietly; she told him how much she loved him, how special he was. He felt her calmness and was content to lie in her arms. He looked up into her face and saw her smile. He smiled back, gave a big sigh and closed his eyes. He was at peace.

'Oh, what peace we often forfeit', goes the old hymn. We live in a frazzled society where everything has to be done at breakneck speed. And it takes its toll on family relationships, physical health, and mental well-being.

Challenge

Let God breathe his still dews of quietness till all your strivings cease.

Pray

'Take from my soul the strain and stress, and let my ordered life confess the beauty of thy peace' (John Greenleaf Whittier, 1807-1892).

323

A place for the Lord

Question time

- Are you good at giving hospitality?
- Or do you prefer to be on its receiving end?

Read Psalm 132:1-5

Comment

David's plan was to build a temple for the Lord. For years, the Israelites had worshipped God on the move and taken a tent – albeit an elaborate one – that was used as a temple. It was un-pegged from one place and moved on to the next stopping place, where it was re-pegged. It was Solomon who eventually built the Temple in Jerusalem. He said to the people, 'I have built the Temple for the worship of the Lord God of Israel.' He then prayed, 'Can you, O God, really live on earth? Not even all heaven is large enough to hold you, so how can this Temple that I have built be large enough?' (1 Kings 8:20, 27).

Christian heritage in the UK is evident by the number of churches that are dotted around the countryside, in towns and in cities. Great cathedrals were built to the glory of God. But what place can we provide for the Lord? The psalmist says he won't rest until he's provided a place for the Lord.

Challenge

God makes it clear in the Bible that he's not so concerned with outward structures but with our inward attitude to worshipping him. Is your innermost being the place where God lives? God wants our worship to be real and that begins within us.

Pray

O come to my heart, Lord Jesus, there is room in my heart for thee.

324

Priests

Question time

🌿 What do you know about your priest or church leader's life outside the pulpit?

Read Psalm 132:6-9

Comment

Today, examples of child abuse and financial misdeeds don't show priests in a good light. The psalmist wants priests to 'do always what is right' (verse 9). Each of us who claims to be a believer in God and a follower of Jesus is called to do what is right. But leaders of disciples have a particular responsibility to represent Jesus, our great high priest, in an honourable way.

Before we start making judgements – and we live in a judgemental world where modern media make it easy to make and/or read judgemental comments about anyone and everyone – we need to remember what Peter wrote in his first letter regarding *all* believers, 'You are the chosen race, the King's priests, the holy nation, God's own people' (1 Peter 2:9).

Each of us has a responsibility to be responsible, but also – and this is something that many would find difficult – to 'teach and instruct one another with all wisdom' (Colossians 3:16). In other versions of the Bible the word, 'admonish' is used. You may be diffident about admonishing someone else in the faith, and how would you feel if you were on the receiving end of admonishment? Before verse 16, Paul makes it clear that if we are God's people we must be compassionate, kind, humble, gentle, patient, tolerant, forgiving – and loving.

Challenge

Whether priest or people in a church fellowship, we should act as one body to build each other up.

Pray

For priests and people, that all may do what is right in the eyes of God.

325
Flourish

Question time

How would you help a child to flourish at school and as they grow up?

Read Psalm 132:10-18

Comment

'We blossom and flourish as leaves on the tree, and wither and perish, but nought changeth thee' (Walter Chalmers Smith, 1824-1908).

This is another of the Messianic psalms, looking ahead to the arrival of David's great successor, the Lord Jesus Christ. It is his kingdom, out of the many kingdoms and empires that come, then go, that will flourish forever. It's a great comfort when we see the world's regimes rise and fall to know that there is a kingdom that outlasts them all.

Jesus spoke a lot about the kingdom of God or the kingdom of heaven. His arrival was hardly king-like, however. Birth in a cowshed was followed by being a refugee as a toddler, he had a humble childhood home, was booted out of his town when a young adult, and lived on the road for the last three years of his life on earth. His only crown was one of thorns rammed down onto his head and he died when in his early thirties. But he was raised to life and his kingdom is still growing millennia later. We blossom and flourish and wither and perish. Our lives on earth are short. His life was shorter than many of ours.

Be encouraged

If we believe and trust in him as the King of the universe and the Saviour of the world then, though we die physically, we will be raised to new life and continue to blossom and flourish. And that blossoming can start as soon as we give our allegiance to him while we live on earth.

Pray

That the seeds of faith that have been sown may flourish and that we may produce fruit for God while we have the opportunity.

326

Harmony

Question time

🍃 How harmonious is your church fellowship?

Read Psalm 133:1-3

Comment

When my children were little they hated having their hair washed. Shampoo seemed to get in their eyes however much they covered their faces and the water seemed to go everywhere, running down their necks, into their ears and mixing with the tears that ran down their faces.

This psalm always makes me laugh as I have a mental picture of Aaron and his beard and it reminds me of those far from harmonious hair-washing rituals. Beards are fashionable at the moment. I can't say I particularly like them but they're a fashion statement for this generation, as they have been in different generations through the ages.

The point of this reference to Aaron's beard is really not so much to do with the beard as with the oil.

Oil was used cosmetically and medicinally but also for important ceremonies, including the occasions when a priest or king was appointed by God. The oil was precious, the ceremony was important. Here the psalmist likens it to the harmonious living which the people of God should enjoy together.

I'm relieved to report that the traumas of hair-washing are long over and the family can now, on rare occasions when it is recalled, laugh about it, and harmony is happily restored. As it should be.

Challenge

Can you echo David's first verse? How can you help the harmony process within your household?

Pray

For harmony in family life and in the life of the church.

Raise your hand

Question time

How do you like to worship God?

Read Psalm 134:1-3

Comment

One of the loveliest aspects of Christianity is that believers are so diverse. Different nationalities, different cultures, different languages, different political allegiances, different habits, gifts, opportunities, features, and so on. Yet all are one in Christ Jesus. Except in worship. Or so it seems sometimes. Although all are one, there is still diversity in the how of worship. We know who we worship but we have different ways of worshipping.

Some people like ritual, dignity and formality with a distinct liturgy. Others like freedom in worship, informality and a kind of free-for-all where anyone can chip in with a prayer, a thought, a Bible

reading or whatever. There are those who can't abide so-called 'happy-clappy' worship, others find plainsong a yawn.

Here in the psalm there is a call to praise the Lord by raising hands in prayer when worshipping in the Temple. I've been to church services where many hands are raised during the singing of hymns and songs, where there are choruses of 'Amen' throughout the prayers, and where the choir sings, sways and claps and actually looks as if its members are enjoying themselves in worship! Whatever next!

Challenge

We're all different. The important thing is not so much how we feel comfortable worshipping God, but that our worship and thanksgiving is real. And for each of us that will be different.

Pray

For acceptance of different ways of worshipping God.

Whatever he wishes

Question time

🍃 If you could wave a magic wand, and have your wish come true, what would you like to see happen?

Read Psalm 135:1-7

Comment

I'd love to see the end of warfare, I'd like to climb mountains on a clear day and admire the views, I'd very much appreciate going to a sports event of my choice, I'd wave my wand to put an end to disease and dis-ease . . . Oh, so many things. The facts are that most of the things on my wish list are not in my control. I can't do whatever I want. I don't have a magic wand to make my dreams come true.

God, on the other hand, can do whatever he wishes (verse 6). It is his universe. It is he who is in charge of the weather, he who owns everything on land, in the sea and in the air, and in the immeasurable realms of space. Look at the descriptions of God in these verses: he is good, he is kind, he is great. He who owns everything is to be praised forever.

Challenge

Take time today to observe God's world, to look at weather patterns. See the swirls of cloud formations on the surface of the globe, think about how the seas with different names are all connected and what happens in one part of the oceans impacts on other parts.

Pray

Praise God for his creation and be thankful that it is he who can do whatever he wishes.

All generations

Question time

What historical family or national event does your family remember together?

Read Psalm 135:8-14

Comment

It's not long since the centenary of the ending of World War 1. How important is it that the sacrifice of soldiers is remembered more than a hundred years after the war? On the eleventh day of the eleventh month there are commemorations to remember. Those who served in the Second World War are also remembered and for the decreasing number who are still alive, it is important that we remember the hardship that they went through in order for us to live in relative peace today.

Thankfully, young people are engaged in remembering too. Children will hear stories of their great-grandparents and great-great-grandparents and will be inspired to work for peace in their time.

They remember with thankfulness what was done so that they can live.

But how much does the young generation know of God? It's sobering to think that they may know more about the world wars than they do about God. My generation, brought up in the 1950s, knew about keeping Sunday as a different day. Church and Sunday school attendance were the norm and their parents knew about God and Christianity and told their children Bible stories.

Challenge

What part could you play in helping children to learn about God?

Pray

Thank God for today's children who are learning about God and pray that, even if the numbers are fewer, the message of God's love will continue to be passed from generation to generation.

330
Idols

Question time

What or who do you regard as the gods of your nation?

Read Psalm 135:15-21

Comment

Here is a call to praise God, to praise the Almighty creator of the universe, to praise God for who he is. How does he compare with the 'gods of the nations'? God is the creator who formed human beings, he speaks, he sees, he hears, and he breathes his living Spirit into his people who trust him.

This is in contrast to the gods that human beings make who have no life. They are just inanimate objects which, although they may be made with precious metals, are of no value because they can't communicate with human beings.

Be encouraged

Thank and praise God that he is alive, that he communicates with us through creation, through his living Word: Jesus his Son our Lord, through his written word, the Bible, through his Spirit who lives in the lives of those who trust and believe in him.

Pray

No wonder the psalmist ends this hymn of praise by saying four times, 'Praise him!' Why not do that right now as you think about God who is alive and active in the world and in our lives.

331
He alone

Question time

🍃 Who is your forever hero?

🍃 Who do you look up to more than anyone else?

🍃 What are the attributes of that person?

Read Psalm 136:1-9

Comment

This is a hymn of thanksgiving to God to whom the psalmist looks up with deep gratitude. What does he see as God's attributes? He is good; his love is everlasting; he is the greatest; he is the mightiest; he performs miracles; he is wise; he is the creator of the universe. No wonder the psalmist sees God as greater than anyone else. Pre-eminent. 'He alone . . .' (verse 4).

We see in this psalm what God does for his world. What does he do for you? How have you felt his goodness, love, might and wisdom? The recurring refrain underlines the eternal nature of God's love.

Be encouraged

Paul wrote to the church in Rome: 'I am certain that nothing can separate us from his love: neither death nor life, neither angels nor other heavenly rulers or powers, neither the present nor the future, neither the world above nor the world below – there is nothing in all creation that will ever be able to separate us from the love of God which is ours through Christ Jesus our Lord' (Romans 8:38, 39).

Pray

The Father, Son and Spirit work as one to demonstrate God's love for the world. Jesus came to earth to offer us God's personal love that will last forever. Give thanks.

332

Eternal love

Question time

Can you think of times in your nation's life when God has been particularly active?

Read Psalm 136:10-26

Comment

These verses show us God's practical side. His love is active in the world and in the lives of its inhabitants. We have here a list of historic happenings in which God was at work.

Think of the ways in which God was active in the life of Bible heroes: Joseph, taken to Egypt as a slave, rising to the position of Prime Minister, being reunited with his family. Moses, rescued from a river, chosen by God to be a leader. Daniel, exiled in a foreign land, thrown to the lions, messenger of God. Peter the fisherman, followed Jesus, denied Jesus, was restored by Jesus, led the early church.

Challenge

Look back over your life and see where and when God was active in his eternal love for you. Have you had a chequered pathway to go along? You're in good company! In Jesus' life on earth he spoke love, demonstrated love, was – and is – love. There is much uncertainty in the political world – think of many governments around the globe; in the physical world – think climate change and pollution; in the personal world – think poverty, physical and mental ill-health. In all areas of life God's love never fades. In 1 John 4:16 we read, 'God is love, and those who live in love live in union with God and God lives in union with them.'

Pray

Praise God that his eternal love is perfect.

333
Greatest joy

Question time

- Have you ever been robbed?
- How did it make you feel?

Read Psalm 137:1-9

Comment

My purse, with bank cards and other personal identification, was stolen from my bag when I was in the local library working at a desk. I felt shaken that someone had violated me by taking what was mine. There was a sense of loss that wasn't just about the money.

Most laments stem from a sense of loss – of one kind or another, and some losses are much worse than others. The Israelites were in exile and mourning the loss of their homeland and of their city. They lament and weep in remembrance of what had been, they weep in their present circumstances, they question how they can possibly sing to God when in such a place of misery.

And yet they recall that God is still their greatest joy. In the book of Lamentations, which is a series of laments, the theme is similar: 'my eyes are overflowing with tears. No one can comfort me; no one can give me courage' (Lamentations 1:16). Sufferers ask why God has abandoned them. Why does stuff go wrong? Why our loss?

Be encouraged

There are times when we need to lament, even though we know God who is our 'greatest joy'.

Pray

If you need to lament, maybe about something in the past that you've never allowed yourself to lament over, do it now.

334

Supremacy

Question time

- Think of human leaders of nations who exercise supremacy over other people.
- Is this a good or a bad thing?

Read Psalm 138:1-8

Comment

It's questionable whether certain politicians are there to serve their people or to build their own power base. Even if they start off with altruistic motives, the pull of power can become too great for some to resist. The thought of supremacy is what drives them and what, in the end, can become their downfall.

God is supreme. We've seen in so many of the psalms how he is supreme and unique in his creation of the world and supreme over human beings. And yet he is deeply devoted and will do anything for his people whom he loves.

Do we give him the honour that he deserves? In the British Houses of Parliament the politicians are known as 'Honourable'. Their honour pales into insignificance when set beside our most honourable God.

Challenge

We somehow have to balance the supremacy of God as the Almighty with his fatherly side. He is the God and Father of our Lord Jesus Christ, but Jesus told us to address God as, 'Our Father', just as he did. What a privilege!

Pray

Talk to God now as the Almighty to whom, one day, all kings and powerful people will bow down, but also as the Father who loves you and is faithful to you.

335
Too deep

Question time

What thrills you about new discoveries in the natural world?

Read Psalm 139:1-6

Comment

I guess we should expect that the God of the universe should have complete knowledge and care of all his creation – including us.

God knows the griffon vulture which can soar to 37,000 feet. He knows the fangtooth, a fish that can be found as deep as 16,500 feet in the ocean. He knows the furthest reaches of space, far beyond human exploration or space probe travel. And yet he knows the tiniest ant and the largest elephant. And he knows you and me. No wonder the psalmist David says, 'Your knowledge of me is too deep; it is beyond my understanding.'

Human beings have, over centuries, discovered more about the natural world. Modern methods, including the use of drones, enable scientists to monitor what goes on in remote areas of land and sea without disturbing the creatures they're researching. People have a God-given curiosity about the planet on which we live, but also a curiosity about what is beyond the blue planet that we call home. And yet it is minimal compared with God's knowledge!

Be encouraged

Are you encouraged or concerned about God's knowledge of you? Not only does God know our thoughts, he understands them. He knows what we'll say, he sees what we do, he surrounds us.

Pray

Praise God for who he is and for the wonder of his knowledge.

Darkness and light

Question time

What do you like about darkness and light?

Read Psalm 139:7-12

Comment

To mark the beginning of Advent a service is held in many cathedrals and churches called 'From Darkness to Light'. The service starts in complete darkness. One candle is lit at the back of the building and then, as the service progresses, lines of candles are lit until, at the end of the service, the whole building is ablaze with the lights of thousands of candles.

Jesus, the Light of the world. This is what John wrote about him: In the beginning the Word already existed . . . Through him God made all things; not one thing in all creation was made without him. The Word was the source of life, and this life brought light to people. The light shines in the darkness, and the darkness has never put it out' (John 1:1, 3-5).

There is no escaping the light. Jesus was one part of the Trinity that existed before time began. However much we may try to evade God, he is still there, and his light shines. Why would we want to avoid the Light of the world? As David says, God is everywhere and wherever David might go, he says God 'would be there to lead me . . . and there to help me' (verse 10).

Challenge

Is there something that you wish to hide from God? Don't live in darkness; live in his light and he will help you.

Pray

That the many people who attend special Advent services may truly see the Light of the world.

337
Baby talk

Question time

Can you guess how many muscles criss-cross your face and head?

Read Psalm 139:13-16

Comment

The intricacies of the human body are mind-boggling. 150,000 km of peripheral nerves, thousands of taste buds, and 50 little muscles that criss-cross the face and head, making it possible for us to smile, grimace, question, express surprise or look sympathetic. And a brain to appreciate it, wonder at it, and thank God for it.

A friend commented on how curious it is that every human being has the same internal organs: heart, lungs, stomach, etc., and yet each person is a different shape and size. Yes, each of us is unique.

God's book has details of you and me in it. If he's got me sussed out, then I should be ready to trust him. His knowledge of me is beyond my understanding, his love and care for me greater than any human being's love and care for me. He is there to lead me, help me and travel with me through these days that he's allotted to me.

Challenge

Take time to read these verses again and bask in God's complete knowledge and care for you.

Pray

I'm awestruck, Lord, not just by the amazing body that you've given me, but by your care for your created work of art. I am your treasure and you love my body, my mind and my soul, my whole being. Thank you.

338
Grains of sand

Question time

🍃 Have you ever tried to count the stars?

🍃 How many could you count?

Read Psalm 139:17, 18

Comment

Scientists and mathematicians have tried to calculate how many grains of sand there might be on earth – and whether there are more grains of sand than stars in the sky. The Milky Way Galaxy alone may have as many as 400 billion stars and there could be as many as 2 trillion galaxies. Sand or stars? The numbers are beyond our understanding. The answers to such mind-blowing calculations are inconclusive but it's estimated that there are likely to be five to ten times more stars than grains of sand. And, wait for it . . . there might be five sextillion grains of sand. That's a lot of noughts.

David had no idea how many grains of sand there might be in the world but he knew it was a lot and so he used that image to tell God how awesome and numerous he found God's thoughts.

With the additional knowledge and mathematical formulae that have emerged in the 3000 or so years since David's time, we should be even more in awe of God's immensity than David was. It was almost like a dream – weird and wonderful. And he concludes, 'When I awake, I am still with you.'

Challenge

Next time there's a clear night, look at the stars. Next time you're at the beach, take a handful of sand and try to count the grains.

Pray

For scientists in their exploration of the universe.

339

Examination

Question time

What are your feelings and concerns about a medical examination?

Read Psalm 139:19-24

Comment

I wonder whether, if you have a favourite psalm out of the 150 that are available to us, 139 is your favourite? Its dimensions are vast, yet it covers the most intimate and intricate subject matter. David finishes with a plea to God to deal with the wickedness in the world, but then asks God to examine *him*. We already know that God knows our minds and our thoughts. But David takes things a step further. He wants God to root out undesirable thoughts, words and actions in his life and take him forward.

When compared with the length of time the universe has existed, and the heights and depths of its geography and history, David brings things back

to the realities of everyday existence. We can live in the vastness but we also live in the nitty gritty of our own lives, in our homes, at work, and in our relationships.

Challenge

We need to follow David's example of keeping close to God and asking him to work in us and guide us in his ways.

Pray

Turn verses 23 and 24 into a personal prayer from you to God. Bring to him the things that perturb you about your own life and lifestyle, and commit your life to him afresh today so he can guide you into everlasting life.

340
Living with God

Question time

How do you deal with the aggravations and difficulties of your life?

Read Psalm 140:1-13

Comment

The realities of living in a fallen world can weigh heavily on us, as they did on David. He was only too aware of the people and situations that burdened him.

Those who have committed their life to God live with the paradox of being in the world of hardship and disharmony, of bewilderment and evil, and yet living in God-space where God is ever present and where we see glimpses of him at work in our lives and in the world.

So, how do you deal with difficulties in your life? Do you bluster on in your own strength, defending your corner, thinking malicious thoughts about those who hurt you, or do you accept such things as being part of living? We can rest in the presence of God while working and living in adverse conditions. And so the psalmist, after his rant, concludes that God is in control and so those who follow his ways will praise him. Do you praise God, even when life is dealing you a poor hand? Remember that you live in the presence of God and he will never leave you or forsake you.

Be encouraged

One of the things the disciples of Jesus were scared of was that he would leave them. He promised that the Spirit would come to be their comforter, companion, teacher and helper. That same promise is there for those who are his followers today.

Pray

Thank you that I need never feel alone because you are with me. Thank you for your Spirit who lives in me to strengthen, help, comfort and encourage.

341

Keep me

Question time

What prevents you from doing wrong?

Read Psalm 141:1-7

Comment

British children learn about Norman castles in their studies of medieval times and, if they're lucky, get the chance to visit one that is still relatively intact. Dover, Windsor, Colchester, have all survived fairly unscathed, each with an impressive keep. Others, such as Kenilworth and Corfe, though worth seeing, are ruined.

In verses 3 and 4 there is talk of a guard and a sentry and the desire that God will keep the psalmist from wanting to do wrong. He needs the fortress that is God's solid foundation and a protection, to keep him. A keep to keep.

In New Testament terms the follower of Jesus builds his life on the foundation of God's word and the Holy Spirit acts as guard and sentry, prompting

us as necessary to know what to say and when, how to smile and why, and teaching us right from wrong.

The Norman castle's keep was often at the centre of the castle in the safest place and surrounded by walls and ditches.

Challenge

How much are you prepared to stay in God's keep and do you ask him, as the psalmist did, to keep you – not just from doing wrong but from wanting to do wrong?

Pray

For a sense of God's presence to guard, protect and guide.

342

Keep trusting

Question time

On a scale of 1 to 10, how good are you at perseverance?

Read Psalm 141:8-10

Comment

It's one thing to keep trusting God when things are going well. It's another to trust him when, in contemporary parlance, life sucks. God's people in exile experienced a rotten time. Read Lamentations 5 to learn more. It's a shocking catalogue of grievances. Is it any wonder that in verse 15 of that chapter we read, 'Happiness has gone out of our lives; grief has taken the place of our dances.'? Verse 19 has a glimmer of hope: 'But you, O Lord, are king forever and will rule to the end of time.' Yet in the very next verse the people cry out again, 'Why have you abandoned us so long? Will you ever remember us again?'

There were no pat answers. Though that is perhaps disappointing, it is also reassuring to think that we're not the only ones for whom life seems dire.

The psalmist uses that same little word as in Lamentations: 'But . . .'. Despite the awfulness of David's experience (yes, it's David again!) he keeps trusting. That word 'keep' again.

Be encouraged

Each of us who is a follower of God, whatever our circumstances, is kept by his power. Keep on keeping going.

Pray

Help me to keep steady in my walk with you, Lord, and never to give up. 'There's no discouragement shall make me once relent my first avowed intent to be a pilgrim.'

343
Ready to give up

Question time

🍃 What have you given up doing because it's just been too hard?

Read Psalm 142:1-4

Comment

A television series showed pairs of people on a race to Singapore from London. They were not allowed to fly and were given only a limited amount of money. The pair who won were not youngsters but a retired couple who had a fierce drive never to give up. Determination, gumption and probably a bit of luck, helped the couple win.

What is your attitude to personal problems? Do you see them as a challenge to be overcome or a setback that is just too wearisome to fight? As we get towards the end of the psalms, we have another set of poems by David. We've already seen how much trouble he's had in his life experiences, how downcast he has got at times and how, on occasions, he has been at the point of giving up.

Look at what he says to God: 'I call to the Lord for help; I plead with him. I bring him all my complaints; I tell him all my troubles.' Are you as honest with God as David is? But just before his moans, he acknowledges that when he's ready to give up, God knows what he should do.

Be encouraged

Way back in Moses' time, God told Moses his name: I AM. Yes, God *is*.

Pray

Thank you, Lord God, that you are permanently present. May I remember that when setbacks occur.

344
All I want

Question time

How often did you say to your parent, 'Oh, but all the other children in my class have a bicycle…, go to a theme park…, have parties…? Or whatever your want of the moment might have been.

Read Psalm 142:5-7

Comment

Are there things in life that you want now? For yourself, for your family, for your neighbourhood, for your nation? Is there someone that you long for – maybe a friend or relative who has moved away or died? Do you long for freedom from anxiety or from the disease that is crippling your body, or from people who are hurtful? It's human nature to want. And it's right that we should share these desires with God but everything, yes everything, in this life is transitory. God is the only lasting constant. So logic says that David's desire for God is the most sensible thing he could want.

Do you want temporary relief from something, or temporary gratification, or temporary things that might make your life happier or easier or less stressful? Probably! But set those wants and desires alongside your desire for God and let him share your life.

Challenge

It's a question of putting God first. He may or may not answer our prayer in the way we want; that's up to him, but keep the communication open.

Pray

Perhaps you can echo David's prayer for help and say to God, with him, 'You are all I want in this life.'

345

Bring to mind

Question time

Think back to an occasion when you saw fireworks. Where was it, who were you with, why were you there, what was the weather like, how did the spectacle affect you?

Read Psalm 143:1-6

Comment

Remember, remember the fifth of November, gunpowder, treason and plot... Whether we really need to remember what Guy Fawkes failed to do in the British Parliament, I'm not sure, but in the interests of democracy it's probably not a bad thing to remember. Of more importance, however, is to remember what God has done for us. Look at verses 5 and 6.

Tomato soup is the best drink for Bonfire Night. Warming, nourishing, filling. As we remember what God has done for us, we should be thirsty for him. The more we remember, the more we want of God.

He quenches our thirst, warms us, nourishes us, fills us – with his Spirit.

Sometimes we need to consciously bring things to mind. David uses various words: remember, think, bring to mind . . .

Challenge

Use the same questions as for the fireworks Question time, to think about what God has done for you in your life, your part in it and God's part in it.

Pray

Some of your memories of God's goodness.

346

Morning reminder

Question time

🍃 Do you have to set an alarm to go off in the morning? 5, 6, 7 o'clock? It's a reminder, a prompt that you need to get up and get going – to school, to work, or if you're lucky, to go on holiday.

Read Psalm 143:7-12

Comment

What's the first thing you do after turning off the alarm? Do you start the day with God? It's not a bad thing to do. Give your bleary eyes a chance to open, and your mind a chance to focus on the new day, and then give your attention to God.

'Remind me each morning of your constant love', says David. Do you need more of a reminder some mornings than others? It's easier if the sun is shining, perhaps, or if you're feeling energetic or if

it's your birthday. Not so easy if you wake with rain pelting down outside, and stress has already reared its morning head.

When we commit each fresh new day to God, whatever the weather or how we feel, we will go forward into that day as a partnership.

Challenge
Trust God, and let him guide you through the day – which he will do, because he loves you.

Pray
'When morning gilds the skies, my heart awaking cries, may Jesus Christ be praised.'

347
Pay attention

Question time
🍃 To whom do you pay attention?

Read Psalm 144:1-3

Comment

My grandfather failed to pay attention to bills that came through the letterbox. He simply ignored them by binning them. Children are told to 'pay attention' by their teachers at school. Parents, according to a recent news item, are being encouraged to talk to, and play with, their children. We're not always very good at paying attention to whatever we should be paying attention to!

Do we pay attention to God? But wait a minute, that's not what this psalm is saying. No, it's saying that God pays attention to *us*! He doesn't ignore us like an unwelcome bill, he doesn't gaze out of his heavenly window and decide whether or not to throw some more stars into space, he doesn't ignore his children like a busy parent might. He

pays attention. And David questions this in verse 3: 'Lord, what are mortals, that you notice them; mere mortals, that you pay attention to us?' There is an echo of Psalm 8 verse 4 here. David is filled with wonder at God's attention.

Challenge

Next time your attention wanders, think of God and how his attention never wanders. He keeps a protective eye out for you, just as he kept a protective eye on David.

Pray

When you're next out walking, pay attention to the details of nature around you. Praise God that each item of God's creation that you see is an indication that he pays attention to his world – including you.

348
Puff of wind

Question time

What is your attitude to life and death?

Read Psalm 144:4

Comment

In Act 5 of *Macbeth*, William Shakespeare wrote, 'Out, out brief candle! Life's but a walking shadow, a poor player that struts and frets his hour upon the stage and is heard no more.'

David likens human beings to puffs of wind and our lives – our days – as a passing shadow. He's alluded to it before in Psalm 39. It's a recurring theme in the Bible, often mentioned in the Psalms but also in Isaiah's prophecy and by Jesus in the Gospels. None of us knows how many days we will have and so we need to live well each day. In the parable of the rich fool Jesus warned about thinking we're OK, that we can live as we wish, eat, drink and be merry. What happens, Jesus says, if you die tonight? What good are all those things you pinned your life on? James and Peter talk about the brevity of life, as does the book of Hebrews.

Do you want to cram as much into life as you possibly can so that you get your money's worth, so that you don't feel cheated because you've missed out?

Challenge

The message of the Bible is that a full life comes from Jesus, it is his word that endures, and that, while alive, we need to ensure we're ready to meet our maker.

Pray

For a realistic attitude to life and death.

349
Reach down

Question time

> In what circumstances might you reach down to grasp a child's hand?

Read Psalm 144:5-8

Comment

We have pictures in the psalms of God's arms embracing us, of him seeing us and observing us and, here, of him reaching down – tearing apart the heavens to grasp us and save us.

Isn't that a picture of what Jesus did? He came from heaven, down to earth, to be with human beings, indeed to become fully human himself, so that he could enjoy our joys, share our sorrows, but above all – in his divinity – rescue us from the 'deep water'. He did that by living and teaching the people of his time, then dying a horrible death for the people of all time. Only he, the holy one from God who *is* God, was able to rescue us and give us the opportunity to be restored into a relationship with the holy God.

I love the thought of God moving heaven and earth to reach down to me! He does it for each one of us, such is his love and compassion.

Challenge

What is your response to God reaching down to you? Do you reach up to grab his hands and hang on tight?

Pray

For a good connection between you and your Saviour.

350

Happiness

Question time

What activity makes you happy?

Read Psalm 144:9-15

Comment

When I can't sleep at night I listen to the radio – and its broadcasts often send me straight back to sleep, which is good. In the morning when I wake I listen to the shipping forecast, a short news bulletin, prayer for the day, the farming programme, then Tweet for the Day – a snatch of birdsong from my radio (and from outside my window). Those programmes provide a bit of sanity before 7 am. And then the nitty gritty of current affairs comes on. This morning I listened to part of a phone-in about divorce, then a political argument where the speakers spoke over the top of each other, interrupted each other and were generally less than courteous.

At that point I switched to a classical music station and its calming influence. A Lent series at my local

church focused on Music for the Soul, a series of talks illustrated with excerpts of music. In moments when I need a break from the computer keyboard I swivel round and sit at the piano keyboard, and play a few hymns, thunderous toe-tappers or quiet reflective pieces. David, the harpist, turns to music to soothe his soul, praise his Lord, and gee him up for what lies ahead.

Challenge
Whatever your nation's shenanigans, can you echo David's words in verse 15?

Pray
For happiness in the Lord.

351

Beyond understanding

Question time

- What's the hardest subject you've ever studied?
- Why was it beyond your understanding?

Read Psalm 145:1-3

Comment

When we think in terms of God, his greatness is – as David points out – 'beyond understanding'. Human beings are blessed with brains that enable us to think, reason and reflect and try to work out answers to everything that we experience on earth. Each of us is blessed with different abilities and gifts, and we use what we've been given as best we can. But however brainy we are, however inquisitive, however deep our thoughts, we can never fully comprehend God and his greatness. Should we even try?

Job tried. He went through more bewilderment and grief than most of us. He tried to fathom God out but said, 'Everyone has seen what he has done; but no one understands it at all. We cannot fully know his greatness or count the number of his years' (Job 36:25, 26).

Paul, who was no ignoramus, had a great deal to say about God but had to admit, 'How great are God's riches! How deep are his wisdom and knowledge! Who can explain his decisions? Who can understand his ways? As the scripture says, "Who knows the mind of the Lord? Who is able to give him advice? Who has ever given him anything, so that he had to pay it back?" For all things were created by him, and all things exist through him and for him. To God be the glory forever! Amen' (Romans 11:33-36).

Be encouraged
Relax! God is great!

Pray
Use these verses as your prayer today.

352
Good to everyone

Question time

🍃 Do you think God is good to everyone? Be honest . . .

Read Psalm 145:4-9

Comment

Well, what do you think, is God good to everyone, or not? You might say, well God has given each person the chance of life on earth so that's him showing his goodness. But what about the baby who is on life support and then dies? Or the child who grows up in a home where abuse is rife and that child is traumatised for life? Or the families who see fellow family members hacked to death in war-torn zones? Or, or, or . . . Can we truly say that God is good to everyone?

We've seen many times how David expresses different feelings towards God – often within the same psalm! Sometimes he tells God how he feels abandoned by him, rejected, thrown out as rubbish. Other times, as here in verse 9, he feels God's goodness and compassion and, in a sweeping statement, he says that God is good to everyone.

Our finite minds cannot know the infinite mind of God, however hard we try – as we discovered in the previous section of this psalm. Is that a cop-out for not knowing how to explain this phrase? Probably, but I have no better answer.

Be encouraged

What I do know is that God wants us to trust him and to act as his ambassadors, showing his goodness in his world.

Pray

For the many people who find it hard to believe that God is good.

353
Royal power

Question time

What aspect of God's royal power do you find most compelling?

Read Psalm 145:10-13

Comment

The thrust of this psalm is praise. This section points us ahead to the arrival of Jesus on the scene a thousand years after David wrote the psalm, and even further ahead to the end of time as we know it, when God's glory will be seen by everyone in all its splendour, when everyone will see that Jesus is the King of kings and that his kingdom will last beyond time as humans know it.

Think about Palm Sunday and Jesus riding into Jerusalem and being hailed and honoured. Zechariah prophesied, 'Shout for joy, you people of Jerusalem! Look, your king is coming to you! He comes triumphant and victorious, but humble and riding on a donkey ... Your king will make peace among the nations; he will rule from sea to sea . . . The Lord will save his people' (Zechariah 9:9, 10, 16).

And in Revelation we read about the completion of God's kingdom, when people from every nation will worship him and tell of his splendour and majesty.

Be encouraged

All of creation will worship him. I love that thought. We have glimpses now of birds singing God's praise. Think of the blackbird on the chimney top, or a robin on the apple tree. Think of blossom on the trees, of fresh growth and beautiful harvests: 'All your creatures' (verse 10).

Pray

Praise God for the glimpses of Paradise that we see here and now.

354
Look hopeful

Question time

- How do you anticipate the arrival of good food to your table?
- Do you picture it in your mind's eye?
- Do you think of the taste?
- Are you excited at the prospect of being fed?

Read Psalm 145:14-16

Comment

A robin looked hopefully towards my husband and me one day. We'd bought take-away coffee and were eating cake, bought at a farmer's market stall, on a bench in a park. The cakes were delicious, so obviously homemade with good ingredients including love, and we demolished them. The robin approached, alas, too late. His head was cocked on one side and a beady eye looked at us somewhat reproachfully. I apologised to him and hoped he'd find some crumbs elsewhere. He flew into a nearby tree and serenaded us, before leaving in search of someone else's crumbs or a juicy worm.

While I wasn't much help to the robin on that occasion, it's good to see bird feeders hanging on trees in gardens. Equally, it's heartening to know that there are food banks and meal centres for people who would otherwise go without food. How often do you see someone look up hopefully to you for help? God very often helps those of us who are in trouble through the goodwill of others.

Challenge

How much are you able to do to be God's helper and a lifter-up of those whose hope is fading?

Pray

For what we are about to receive, may the Lord make us truly thankful.

355

Near

Question time

What are the benefits of having family or friends nearby?

Read Psalm 145:17-21

Comment

'Be near me, Lord Jesus, I ask thee to stay, close by me forever, and love me I pray. Bless all the dear children in thy tender care, and fit us for heaven to live with thee there.' We're used to hearing little children singing this Christmas carol and we smile at their sweet young voices but how many of them actually know that Jesus can be near them?

David frequently calls out to God. He has a close relationship with his Lord and knows that God is near him wherever he is, whether on a hillside with his sheep, on the throne of his kingdom, or battling life out in the world of other human beings. How near does God feel to you today?

When I'm too weary for words and prayer doesn't come easily, I use the words of that last verse of 'Away in a manger' as a prayer. Sometimes I don't know how to pray for my loved ones. In their trials it's hard to know how to help. As a friend says to me sometimes, 'I just have to give my children to God.' Sometimes we feel helpless in trying to solve the testing times of other people, especially when they're close friends or family.

Be encouraged

It's comforting to know that God loves our friends and family members and cares for each of them. And even if they don't call out to God themselves, we can call on him on their behalf and entrust them to his care.

Pray

For specific people who need to feel God's nearness.

356

Dust

Question time

🍃 What is your reaction to seeing dust in your home?

Read Psalm 146:1-4

Comment

It always surprises me how much dust is collected in my vacuum cleaner from a quick going-over of the carpets in my home. The dust isn't obvious in the carpet but enough is sucked up to fill the equivalent of a jam jar. The dust is thrown away. Done and dusted you might say.

Human beings appear in the world and then leave. Their time is limited. The psalmist gets his priorities right. He wants to praise the Lord while he lives and for as long as lives because he knows that, after death, his body will be reduced to mere dust.

We may expect great things from human leaders but the psalmist points out that we can't trust political or church leaders or any other sort of leader to save us. They are fallible human beings with a limited shelf life. And they, like the rest of us, will return to dust. Isaiah makes this clear in talking about God: 'He brings down powerful rulers and reduces them to nothing . . . When the Lord sends a wind, they dry up and blow away like straw' (Isaiah 40:23, 24).

Challenge

Who then, may we trust to save us? God alone. And we know that because of Jesus the Saviour.

Pray

Let's praise God as the psalmist does while we have breath, before we're reduced to dust.

357

Sight

Question time

🍃 Close your eyes and try walking around your home. What made it hard – or easy?

Read Psalm 146:5-10

Comment

George Matheson (1842-1906) started to lose his eyesight in his late teens when a student at Glasgow University. His sight completely left him, as did the girl he was to marry who declared that she didn't want to be the wife of a blind man. A double blow that led him to place his hope and trust in God's love for him, demonstrated by Jesus. Matheson went into Christian ministry, which included preaching at Balmoral to Queen Victoria. When Matheson was 40 he wrote a hymn that emerged from a time of great mental suffering.

At the end of verse 7 of this psalm we read, 'The Lord sets the prisoners free and gives sight to the blind.' Not just physical sight but spiritual sight too,

something that Jesus fulfilled during his time on earth.

Matheson's hymn has touched the lives of many who have experienced tragedy and loss in their own lives. It begins, 'O Love that wilt not let me go.' The second verse reads, 'O light that followest my way, I yield my flickering torch to thee; my heart restores its borrowed ray, that in thy sunshine's blaze its day may brighter, fairer be.' That is the testimony of Matheson, it is the testimony of those who have received spiritual sight from God. Praise the Lord!

Be encouraged
That God never loses sight of you.

Pray
For those who have physical sight impediments and for those who care for them.

358

Star-naming

Question time

🍃 What comes to mind when you think of Jesus as the Light of the world?

Read

Psalm 147:1-6

Comment

I'm glad that Orion is mentioned in the Bible by name. It's one of the few constellations that I recognise and can say, 'There's Orion!' But God knows the names of all the stars in the sky – and we've already seen how many noughts that involves. Oh yes, great and mighty is our Lord, indeed!

The Bible mentions the stars in the sky on many occasions, but also uses stars to illustrate the great light of the world, Jesus Christ. As far back as Numbers we read, 'I look into the future, and I see the nation of Israel. A king, like a bright star, will arise in that nation' (Numbers 24:17). Isaiah points to Jesus: 'The people who walked in darkness have

seen a great light' (Isaiah 9:2) and, 'Arise, shine, for your light has come, and the glory of the Lord rises upon you' (Isaiah 60:1, NIV). Jesus says, 'I am the light of the world' (John 8:12). And in the last chapter of the Bible – Revelation 22:16 – Jesus says, 'I am descended from the family of David; I am the bright morning star.'

Be encouraged

Jesus is the star of God's show. He is greater than all the stars in the sky. It is to him that we sing praises. It is good, pleasant and right to praise him.

Pray

Praise God for Jesus, the Light.

Message

Question time

How do we receive messages?

Read Psalm 147:7-20

Comment

Think how the early letters of the church would have been delivered to the Mediterranean churches – by runner, by horse and cart perhaps. It would have taken days or weeks. Think of how letters were transported by ship until aircraft could take them to recipients around the globe. Then came the postal system. Now we can receive messages instantly on our technological devices. Some messages are trivial, some are important.

God's message, as we near the finishing line of the Psalms, is of immense importance and impacts the lives of all who hear it. What is the message and how do we respond?

God communicates good news. He tells us he loves us, he gives us rules for living in harmony with the other inhabitants of his created world, he points out that he is holy and we need to be put right with him so that we can have a relationship with him. He tells us that he sends a Saviour who offers forgiveness of sins and a new life of joyful fellowship with the creator.

Challenge

How will you respond to God's message today and how will it impact the rest of your life?

Pray

That God's message will be heard and received by those who don't yet know it.

360
All together now

Question time

🍃 Have you ever been to a concert? School concert, pop concert, classical concert, opera . . . ?

Read Psalm 148:1-14

Comment

The Last Night of the Proms is a noisy, joyful concert marking the end of a long series of promenade concerts that happen daily in London throughout the summer. The excitement of the Last Night reaches fever pitch with flag-waving, hooters hooting, whistles whistling and voices joining with musical instruments to make a joyful noise in praise of music-making. Young and old, promenaders and sitters, plebs and posh, are united in song.

This psalm is a song of praise where everyone and everything come together to praise God. It's not just people. Angels, everyone in heaven, sun, moon, stars, sky, sea, weather, animals and birds, trees and plants, rich and poor, rulers and people, adults and children. The psalmist mentions everything and everyone that he can think of and all, singly and collectively, acknowledge God's greatness.

What will worship be like in heaven? I've been asked. Noisy but tuneful, I imagine, with perfect harmonies in music and in relationships. Nobody will say, 'I don't like happy-clappy', or 'I don't like plainsong', or 'I don't like Victorian sentimentality', or whatever. Like the Last Night of the Proms but even better.

Challenge
Get practising for heaven's concert of praise.

Pray
For harmony between worshippers now whose musical tastes differ.

Honours for the humble

Question time

Why would God take pleasure in you?

Read Psalm 149:1-9

Comment

One of my grandchildren loves bashing the drums, one likes dancing, others like singing or playing flute or piano. The thought of these young music-makers practising their praise fills me with delight. In Zephaniah we read, 'The Lord will take delight in you, and in his love he will give you new life. He will sing and be joyful over you, as joyful as people at a festival' (Zephaniah 3:17, 18). I'm so glad God likes music but I guess that's all part of his creativity which he has passed on to us too and for which we can be thankful. The psalm tells us that God takes pleasure in his people (verse 4) and honours the humble.

Jesus told us to come like children to him, eager and uninhibited. Let's do that and enjoy his company and praise him in whatever way we can.

Challenge

Find a drum to bash, fiddle on the fiddle, pluck the strings of a harp or guitar, and leap and dance for joy because of who God is.

Pray

For children learning to play musical instruments.

362

Music-making

Question time

🍃 Why is it significant that the psalms end with praise?

Read Psalm 150:1-6

Comment

If you haven't yet tuned your instruments, now's the time to do so. Polish the trumpet, dust off your lyre, practise scales on your flute, and if you don't have cymbals, get out some saucepan lids. And don't forget to lubricate your vocal cords with a bit of gargling. Now is the time for that mega music festival in honour of the Lord. What a fitting way to end the psalms. Praise the Lord! Praise him at your place of worship – cathedral, parish church, free church, house church, and in the bath. Let your praises ascend to the skies, reverberate around the houses. Let those around you hear your praises, see your joy, sense your thankfulness to God.

Fanfares on trumpets herald the arrival of important personages on special occasions. TV audiences see royal weddings or commemorative services, choirs sing, and everyone is eager with anticipation of the arrival of the star.

Be encouraged

When we praise God we are worshipping him as the creator of the universe, as the Saviour of the world, as the Spirit who lives in us to aid us in our worship, our understanding, and is our comforter and companion. All these we celebrate – and so much more.

Pray

How great is the God we adore, our faithful and unchanging friend.

363
Subject matters

Question time

- What was your favourite subject at school?
- What subject would you most like to study now?

Read Psalm 119:49-56

Comment

We've read all 150 psalms and revisited part of the longest one. It's time now to do some summarising. The psalms cover many subjects: praise, thanksgiving, trust, wisdom, lament and vindication. There are psalms about God as king, royal tributes, psalms that point forward to the Messiah and songs about Zion – the city of God. The reading today, which we covered earlier in this book, features some of the emotions arising from those subjects: hope, suffering, comfort, promise, remembrance, anger, reflection, happiness, obedience.

Challenge

Is there a particular emotional response that you need to build on – hope, for example, or that you need to ask God to take from you – anger, maybe?

Pray

Praise God for the variety of subjects in the psalms and their relevance for us today.

364

Favourites

Question time

Which has been your favourite psalm as you've read through the book?

Read Reread your favourite psalm or verses from a psalm.

Comment

It's likely that you'll have difficulty choosing a favourite psalm! One may speak to you on one occasion, another on a different day. It depends on your circumstances, your feelings at the time, your concerns or joys. You might need encouragement or need to be challenged. You might be moved by reading a particular psalm and want to share it with someone else. That's a good thing to do! We're not to be isolated as God's followers. We learn on our own and in the company of others. We pray in quiet places in an intimate relationship with God, we praise him in the company of a gathering of other worshippers.

Love songs

365

'There is something wonderful in music. Words are wonderful; music is more wonderful. It speaks not to our thoughts but straight to our hearts and spirit. It surprises us in the most tender of places. Where there has been pain bitter beyond tears, it reaches to the very root of our souls. It is the sunshine and the moonlight; the song of the skylark and the stars. Music is the speech of the Angels that fills the universe – the love songs of God himself, who sings his heart out.'

This anonymous piece sums up what the psalms are all about. Words and music combine to express every emotion known to human beings. Thank God for writers and composers, for their gifts that reflect the creativity of the creator. Let's use the psalms to speak and sing our own thoughts to God and enjoy the love songs that, in turn, he sings to us.

'Of all the creatures both in sea and land
Only to Man thou hast made known thy ways,
And put the pen alone into his hand,
And made him Secretary of thy praise.'

'Providence', lines 5-8, George Herbert (1593-1633)

Be encouraged

To share what you've learnt from the psalms with your family or with a friend or neighbour. God speaks to us as individuals but also through our shared humanity with others.

Pray

Thank God for your favourite psalm. Ask him to give you opportunities to share with others the insights he has given you.

Thank God for the psalmists and their poetry that resonates with the complexities of our life experiences and points us to the God who loves and cares and to whom we can ask questions, vent feelings and offer praise because he is great, constant and everlasting.